INNOVATION AND
MARKET STRUCTURE

INNOVATION AND MARKET STRUCTURE

Lessons from the Computer and
Semiconductor Industries

NANCY S. DORFMAN

Ballinger Publishing Company • Cambridge, Massachusetts
A Subsidiary of Harper & Row, Publishers, Inc.

International Standard Book Number: 0-88730-185-1

Library of Congress Catalog Card Number: 86-21619

Printed in the United States of America

Library of Congress Cataloging-in-Publication Data

Dorfman, Nancy S.
    Innovation and market structure.

    Includes bibliographies and index.
    1. Computer industry—Technological innovations.
2. Semiconductor industry—Technological innovations.
3. Technological innovations—Economic aspects.
4. New business enterprises. 5. Research, Industrial.
6. Competition. I. Title.
HD9696.C62D67   1987   338.4'7004   86-21619
ISBN 0-88730-185-1

CONTENTS

LIST OF FIGURES AND TABLES

ACKNOWLEDGMENTS

Research for this study was supported in part by a grant from the National Science Foundation (Grant number PRA 8300600) during parts of 1983 and 1984 at the Center for Policy Alternatives, Massachusetts Institute of Technology. A number of individuals deserve special thanks for their contributions. Matthew Giamporcaro, then an engineering student at the Massachusetts Institute of Technology, provided invaluable assistance in getting the project underway during the summer and fall of 1983. As a research assistant, he worked imaginatively and intelligently to assemble material from which information on major innovations was drawn and to develop preliminary surveys of innovations. He supplied valuable instruction on technical issues as well and constructive and insightful comments on early drafts of chapters. Jun-Tsiang Lam, also an engineering student at MIT, assisted in assembling information on innovations in magnetic disk storage.

An advisory group of four academic economists provided constructive criticism, insights, and encouragement. The group included Richard R. Nelson at Columbia University, Edward B. Roberts at MIT, Myles Boylan at the National Science Foundation, and John A. Hansen at Fredonia State University College in New York. The members were inordinately generous with their time and their interest. Chapters 1, 2, and 10 were prepared after the group was disbanded, and substantial revisions of all of the chapters were subsequently undertaken. Bo Carlsson,

Chairman of the Economics Department at Case Western Reserve University, was exceptionally helpful in reviewing and commenting on a later draft of the manuscript.

Arthur L. Norberg, Director of the Charles Babbage Institute and member of the Department of Computer Science at the University of Minnesota, and I. Bernard Cohen, Victor S. Thomas Professor, Emeritus, of the History of Science at Harvard University, reviewed early drafts of Chapters 3 through 9 and provided detailed and extremely useful comments. Richard B. Adler, Associate Head of the Department of Electrical Engineering and Computer Science at MIT, spent several hours discussing with me the history of technology in the semiconductor industry and evaluating the importance of innovations that are included in Chapter 8.

Finally, I wish to express my appreciation to the International Data Corporation of Framingham, Massachusetts, a leading market research organization specializing in the computer industry. Officials of that organization generously provided me with access to their extensive library, including comprehensive files on individual firms in the industry, as well as to copies of reports that the company had prepared covering numerous segments of the industry dating from the early 1960s. Their *EDP Newsletter,* cited throughout this volume, provided a running history of market activity in the industry.

Needless to say, I accept full responsibility for the contents of this book.

Nancy S. Dorfman
Center for Technology, Policy and Industrial Development
Massachusetts Institute of Technology
Cambridge, Massachusetts
September, 1986

1 THE MARKET CONDITIONS FOR INNOVATION: INTRODUCTION

This study examines the history of innovation in two major industries that for over 30 years have shared in one of the most dramatic technological revolutions of all time. The electronic computer and the transistor came into the commercial marketplace almost simultaneously in 1951 and 1952, and quite independently of each other. A more serendipitous pairing of technologies could not have been imagined. Before the decade was out, the computer had been transistorized, commencing a synergistic development that led from the first commercial computer, UNIVAC I, which contained 5,000 vacuum tubes and weighed 5 tons, to todays' microcomputer, which sits on a desktop, sells for a few hundred dollars, and outperforms its ancestor. At the same time, the solid state revolution paved the way for powerful single processors that performed over 10 million instructions per second by the early 1980s.[1] In place of vacuum tubes in these machines are the descendants of the transistor: silicon chips, about a half-inch square, each containing the equivalent of thousands of vacuum tubes.

As the wheels of progress spun, hundreds of newly founded enterprises were drawn into the mainstream of competition to design and produce new electronic products. Their success cast new light on a debate that has engaged economists for more than a generation. The question concerns the relative importance in engineering technological progress of large, established corporations compared with small, entrepreneurial firms.

1

The purpose of the present study is to compare the roles of new commercial enterprises with those of large, established firms in spearheading technological progress in different branches of the computer and semiconductor industries since they evolved in the late 1940s and to understand how the structural characteristics of the different markets shaped those roles. For this purpose five industry sectors have been singled out: mainframe computers, minicomputers, computer printers, magnetic disk storage devices, and integrated circuits.[2] They were selected to provide a spectrum of experience ranging from markets in which established firms thoroughly dominated innovation to those where new enterprises were largely responsible for technological progress.

AN HISTORIC DEBATE

On the eve of the technological revolution that was ushered in by the transistor and the electronic computer, circa 1946–47, a revolutionary doctrine was announced by one of the world's most eminent and influential economists. It lit the fire of a debate that has preoccupied economists and public policy experts up to the present day. The issue concerned the relative importance in driving economic progress of large, oligopolistic firms, compared with the classical "atomistic" enterprises that operate in perfectly competitive markets. Joseph A. Schumpeter, writing in *Capitalism, Socialism, and Democracy* in 1942, announced the revisionist theory that

> the large scale establishment or unit of control—has come to be the most powerful engine of (economic) progress and in particular of the long-run expansion of total output not only in spite of, but to a considerable extent through, this strategy (of monopolistic practices) which looks so restrictive when viewed in the individual case and from the individual point of time. In this respect, perfect competition is not only impossible but inferior, and has no title to being set up as a model of ideal efficiency.

Elsewhere in the same book:

> As soon as we go into details and inquire into the individual items in which progress was most conspicuous, the trail leads not to the doors of those firms that work under conditions of comparatively free competition but precisely to the doors of the large concerns . . . [This is because the] fundamental impulse that sets and keeps the capitalist engine in motion comes from the new consumers' goods, the new methods of production or

transportation, the new markets, the new forms of industrial organization that capitalist enterprise creates.[3]

In Schumpeter's 1942 treatise the large firm dislodged the small entrepreneur, who had claimed center stage in his earlier work. Economic progress replaced allocative efficiency as the critical force in maximizing total output. Competition based on price became less crucial than competition based on innovation, and large firms with a degree of monopoly power were singled out as the economic units with the incentive and the wherewithal to compete on these terms.[4]

Schumpeter received support from J.K. Galbraith in 1952, just as the computer and the transistor were arriving on the commercial market for the first time. In *American Capitalism* Galbraith declared:

> There is no more pleasant fiction than that technical change is the product of the matchless ingenuity of the small man forced by competition to employ his wits to better his neighbor. Unhappily, it is a fiction. Technical development has long since become the preserve of the scientist and engineer. Most of the cheap and simple inventions have, to put it bluntly, been made. Not only is development now sophisticated and costly but it must be on a sufficient scale so that successes and failures will in some measure average out. Because development is costly, it follows that it can be carried on only by a firm that has the resources associated with considerable size.[5]

Schumpeter and Galbraith were not alone in their view of the pivotal role of the large-scale organization, but neither were they unchallenged. The most compelling counterattack came from Jewkes, Sawers, and Stillerman in a 1958 book, *The Sources of Invention*, which analyzed 50 case studies of twentieth-century inventions (the 1969 edition added a survey of 10 more recent inventions). In that book, which has become a minor classic, they specifically addressed the effectiveness of large corporate research establishments compared with the small, independent inventor and concluded:

> Against the claim for the efficiency in development of the biggest and the most securely established industrial organizations may be set, therefore, the advantages of the attack from many angles. The tasks of development are themselves of such diversity and of so varying a scale that it may be a great and a dangerous over-simplification to suppose that they can always be best handled by any single type of institution. It may be that the happiest situation for a community, the condition most effectively contributing to general liveliness, will be found where the variety in form and outlook in industrial institutions matches that of the problems with which they have to deal;

firms of varying size, some disposed to pursue plans deliberately and with an eye on the distant future and others inclined to plunge heavily for quick results; some mainly concerned with holding an established status and others prepared to dare much to restore a lost position or to break into a new industry; some that regard their forte as lying in rapid innovation and others which feel that their strength is found in following up and improving. It may well be that there is no optimum size of firm but merely an optimum pattern for an industry, such a distribution of firms by size, character and outlook as to guarantee the most effective gathering together and commercially perfecting of the flow of new ideas.[6]

Jewkes and his collaborators were concerned with invention, rather than innovation, which includes the successful production and marketing of an invention. But other case studies of individual firms and industries supported the thesis that large industrial corporations do not have a monopoly on innovation. Writing in 1967, Nelson, Peck, and Kalacheck called attention to the importance of independent inventors operating in separate market niches from those of the corporate industrial laboratory.[7] Scherer, at about the same time, concluded that "giant firm size is no prerequisite for the most vigorous inventive and innovative activity."[8]

More recently, economists have searched for insights regarding the so-called Schumpeterian hypothesis by formally modeling the innovative process, but such models, of necessity, require rather restrictive assumptions. On the basis of one such model, Nelson concluded, "In short, Schumpeterian competition would appear to involve a wide range of phenomena with a variety of different structural possibilities. The simple proposition that, under Schumpeterian competition, large firms with considerable market power are necessary in order for there to be rapid industrial innovation, or that such a structure naturally will emerge, or both, would appear to require rather special assumptions to be true."[9]

Perhaps the most extensive efforts to test the Schumpeterian hypothesis have been based on statistical analyses of the relationship between innovation on the one hand and size of firm or market structure on the other. These studies, taken as whole, point strongly to the conclusion that the relationship is extremely subtle and complicated and that the statistical data that are available for testing it leave much to be desired.

The outline for the present study was motivated in part by the overall inconclusiveness of these often imaginative and meticulous studies, but also by the growing focus of public attention on the small, entrepreneurial company, characteristically portrayed as the knight in armor who will slay the dragon of Japanese technological proficiency. The debate appears to have moved 180 degrees since Schumpeter wrote in 1942. Perhaps we can have our cake and eat it, allocative efficiency and maximum economic progress too, thanks to the innovative energy of the small, entrepreneurial firm.

To help separate myth from reality in this vision it would be useful to undertand better the particular roles that small, entrepreneurial firms play in promoting innovation in different markets and the characteristics of individual markets that shape those roles. The question of whether large, established companies are more or less innovative than small new ones may not have an answer independently of the market conditions under which the firms operate. The tack taken here is to avoid asking, in a general sense: Who is more innovative? The group of industries selected for study is not intended to constitute a representative sample, and it is strongly emphasized that the purpose is not to draw inferences concerning that debate. Instead, industries were chosen to provide a sufficient range of patterns of innovation, from a predominance of small new enterprises to their virtual absense, to provide a basis for exploring the reasons for the varying performance of such firms as innovators in different industries.

The importance of the question should not require much elaboration in an era in which government efforts to promote competitiveness abroad and productivity at home have become a focus of policy debate. Two of the main actors in the script that is about to unfold here, IBM and AT&T, have in recent years been the targets of major antitrust suits filed by the U.S. Department of Justice. Legislation passed in the early 1980s mandated that a share of all federal research and development (R&D) expenditures be allocated to small firms, and special tax laws have been passed to make it easier for them to compete. Much hope is pinned on the success of new "high tech" firms at the same time that lagging productivity in older industries populated by small firms, like shoe and furniture manufacturing, is cause for despair. Studies like this one will, it is hoped, help to provide a basis for structuring public policy, if any is needed, to encourage innovation.

Theoretical Arguments

The justification for the theory that large firms are significantly more innovative than small ones is derived from four principle premises: 1) the large firm's presumed greater incentive to innovate, 2) its more adequate financial resources with which to do so, 3) its ability to spread the risk of R&D, and 4) its ability to exploit economies of scale in R&D.

Schumpeter argued that in order to innovate a firm must first have an incentive to invest the necessary resources under what are likely to be more than normally risky circumstances. The necessary resources include not only the usual investment in producing and marketing but the additional investment that is required for research and development. The incentive must include, therefore, the prospect that the innovator will be able to monopolize the sale or use of the innovation long enough to assure it an economic rent that will justify the investment in R&D. By definition, this would not be possible in the perfectly competitive markets that are populated by numerous small enterprises since such firms can earn no more than a "normal" profit on investment in production. Monopoly power is usually associated with the advantages of size and maturity that protect a firm from competition that would force it to sell at a price no greater than average cost of production.

The second reason to expect the role of innovator to fall to large companies was emphasized by Galbraith when he argued that the high threshold cost of R&D that must precede innovation in the modern economy precluded innovation by small firms. "Because development is costly, it follows that it can be carried on only by a firm that has the resources which are associated with considerable size."[10] The abnormally high profits of the monopolist can help to provide these resources. Galbraith's case is even stronger when one considers that most innovators need capital not only to support R&D but to support production and marketing of the innovation as well since sale of patent rights cannot generally be relied on to capture a significant share of the surplus.

The third advantage of large companies derives from the considerable uncertainty of the success of the R&D effort and ultimately of the production and marketing of an innovation. The greater the number of innovative projects undertaken by a single company, the greater the chance that successes and failures will average out. Only a large company can be diverse enough to avoid putting all of its eggs in one basket. Nelson pointed to a related reason that large diversified firms may enjoy greater returns to R&D than small firms: the greater likelihood that a firm will find applications for the results of R&D the more varied its range of products.[11]

The fourth argument favoring large firms is the possibility of returns to scale in R&D. In addition to these four arguments, it is sometimes contended that large firms are in a better position than small ones to attract highly qualified personnel, not simply because of their greater financial resources but because they are able to offer better research facilities, greater job security, and prospects of upward mobility.

These are, then, the arguments generally put forth in support of the notion that large firms fuel the engine of technological change. But there is another side to the story. There are a number of reasons that small enterprises might be expected to be more innovative than large.

First, there may be diseconomies of large-scale organization in mounting strategies for developing and marketing new products. The multiple levels of decision makers who must approve policies to innovate within a large bureaucratic organization and the inferior communications between research, production, and marketing departments are frequently cited in defense of this proposition.

Second, small companies have less capital tied up in the old technology than do large firms, and new companies have none at all. The larger the company, the greater the capital it is likely to have invested in equipment and inventories that could be made obsolete by the introduction of a new product or process. The less its fear of competition, the longer a company can afford to delay introduction of a new product or process that competes with its current line.

Third, a strong case can be made that, contrary to the earlier assertion, small firms have an advantage in acquiring the talented scientific, technical, and managerial personnel needed to produce innovations and in inspiring high performance. Anecdotal evidence abounds that the bureaucracy that characterizes so many large enterprises is biased against hiring young talent with new ideas and giving them much rein. This bias was manifested in the leisurely pace at which the research departments of major vacuum tube companies refocused their staffing toward solid state electronics after the invention of the transistor and by the reluctance of IBM's tabulating machine department, at about the same time, to move into computers. In addition, established corporations can rarely offer potential innovators the financial rewards of a genuine partnership in a successful innovative undertaking that a small, new enterprise can provide. Profit sharing can offer a greater incentive to individual effort in a small, privately held company compared with a large, publicly held corporation where the effect on stock values of a successful internal venture is strongly diluted. The steady flow of entrepreneurs leaving jobs with new ideas in hand to found companies of their own attests to the seductiveness of the entrepreneurial role.

Theoretically, then, there are forces that can tip the scales in favor of either smaller or larger firms depending on the circumstances. There is no basis for assuming that the scales will always tip in the same direction. The empirical evidence supporting any one of these arguments is far from definitive. But it ought to be possible to say something about the specific kinds of circumstances in which one or another argument is likely to be decisive. Most of the empirical work in this field has attempted, rather, to test various versions of the hypothesis that large or monopolistic firms are, in general, more innovative than others. The aim of the present study is to understand the particular kinds of markets in which small new innovators are most likely to find success.

Empirical Studies

Empirical studies of the relationship between innovativeness and market structure have been so thoroughly and thoughtfully reviewed by Kamien and Schwartz as recently as 1982 that more than a cursory summary would be superfluous here.[12] Other useful reviews of these studies have been published by Rothwell and Zegvel, the Senate Select Committee on Small Business, and Zerbe.[13] Much of the work is based on statistical regression analysis that uses a measure of innovative output or input as the dependent variable and evidence of firm size or monopoly power as the independent variable.[14] On the whole, the very large body of research reviewed by Kamien and Schwartz has yielded results that tend to be inconclusive (not statistically significant) or contradictory (disagreement among results of different studies). There are serious conceptual problems in quantifying concepts such as innovation or monopoly power, and measures of the appropriate variables are generally available only for limited groups of firms or industry categories and rarely for a representative range of firm sizes.

In the absence of any acceptable body of data covering the number or value of innovations by firms or industries, the number of patents issued to firms, individually or by industry, is the most commonly used proxy, and its shortcomings are obvious: all patents are by no means of equal importance, different firms within an industry and between industries have strongly varying propensities to patent their inventions, and all patents are not followed up by innovations. Occasionally subjective measures of innovation have been substituted for patents within relatively small groups of industries.

Beyond the measurement of innovations is the problem of measuring firm size (assets, sales, value added, or numbers of employees, which are not perfectly correlated) or monopoly power (concentration ratios or product differentiability). Studies that relate innovative input or output to firm size generally must rely on data from samples of fairly large firms, such as the Fortune 500 or the x largest firms in a given industry, leaving out genuinely small or new enterprises altogether. The influence of market power on innovation is usually evaluated from the relationship between innovative input or output and industry concentration ratios (the percentage of total sales in an industry attributable to the 4, 8, or 20 largest firms). Census statistics on concentration ratios are available in no greater detail than four-digit SIC classes, and experience indicates that four-digit industries can contain numerous products whose cross elasticities of demand are close to zero.[15] But concentration ratios do not in any case provide consistent measures of the ease of entry in different industries nor the degree of monopoly power shared by the top firms. The four-digit industry Electronic Computing Equipment contains mainframe, mini- and microcomputers along with peripheral equipment (accessories) for all of them. Historically, as we shall see, different firms have specialized in different branches of this industry and even in different price ranges within branches. By contrast, the semiconductor industry is divided into more homogeneous sectors; integrated circuits makes up a four-digit class by itself. But even there, specialization exists among firms. Concentration ratios do not reflect the degree of foreign competition, which is compelling in integrated circuits, nor do they indicate the turnover among the top four companies. All of these factors could help to account for the unsatisfactory results of the statistical analyses. Kamien and Schwartz mention, also, that most studies do not succeed in adequately controlling for factors other than size or monopoly power that influence innovativeness.

THE PRESENT STUDY

Objective

The present study departs in several respects from most of its predecessors. The objective is not, as mentioned, to test a theory but to identify the market conditions under which small, new firms innovate. To a generation for whom names like Digital Equipment, Intel, and Apple are household words, a theory of innovation that does not account for the performance of small, new innovators cannot claim to be a fully developed one. Those firms and hundreds of others like them came into the world by innovating. But the same generation has seen giants like IBM and AT&T come forth with one major innovation after another as well. Clearly, as Nelson[16] and others have recognized, more complex and subtle forces are at work in setting the stage for innovation than size or monopoly power of enterprises. This study looks at only one group of industries. Similar questions will have to be asked of others in the process of building a theory.

Size versus Age of Firm

A further departure of this study is its focus on the age of firms rather than size alone in analyzing patterns of innovation. Instead of drawing a line between large and small firms the analysis distinguishes between new firms and well-established firms. This departure was motivated by the appearance of a natural dichotomy along this line that separates groups of innovative firms. Innovations have generally been initiated by either large established companies or relatively new ones. The small mature firm was almost conspicuous by its absence among innovators.

A second reason for drawing a line on the basis of age of firm was pragmatic. This study is based on records of individual innovations and the particular firms that were responsible. It is much easier to ascertain the date of birth of a company than to determine its size at the time that it introduced a particular innovation. Moreover, successful new innovators that start out small tend to grow very fast. Often they continue to innovate. A snapshot of its size on any particular date does not capture the salient characteristics that set such a firm apart from established oligopolists on the one hand or established small firms on the other.

The study was begun with the idea of defining a "new" firm as one that had not become established in any market prior to the creation of the market in which it became an innovator. All of the industries studied were created after 1950 and companies like IBM, AT&T, RCA, and General Electric were major corporations in industries related to computers or semiconductors before those industries came into being. On the other hand, Digital Equipment (DEC) in minicomputers, Intel in integrated circuits, Shugart in floppy disks, and Diablo in the low-cost computer printer industry, to name just a few, were either new companies at the time their markets were created or were founded still later. They did not diversify from related industries that were already well established. Although this method of classifying firms, rather than by years since birth or size alone, seems to be the one that most successfully separates the large, established companies that Schumpeter and Galbraith celebrated from other innovators, it is not without ambiguity. For one thing, as time goes on a new firm becomes not only older but, more troublesome; if it is successful it becomes large and in some important respects comes to resemble the large, established firm more than the new one. In addition, there is an occasional small company like Texas Instruments that had established itself as an innovator in a totally unrelated industry (oil exploration equipment) before moving into electronics. It has aspects of both old and new companies. But, because most new firms that introduced one or more significant innovations, introduced at least one of them within a few years of its formation, there is, on the whole, less room for ambiguity than one might fear in adopting this method of classification.

The Selection of Industries

The five industry sectors chosen for this study were selected to provide an opportunity to examine the complex web of market forces that affect the willingness and ability of different classes of firms to innovate. They range from industries in which small new firms dominated innovation to those in which they were virtually absent. As the study proceeded it became evident that, in terms of the characteristics that influence the propensities of firms of different sizes and ages to innovate, more than five industry sectors had in effect been chosen to study. Relevant characteristics in some industries changed over the 30-year time span, and within industries important differences in structure were sometimes found between the high and the low price and performance sectors of markets.

Each industry is examined from the date of its inception to the early 1980s, and during these periods, each underwent an exceedingly rapid rate of innovation, although the pace of technological progress was faster in some than in others. Government-sponsored research during and soon after World War II had paved the way for technological opportunities, unprecedented in their scope, that were uncorked by developments in solid state and computer electronics near the end of the 1940s. As the electronics revolution progressed, demand pull from the commercial market added its weight to technology push to spur innovation. (Advances in computer peripheral equipment are a prime example.) The intensity of technological progress in these industries enhances the opportunity to observe the participation of different kinds of firms in the innovative process. On top of superb opportunities for innovation, most of the industries exhibited high elasticities of demand with respect to improvements in price or performance. The result was that extraordinarily high rates of growth in demand accompanied technological change, making for rapid rates of recovery of capital invested in innovation.

Finally, a common feature of the industries is that patents have not afforded much protection to innovators for a variety of reasons that will be discussed in later chapters. The exact extent to which the ineffectiveness of patents is paralleled elsewhere in the economy is unknown, but there is evidence that the condition is far from unique.

Defining and Evaluating Innovation

An innovation is a product or process that is, in a technological sense, new and has met the market test. A product innovation must be regarded as superior, at a price that will at least cover average cost, to all available substitutes by enough customers that its sale will yield at least a normal profit on investment, including investment in R&D, production, and marketing. A process innovation must facilitate production of a product that is superior in quality relative to its cost, compared with what other available processes can do. To simplify exposition, the term "new product" will include process innovations throughout the study except when the distinction is important to clarity.

Some innovations that meet these criteria are trivial while others are of momentous consequence. Even though it may be possible to envision, in principle, objective methods for comparing the values of different innovations, in practice the necessary information to implement such methods would be either impossible or prohibitively costly to obtain for a sample of any reasonable size. It might even be troublesome to obtain agreement on the principle.

In addition to the fact that all patents do not lead to innovations and all innovations are not patented, patent statistics give each one the same weight. Thus, although they represent the most complete body of data that we have relating to innovations and the individuals or firms that were responsible for them, patent statistics are seriously flawed for our purposes. The alternative is to identify actual innovations, one by one, and assign each a value. This is the approach taken here, in effect. It, too, has its shortcomings. In return for any reasonable effort only a small sample of such innovations can be identified. Recognizing this, the study is confined to identifying only what seem to be major innovations in each industry and giving them, with few exceptions, equal weight. But two problems still remain. A basis is needed for deciding what constitutes a major innovation, and even then we cannot be certain of success in assembling a complete list of such innovations.

These difficulties are mitigated by the fact that the present analysis needs only a description of the pattern of distribution of innovations between the two different classes of firms in each industry: Were innovations attributable overwhelmingly to large established firms, small new enterprises, or some combination of the two? The objective is not to measure the relative innovativeness of different classes of firms but to distinguish the markets in which small new firms had both the ability and the incentive to innovate from those in which they did not. Even allowing for errors of judgment and oversight, the pattern in each industry has emerged clearly. In order that the reader can have confidence in the assessment of these patterns it seemed appropriate in some industries to rather tediously describe the nature of technology and the way in which it unfolded as one innovation followed another. On the other hand, in general purpose mainframes, for example, a thorough account of innovations and innovators was not necessary because the virtual absence of small, new enterprises ruled out a significant role for them in the innovation process. The growth of the minicomputer industry, by contrast, was demonstrably driven by new enterprises, leaving little doubt as to the sources of innovation. In other industries, a more complete accounting of innovations and innovators was necessary. While there is room to question the wisdom of including or excluding specific innovations, it is unlikely that many readers will quarrel with the conclusions regarding the relative performance of either old or new firms as a class in any given industry.

Information concerning the development of technology and innovation in each industry was drawn mainly from four kinds of sources: scholarly texts and journals that provide histories and analyses of technology in the various industries during different stages of their development; articles in trade journals, especially articles that review the development or state of the art of a specific technology; the International Data Corporation of Framingham, Massachusetts, a leading electronic data processing (EDP) market research organization, which generously made available its historic files of the computer industry dating from the early 1960s; and a number of useful books dealing with innovation in various sections of the electronics industry more generally. Information regarding the firms that were responsible has come from the same or similar sources for the most part. Finally, I have spoken with a number of experts in the technical and business areas related to the substance of the study.

METHOD AND ORGANIZATION

Each of the five industries is analyzed within a framework of industrial organization theory, using the foundation laid out in Bain's *Barrriers to New Competition*[17] as a point of departure for examining the market conditions that determined whether small, new enterprises were able to innovate without facing insuperable cost disadvantages and had an incentive to do so. Because neither the doctrine concerning barriers to entry nor any other established economic theory at the present time can claim to fully explain those conditions, and because the data that are available are in any case inadequate for testing a fully developed theory, the theoretical framework is employed here as a guide in developing informed judgements and new insights rather than as a basis for rigorously drawn inferences.

In Chapter 2, that analytic framework and its application to the present problem are discussed in some detail. Chapters 3 and 4 are concerned with the computer industry in general and the mainframe industry in particular. During the first 20 years of development of the electronic computer, which began in the mid-1940s, the computer industry was, for practical purposes, dedicated to producing the large, general purpose mainframe. Chapter 3 begins, therefore, with the formative years of the mainframe and its entry into the commercial market in 1951 and continues with the development of the industry until the mid-1960s, when structural changes in the market occurred that paved the way for new products and many new enterprises. Chapter 4 presents an overview of those developments from the mid-1960s to the early 1980s, together with a continuation of the history of the mainframe industry. In Chapter 5 the minicomputer industry is taken up, and in Chapters 6 and 7 two computer peripherals industries, electronic printers and magnetic disk storage devices, are examined. Chapters 8 and 9 cover the semiconductor industry as it developed from the transistor to very-large-scale integrated circuits.

Each of the industry studies is presented within roughly the same format, beginning with a history of the development of the industry and the technology from its inception until sometime in the early 1980s. Then the major innovations and innovators are identified, to the extent necessary for our purposes, with special attention to whether innovators were new or old firms. Finally, the development and structure of the market is analyzed with the objective of explaining the importance of small, new firms as innovators, using the framework set forth in Chapter 2. Chapter 10 presents the general implications of the industry analyses for distinguishing and understanding the roles of new and old enterprises in innovation and the relationship of these roles to market structure.

NOTES

1. Humberto Gerola and Ralph E. Gomory, "Computers in Science and Technology: Early Indications," *Science* (July 6, 1984):11–18.
2. The first four are part of the Electronic Computing Equipment industry which the Census Bureau places in the Standard Industrial Classification (SIC) 3573, and the fifth makes up SIC 3674, Integrated Circuits.
3. Joseph A. Schumpeter, *Capitalism, Socialism, and Democracy*, 3d ed. (New York: Harper & Row, 1950), pp. 106, 82, 83.
4. Ibid., pp. 89, 90.
5. J.K. Galbraith, *American Capitalism* (Boston: Houghton Mifflin, 1956), p. 86.
6. John Jewkes, David Sawers, and Richard Stillerman, *The Sources of Invention*, 2d ed. (New York: Macmillan, 1969), p. 168.
7. Richard R. Nelson, Merton J. Peck, and Edward D. Kalacheck, *Technology, Economic Growth, and Public Policy* (Washington, D.C.: The Brookings Institution, 1967).
8. F.M. Scherer, Hart Committee; Economic Concentration, Hearings before the Sub-Committee on Anti-Trust and Monopoly of the Committee on the Judiciary, U.S. Senate, 87th Congress, Part 3, p. 1,200, cited in Jewkes, Sawers, and Stillerman, *Sources of Invention*.
9. Richard R. Nelson, "Competition, Innovation, Productivity Growth, and Public Policy," in *Towards an Explanation of Economic Growth: Symposium 1980*, ed. Herbert Giersch (Tubingen: Mohr, 1981), pp. 158–59.

10. Galbraith, *American Capitalism*, p. 87.
11. Richard R. Nelson, "The Simple Economics of Basic Scientific Research," *Journal of Political Economy* 67 (1959):297–306.
12. Morton I. Kamien and Nancy L. Schwartz, *Market Structure and Innovation* (Cambridge, England: Cambridge University Press, 1982).
13. Roy Rothwell and Walter Zegvel, *Innovation and the Small and Medium-Sized Firm* (Boston: Kluwer-Nijhoff, 1982).
14. The use of innovative input (expenditures for R&D or employment of research-related personnel) as a dependent variable derives from the theoretical argument that the relative innovativeness of different firms depends on their ability and incentive to invest in R&D.
15. The Standard Industrial Classification of Industries (SIC) employed by the U.S. Bureau of the Census groups manufacturing into 20 two-digit categories and each of those in turn into increasingly smaller and more homogeneous three-, four-, and five-digit groups.
16. Nelson, "Towards and Explanation of Economic Growth, pp. 151–79.
17. Joe S. Bain, *Barriers to New Competition* (Cambridge, Mass.: Harvard University Press, 1956).

2 THE FRAMEWORK FOR ANALYSIS

In order to innovate, a firm must either gain entry to the market for an innovation or transfer the right to produce it to another firm that can enter or has already done so. When patents do not afford protection from imitators, the sale or licensing of production rights rarely offers an innovator much promise of a return on its R&D investment. In the industries studied here, and perhaps most others, entry is generally required in order to exploit an innovative opportunity.[1]

The need for entry directs us to the economic doctrine that is concerned with the structural characteristics of markets that deter new entrants. These barriers to entry impose costs on potential entrants, new or old, that are not imposed on incumbents, with the consequence that new firms can be discouraged from entering even when incumbents' prices are above the competitive level. They result in above normal profits for incumbents and a loss in social welfare; but, more specifically for our purposes, they deter innovation by new entrants except when the cost and performance advantages of an innovation are great enough to overcome the barriers.

In addition to the ability to avoid or overcome barriers that would prevent it from producing competitively, an innovator must have an incentive to invest in whatever R&D is required and assume the more than ordinary risk involved. This incentive rests on the expectation that the cost at which potential competitors can produce an imitation will be high enough relative to the innovator's costs to allow an adequate return on investment.

In the two major sections of this chapter we consider, first, how the theory of market barriers applies to small new innovators and, second, whether the markets from which they are not barred are likely to afford them sufficient incentive to innovate.

BARRIERS TO INNOVATION BY SMALL, NEW FIRMS

Traditional economic theory of barriers to entry offers a point of departure for identifying the characteristics of markets that determine whether small new firms will be capable of entering and innovating, but it does not go far enough. First, the theory is concerned with market performance and, from that perspective, the class of firm that is able to gain entry is not relevant so long as firms most favorably positioned to compete are not barred. It is well recognized that newly founded firms often face obstacles to entry into a market that firms already established in other markets do not.[2] The present effort is concerned with conditions that would deter or prevent a small, new firm from innovating independently of their effects on entry of better established firms or on market performance. From this perspective, cost disadvantages of small, new enterprises in a particular market relative to established firms outside as well as inside of that market must be considered. Finally, while conventional theory emphasizes entry into established markets, innovation often creates new markets. Therefore, it will be necessary to consider specifically how the newness of a market influences entry barriers.

Seminal work on the concept of barriers to entry dates from Joe E. Bain's *Barriers to New Competition,* published in 1956. There, Bain laid out the structural characteristics of markets that determine the potential for new competition from outside, as distinct from rivalry from within, the market and evaluated the importance of barriers that deter entry in a sample of industries.[3] In this context, a "new firm" is a legal entity new to the industry that adds additional production capacity to the industry total. Such firms are called "new entrants" here in order to distinguish them from the newly founded firms that are referred to as "new firms" in this study. According to Bain, any of three market conditions constitutes a barrier:

1. Economies of (large) scale are more than negligible—that is, output of a firm of minimal optimal scale represents a significant fraction of total output.
2. Incumbents have one or more absolute cost advantages relative to potential entrants.
3. Incumbents have an advantage over potential entrants in differentiating their products.

A barrier does not necessarily prevent entry, but the higher any barrier the greater the amount by which prices charged by incumbent firms can exceed the competitive level without encouraging new entry. Incumbents may opt to maintain prices high enough to permit some entry, or a potential entrant that has an advantage over incumbents with respect to one of the conditions of entry may enter successfully in spite of disadvantages with respect to the others. A firm with, say, a sufficient product differentiation advantage achieved through innovation might not be deterred by economy of scale or absolute cost barriers. Following this theory, in order to innovate, a small new firm would have to pursue one or more of four strategies.

1. Enter a market whose structural characteristics offer established firms, whether or not they are incumbents, at best limited advantages overall.
2. Produce a new product or process sufficiently superior to overcome the firm's disadvantages.
3. Enter a market in which the price is maintained sufficiently above minimum average cost to permit it to compete.
4. Enter a market in which large, established firms do not choose to compete.

Bain's formulation of the theory was not the last word. Other economists, most notably Stigler and Baumol, have argued that economies of scale do not always constitute an entry barrier.[4] However, their differences with Bain concern not whether the conditions deter entry but whether the deterrence results in a loss of social welfare.[5] Baumol, Panzar, and Willig define an entry barrier as "anything that requires an expenditure by a new entrant into an industry, but imposes no equivalent cost upon an incumbent." Stigler essentially agrees.[5]

Independently of whether economies of scale in themselves lead to suboptimal performance, they are a deterrent to entry by firms that are handicapped in raising capital due to the absolute cost barrier, and small new firms are handicapped in this respect. Borrowing from Baumol, a deterrent to entry by small new firms can be defined as *anything that requires an expenditure by small, new firms entering an industry but imposes no equivalent cost upon some other potential entrants or on incumbents.* The deterrent will result in a loss in social welfare only when a small, new firm is the most efficient potential entrant.

We consider now the sources of the three classes of barriers and how they affect the ability of small new firms to innovate in a market. The three are not entirely independent. Product differentiation advantages can result from economies of scale in sales promotion, for example. Cost advantages in raising capital may derive from size of firm or from the scale on which capital is raised. The heading under which each is discussed will, as a consequence, occasionally be arbitrary.

Economies of Scale and Scope

Economies of scale exist when the average cost of production falls with increasing design capacity of the firm, assuming all possible adaptations have been carried out to make production at each scale of output as efficient as possible, that the state of technology and factor prices are given and plants are built to produce a particular scale.[6] They can deter entry in either of two ways. What Bain calls the "percentage economies of scale effect" operates when the size of firm that is necessary to achieve minimum optimal scale (MOS) represents a significant percentage of the total capacity of the industry and, in addition, unit costs rise steeply as scale of plant falls short of MOS. MOS is a "significant" percentage of market output or capacity if the addition of the output of a firm of MOS will result in a noticeable reduction in the industry's selling price unless incumbents cut back on production. Under these circumstances, incumbents can generally maintain their prices somewhat above MOS without encouraging entry.

But a firm that is constrained by absolute cost barriers to enter on a small scale cannot be said to be deterred by the percentage effect except in very small markets inasmuch as its output would not be a sufficient proportion of the industry total to noticeably depress the market price. Small firms can be deterred by economies of scale, however, due to the "absolute capital cost effect." It operates independently of the percentage of the market represented by the output of a firm of optimal scale whenever MOS requires a substantial investment of capital, either because the desired plant size is large or because scale economies are achieved by employing capital intensive means of production.[7] (The two often go together.) It may be a deterrent even when the percentage effect is not, or the other way around, and, unlike the percentage effect, it can be associated with economies of scope as well as scale.

The high fixed capital costs that are associated with economies of scale are a deterrent to firms that are at a disadvantage in raising capital, and small new enterprises are handicapped relative to many established firms in the amount of capital they can raise and the price they pay for it as a consequence of diseconomies of both small scale and immaturity. The latter creates an absolute cost barrier.

Any notion of the actual extent of economies of scale in most industries is extremely hard to come by. Most students of the subject would probably agree with Scherer et al. that "estimating MOS values for real-world industries poses numerous conceptual and practical problems."[8] Nevertheless, Stigler was convinced that "in the manufacturing sector there are few industries in which the minimum efficient size of firm is as much as five percent of the industry's output and concentration must be explained on other grounds."[9] Bain essentially agreed. Such hard data as exist usually pertain to technical coefficients of production. Economies of scale in finance, marketing, R&D, and management are still more elusive. I am aware of only one quantitative study of economies of scale in the industries examined here. It pertains to the technical coefficients of production of a single IBM mainframe computer, discussed in Chapter 3. In general we must rely on qualitative judgments to assess their importance and, for this purpose, it is useful to have in mind the major sources from which economies of scale derive.

At the heart of most scale economies are the inherent lumpiness of factors of production (most notably fixed capital but also management and labor) and the advantages of specialization. They can, in principle, occur in any of the activities of a firm: the technical production process, management, physical distribution, selling, purchasing, bearing risk, raising capital, and R&D. (In some activities diseconomies of scale occur as well.) The influence of scale economies in any one of the activities on the overall production function depends, of course, on the significance of the activity as a proportion of total cost of the product. Scale economies may be specific to the number of plants, or to the size of the firm as well as to the scale of a single plant, but economies from increasing the number of plants derive mainly from opportunities to minimize costs in transporting raw materials or finished products,[10] and in industries like those we consider, whose transportation costs are a small fraction of the value of the product, they are at best minimal. Finally, economies of scope may be available to a firm producing two or more different products when complementarities occur in production, marketing, or other functions.

Technical Coefficients of Production.   With increasing scale of plant it is possible to break down tasks into more specialized, and therefore efficient, functions and to utilize more fully production units that cannot economically be broken down into smaller units. When economies of scale are available in the construction of plant and equipment or when a high threshold of facilities is required, the ability to keep large or specialized units of production more fully employed reduces average costs. Large units may also require proportionally fewer workers to operate and further scale economies may be achieved by reducing the set-up time required in shifting from one operation to another and in reducing the number of standby factors that are needed to cope with emergencies and maintenance (economies of massed reserves). If there is a compelling advantage in vertical integration of production processes within a firm, optimum scale must be large enough to employ at least one unit of MOS in each of the integrated processes.

There appears to be a consensus that in most manufacturing industries technical economies can be fully exploited at a relatively small scale of plant. This is even more likely to be the case in newly developing industries where standardization of products and processes has not arrived and technological change is so rapid that sinking funds into dedicated production facilities is not justified. Increasing long-run average costs may be associated not only with an increasing rate of output per unit of time but, as Silberston emphasizes, with the total volume of output over time.[11] When a cost is fixed in relation to cumulative output (product design is a good example), its average per unit of product falls as cumulative output rises.

Research and Development.   Since the industries examined here are among the most R&D intensive in the economy, scale economies in R&D can lead to significantly declining long-run average costs in the overall production function. Because R&D is itself a fixed cost, it is especially important to distinguish between the two sources of scale economies mentioned by Silberston: increasing returns to R&D as R&D input or output increases, on the one hand, and declining costs of R&D per unit output of the firm as the fixed cost of R&D is spread over cumulatively increasing units of the final product.[12] The extent to which economies of scale exist in the first sense is controversial. In principle, they could result from the same sources as in the technical production function. Because larger firms generally produce a more diverse range of products, increasing returns can also accrue from economies of scope due to complementarities in R&D pertaining to different products. In addition, as Nelson points out, the more diversified the firm's output, the greater the chance that an R&D result will find application within the firm.[13]

The problem of evaluating economies of scale or scope is especially intractable in R&D because of the virtual impossibility of measuring R&D output. In the absence of a direct measure of economies of scale, investigators have often focused on the supposed consequences of the phenomenon, namely an increase in R&D expenditures or employment as a percentage of output of the firm as size of firm increases. Fisher and Temin have shown formally that this relationship cannot by itself be used to test the hypothesis regarding economies of scale,[14] and statistical studies have led to ambiguous and often contradictory results that frequently defy interpretation.

Kamien and Schwartz, reviewing numerous attempts to measure the relationship between size of firm and R&D activity, concluded that scale economies exist in the innovation production function up to a modest size of firm and diminish thereafter.[15] Nelson noted, however, that R&D intensity as a function of size varies noticeably among industries and that the variance among firms within a given industry is often quite large.[16] Schmookler pointed out that differences in R&D output may be associated with factors other than firm size, such as quality of staff, that are themselves correlated either positively or negatively with size of firm.[17] Some studies concentrate on only a few industries and, more important for the present study, R&D statistics are not available for very small firms. It is obvious, however, that many R&D projects cannot be completed at all on a small scale and, once a product line is established, the minimum R&D necessary to prevent the firm from falling behind advancing technology can be substantial.

Although, on balance, we are left in the dark concerning the nature of the R&D production function, we can be certain that returns to scale exist in the second sense, namely as the fixed cost of R&D is spread over cumulatively increasing units of the product, R&D cost per unit of product declines. The same can be said for the design of integrated circuits and systems software.

Marketing and Maintenance.   Marketing and maintenance offer opportunities for scale economies, mainly in travel costs of personnel when it is conducted by personal sales representatives and when potential customers are numerous and widely dispersed. But the availability and use of third-party service organizations and distributors can extend the advantages of large scale to small producers. It is not well established that there are economies of scale in advertising, and advertising is not, in any case, an important selling tool in most producer durables industries. The advantage of size in transferring a favorable image to new products represents an economy of scale in product differentiation. A diversified firm can sometimes exploit economies of scope in direct marketing. They can be especially fruitful in marketing complementary products, such as components of integrated computer systems.

Management.   Economies of scale or of scope arise in management for the same reasons they appear in production: specialization of labor and indivisibilities in the performance of certain functions. But, perhaps more than other activities, management is subject to diseconomies of scale when it comes to coordinating decisions, maintaining communication and providing incentives to members of the staff. Where markets or technology are changing rapidly and swift response is necessary to exploit new opportunities, small-scale management may have an advantage.

Bearing Risk and Raising Capital.   The greater the capital required for entry, the greater the handicap to firms that pay a relatively high price for it or face severe limits on the amount of capital they can assemble. There is ample evidence that small, new firms are subject to both of these disadvantages. The question that concerns us in this section is the extent to which they are a function of scale. Newness is also a handicap in the capital market but it represents an absolute cost barrier rather than a diseconomy of small scale.

Small firms, by virtue of their size, may be handicapped in the capital market either because their size subjects them to greater business risk or because they are deprived of economies of scale in processing loans and floating securities. Business risks can be associated, positively or negatively, with a firm's size. Their main sources are unforeseen reductions in market demand due to cyclical or product-specific forces, increased competition, and changes in technology. Insofar as large firms operate in stabler markets where they face more limited competition, these risks will be smaller than otherwise, but not directly as a function of scale. The fact that larger firms tend to be more diversified also reduces their business risk. So long as investors are free to diversify their portfolios, modern portfolio theory argues that diversification of a firm's product menu will not reduce the risk premium demanded by investors, but nevertheless, management may wish to diversify its own portfolio and be willing to enter markets for this purpose under conditions less favorable than would a firm with no other assets.[18] An additional business risk to which small firms are singularly vulnerable is the loss of management through death or withdrawal since such firms typically depend on the leadership one or a handful of persons without a broad-based distribution of responsibility.

Small firms, on the other hand, are in many ways better equipped to cope with change. Large firms tend to employ more specialized equipment, which is less easily adapted to shifting demand, and, because economies of scale are frequently realized through capital intensive means of production, they are handicapped in cutting costs when demand falls. E.A.G. Robinson summed up their inflexibility this way:

> The more elaborate a firm is, the more highly specialized in equipment, the better adapted in lay-out to the existing rhythm of production, the more expensive and difficult will be its re-equipment, the more complicated the task of moving and adjusting to their new functions heavy and capricious pieces of machinery. . . . The smaller firm may be never so well adapted, but will be never so ill adapted, and will enjoy, therefore, a certain advantage when changes of product are frequently necessary, and reorganization is expensive.[19]

The main effects of scale on the availability of capital to small firms appears to derive, then, more from diseconomies in acquiring funds in the capital market rather than from the greater business risk to which the capital is subjected. These effects influence both the amount of capital they can assemble and the price they pay for it. Small firms have limited internal sources of funds and the value of their assets does not usually permit them to borrow extensively. At the same time, they pay more for the capital they do acquire. Some are unable to raise capital through public sale of securities at all, but this restriction may have more to do with the particular industry than firm size.

The higher cost of capital is chiefly related to the cost of flotation. Because the cost of issuing new securities is more or less fixed independent of the size of the flotation, the cost per dollar of capital is inversely proportional to the size of the issue. A study in the early 1960s found that the main difference in the cost of funds to small, compared with large, firms was in the flotation cost rather than the interest cost,[20] confirming an earlier investigation in the 1950s that concluded that the cost of floating new bond issues as a percentage of their selling price was eight times as great for issues under $1 million as for issues over $20 million, and four times as great in the case of common stock issues.[21]

Absolute Cost Barriers

The absolute cost barrier deters entry of new firms into a market when their unit costs of production (including distribution, R&D, and so forth) are higher at every scale of operation than those of incumbents or other established firms that are potential competitors. In other words, new firms' production functions lie above those of the latter. A firm may derive an absolute cost advantage from any of four sources: 1) control of strategic factor supplies, 2) ability to secure factors of production at lower prices than potential entrants due to market imperfections, 3) control of superior production techniques, and 4) conditions in the market for investable funds that impose higher capital costs or more severe capital rationing on other firms.[22] In addition, as Hines observed, new enterprises may face handicaps in competing with firms that are already established due to their lack of experience, lack of a going organization or of developed channels of marketing, purchasing, and information.[23]

Factor Supplies and Prices.   The first absolute cost barrier played no role in the markets examined here, there being no strategic materials of importance to production that were not available to potential entrants. The single critical scarce factor of production is skilled and talented technical personnel. The market for this and other resources is a notably competitive one, which would appear to rule out number 2 as well. Some firms are demonstrably better able to attract extraordinary talent than others, but incumbents or other established firms do not necessarily hold the advantage. Small, new enterprises often provide a more stimulating research environment and greater potential rewards, both financial and psychic, and offer entrepreneurial opportunities to individuals who might be unwilling to accept positions within the hierarchy of a large, going organization. Only small, privately held companies are in a position to offer founders and employees chances to make substantial fortunes through stock options or other profit sharing devices, and the federal government's tax treatment of stock options has favored privately held companies in the 1970s and 1980s. On the other hand, large, established firms can satisfy the demands of specialists who prefer stability, job security, and the opportunity to involve themselves in long-run and costly research. Competitive advantages in attracting personnel of very high caliber may be attributable as much to idiosyncracies of individual organizations as to general characteristics such as size or age of firm.

Production Techniques.   Control of superior production techniques generally rests on control of patents or proprietary information. Patents can be fairly ineffective in protecting production techniques when their holders are obliged to cross license liberally, either because they need to employ numerous other patented products or processes themselves or as a consequence of antitrust pressures. Moreover, when the speed of technological change makes patents obsolete faster than they can be obtained or successfully contested, their usefulness is quite limited. Certain types of inventions are not patentable (this was the case with computer software and circuit design until fairly recently), nor can process technology that rests heavily on experience be readily patented. Finally, patent applications reveal proprietary information that may be of value to actual or potential competitors.

Unpatented knowledge or know-how that is gained from experience in production can give an incumbent a cost advantage, the more so the steeper the experience curve. Its effectiveness as a deterrent to entry depends, inversely, on the ease with which it can be transferred to potential competitors, for example by defectors from the company, and on the speed with which the learning obsolesces.[24]

Capital Costs.   New firms face a disadvantage vis-à-vis established companies in the price they pay for capital and the amount they can raise by virtue of their age in addition to their small size. Demsetz attributed the higher cost to the expense investors must incur in acquiring information which a long-lived firm can reduce on the basis of a history and a reputation.[25] New firms also lack accumulated reserves, and, finally, new management's inexperience increases the actual risk of failure.[26] A partial substitute for a business record can be a management team with an exemplary record of performance elsewhere, however.

For our purposes the question of whether higher cost and stricter rationing of capital are more closely related to a firm's small size or to its immaturity is not paramount, since the firms we focus on are characterized by both. During some years of the 1960s and 1970s the popularity of small, new electronics firms in the capital market may actually have made it possible for them to obtain funds at a lower cost than others. With the emergence of a public market for venture capital in the 1960s and an accumulation of spectacularly successful new electronics firms, the availability of funds improved. But, under any circumstances, the total amount of capital that a start-up firm can raise is severely limited. The venture capital market exists to assemble relatively small packages of funds to invest in enterprises that hold promise of quick returns.[27] This objective bounds the nature of the innovations that a new firm can undertake and requires it to follow strategies to minimize the amount of capital needed during start-up (i.e., the maximum net accumulated cash outflow that is sustained before cash inflow exceeds outflow). That amount can be expressed as a function of the scale of output, the scope of output and the average value of product (which together determine the total value of output per unit of time), and of the capital employed per dollar of output. The purpose of expressing the determinants of capital requirements in this somewhat unconventional way is to facilitate association of the determinants with industry characteristics about which some inferences can be drawn in a study such as the present one, in contrast to studies that investigate the internal operations of individual firms. The first three are associated, respectively, with economies of scale and of scope and with the nature and packaging of the product, while the latter is associated with the advantages of capital intensive means of production, vertical integration, investment in R&D and in other intangibles, such as advertising, and the need for working capital.

It was concluded earlier that the most significant source of scale economies in the industries examined here is likely to be the fixed cost of R&D spread over increasing units of production. The greater the requirements for R&D, the greater the minimum optimum scale of production. But, in addition, R&D is itself a long-term capital cost that must be met regardless of the scale of production. Large R&D requirements thus doubly influence the amount of capital needed, by raising MOS and also the capital intensity of any given scale of output. A firm can rarely innovate without investing in R&D, but it can focus on industry sectors, products, and types of innovation that reduce the investment, the recovery period, and the risk. R&D expenditures can sometimes be limited by transferring to new applications the results of R&D that has been conducted elsewhere, often accomplished with the transfer of personnel. Moreover, fundamental advances in science and technology from time to time produce an outpouring of opportunities for the application of new knowledge to the development of commercial products that do not, themselves, require a great deal of further research. This was demonstrably the case in solid state electronics and computers beginning in the 1950s.

Production cannot take place without a major investment in fixed plant and equipment in industries like public utilities, while in others, like computers, capital intensive techniques do not afford compelling advantages. During the early stage of a product cycle the rapid obsolescence of technology can make investment in more than a minimal amount of specialized equipment uneconomical. We will see that this stage can last anywhere from two years to two decades.

By disintegrating the production process, capital costs can be converted into variable costs and, at the same time, value added reduced as a proportion of total value of output. The practicality and cost effectiveness of integration vary from industry to industry, depending on the extent to which the production process can be broken down into discrete stages and on structural characteristics of markets that influence the availability of merchant suppliers of discrete inputs. Vertical disintegration entails a loss of secrecy, however, and Scherer found quality control as well to be an important motive for integration in a sample of 12 industries.[28] The assurance of a reliable supply of components in rapidly growing market drove large electrical equipment manufacturers to integrate upstream in the mid-1970s, usually through mergers, and finally, integration is increasingly advantageous as the complexity of interrelationships between stages of production increases.

Working capital averages a higher percentage of total capital assets for small manufacturing firms than for large, but it usually involves less risk than long-term capital. Lenders will generally extend less credit for a given amount of collateral to small, new enterprises than to established firms, and banks may require them to hold larger balances on deposit for a given size of loan. Working capital requirements are fairly limited in industries like electronics where large supplies of finished products need not be stocked to meet fluctuations in demand and there is no call to accumulate raw materials to hedge against seasonal or cyclical fluctuations in supply. The extension of credit or leasing of equipment to customers raises working capital needs, however, whereas sales to government agencies who provide short-term financing through progress payments advanced during the production process can reduce them.

A negative cash flow during the start-up phase of producing and marketing a new product is common to both old and new firms, but an established enterprise has marketing and purchasing channels in place as well as an organized management to speed the process along as well as greater liquidity to help it sustain temporary losses.

Product Differentiation

Product differentiation results from preferences on the part of consumers for the product of an incumbent over potentially similar substitutes. It is a deterrent to entry by small new firms whenever it is based on characteristics of the product or of an established producer that they can duplicate only at greater cost.[29] Product differentiation can result from differences in the design or physical quality of competing products, from efforts of sellers to distinguish their products through packaging or branding or offering auxiliary services to buyers, and from advertising or sales promotions.[30] We want to distinguish here between a "physical product differentiation" barrier and a "subjective product differentiation" barrier as they apply to small new firms. The former results from the inability of such firms to produce at the same unit cost a physical imitation of an incumbent's product (including services that may accompany it) because of factors other than economies of scale or absolute cost barriers. The second results from the inability of such firms to generate the same degree of consumer confidence in the desirability of their products as can incumbents or other potential entrants for a given cost.

A product differentiation advantage based on physical characteristics usually derives from patents or trade secrets pertaining to product design. Patents do not always provide effective barriers to physical imitation for reasons that were mentioned earlier with respect to patents on process technology. Trade secrets are sometimes more effective barriers but not always for very long. Their conspicuous success in creating barriers to competition in some sectors of the computer industry derives from complementary relationships between the customer's software and a vendor's equipment, or between different components of a system, when circuit design is proprietary.

Subjective product differentiation is generally based on the confidence that an established firm is able to instill in potential customers concerning the quality and reliability of its product and the prospects that the firm will survive to provide service, replacements, and product enhancements when necessary. Its source is often a reputation accumulated over years of promoting and supplying the same product or a related one. Because a reputation cannot be built overnight, new firms are handicapped in competing with older firms, and the larger the firm the more broadly its reputation is likely to be spread. The more inscrutable, complex, and costly the technology, the less sophisticated the customer, the less frequent the customer's purchases; the greater the customer's need for future servicing and product enhancements, the greater is the seller's opportunity to exploit an image. For producers that supply other producers, a track record is important to demonstrate an ability to meet specifications and delivery schedules.

Lacking an established reputation, an innovator may achieve a subjective product differentiation advantage by virtue of being the first mover, thereby deterring later entrants. Schmalensee[31] observed that goods whose quality is best understood by the customer through experience with use are especially likely to confer this advantage, the more so the greater the cost and risk of acquiring the experience. We will encounter it again in considering incentives to innovate.

In markets for new products the ability to set standards can also confer a product differentiation advantage. Where standardization is important, customers may be reluctant to accept the product of the first mover unless they perceive that the firm has the clout to make its standard stick.

THE INCENTIVE TO INNOVATE

In order to innovate, a firm needs an incentive to invest the resources necessary to develop the innovation, over and above those that will be required to produce and market it, and to assume the more than ordinary risks involved. Under perfectly competitive conditions a firm can expect its earnings from the sale of a product to afford a "normal" rate of profit on its investment in plant, equipment, and other assets that are used in production and marketing, but if it is to have an incentive to invest in the R&D for a new product it must expect to receive a price sufficiently greater than the unit cost of production to include a return on R&D as well, and that return will have to be as great as the firm could expect to earn on any other use of the resources, including compensation for the often very considerable risk that is involved in launching a new product.

The prospect of above normal earnings on producing and marketing an innovation rests on the likelihood that the innovation will result in an increase in the potential surplus of the total value of product over the total cost of production (the sum of producers' and consumers' surplus), net of the cost of R&D, and that the innovator will be able to appropriate some of that surplus. Whether the return will justify the innovator's investment in R&D depends on the increase in potential surplus per dollar of investment in R&D and on the proportion of the surplus that can be captured. Figures 2–1 and 2–2 illustrate how the potential surplus would come about in a simplified case of a cost-cutting innovation. A different example could be developed for an innovation that increased the value of a product with results similar in their essentials.

Figure 2–1.   Industry Demand and Supply before Innovation.

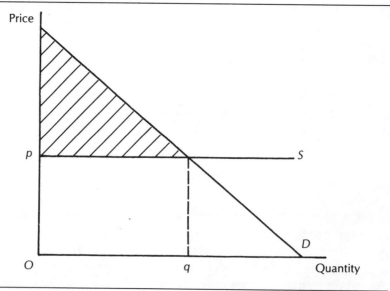

In Figure 2–1, D is the industry demand curve for an existing product before innovation occurs, and S is the supply curve, representing long-run average cost of production to firms in the industry, including a normal return on investment, at each level of output before the innovation takes place. To simplify exposition it is assumed that firms have identical linear production functions. In a perfectly competitive market, q units will be sold at price p in equilibrium, and a surplus will accrue to consumers equal to the area of the shaded triangle. (The consumers' surplus is the sum of the values of each additional unit of the product, measured by the price consumers would be willing to pay for it, minus its market price.) If the supply curve were drawn with an upward slope, a surplus would accrue as well to producers. The price p is equal to average cost of production.

In Figure 2–2, the curve S' depicts the industry supply curve after a fall in average cost of production due to a cost-cutting innovation, where average cost does not include the cost of R&D necessary to bring about the innovation. The innovation increases the potential surplus that is available to consumers and producers combined by an amount equal to the area $p'pAC$. If the innovator had no competitors and supplied the entire market demand q at the old price p, the innovator would capture potential surplus equal to $pp'AB$ in return for its investment in R&D.

Figure 2–2. Industry and Supply after a Cost-Cutting Innovation.

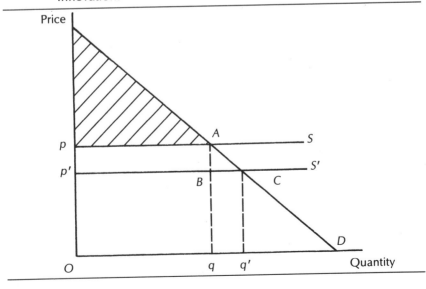

The remaining potential surplus ABC would be lost to society. (Only a perfectly discriminating monopolist could capture the entire increase in surplus.) This would not necessarily be the optimal strategy, of course; that would depend also on the elasticity of D.

Under perfectly competitive conditions, if potential competitors have the same production function as the innovator and can reproduce the innovation without any investment in R&D themselves, the price will fall to p', equal to the new average cost; the quantity sold will incease to q', and all of the potential surplus will accrue to consumers with none remaining to compensate the innovator for its R&D. To the extent that potential competitors must incur some minimum R&D cost in order to replicate the innovation, the price that the innovator can charge without losing sales to competitors will exceed p'. If they must incur R&D costs as great per unit of output as the innovator's, the competitive price will not fall below the level that provides a return on the innovator's R&D as great as competitors would demand. Because R&D is a fixed and nondepreciating cost, its cost per unit of product will, of course, be smaller the greater a firm's cumulative output.

The incentive for the innovator to invest in R&D depends, then, primarily on 1) the value of the potential increase in total surplus per dollar of its investment in R&D, and 2) the difference between the innovator's unit cost of producing the innovation once it is developed and the unit cost to potential competitors of reproducing it, including their R&D. (Under less than perfect competition it would depend also on the elasticity of D, which determines the optimum price of the monopolist.) The first of these can be described, in turn, as dependent on the value of the opportunity for an innovation that is exogenous to the firm and the innovator's efficiency in developing, producing, and marketing it.

To help clarify these relationships, let us call Y_i the expected present value of the potential increase in surplus ($p'pAC$ in Figure 2–2) for an innovation by a firm i, I_i the present value of i's investment in R&D, and P_i the proportion of the surplus i can expect to capture. Then, in order for i to have an incentive to invest in the innovation, $(P_iY_i-I_i)/I_i$ must be as great as i could expect to earn on any alternative investment involving similar risk. The value of an exogenous opportunity for innovation is defined here to be equal to $(Y_l-I_l)/I_l$ when l's costs are as low as any other firms. $(Y_i-I_i)/I_i$, therefore, depends on the value of the exogenous opportunity for innovation and on i's cost of developing, producing, and marketing it relative to that of the most efficient firm. P_i, as we saw, depends on the unit cost to potential imitators of reproducing the innovation after it is on the market relative to i's costs net of R&D.

The number and values of exogenous opportunities for innovation vary from one market to another. Few would argue with the proposition that in semiconductors and computers they were significantly greater than in many other industries during the past 35 years. Because small new firms are confronted with greater cost disadvantages in some markets than in others, their showing as innovators during any historical period will depend in part on the distribution of opportunities for innovation among different markets at that time.

Given $(Y_i - I_i)/I_i$, P_i determines whether the expected return on the innovator's investment will provide an incentive to innovate. P_i depends on the cost advantage over potential imitators that the innovator can expect for any given period of time, which, in turn, depends on barriers to their entry in the market. How can a firm that lacks the advantages of scale or maturity count on preventing imitators from appropriating the surplus needed to assure an adequate return on its investment?[32] By avoiding markets in which they face significant cost disadvantages, small, new innovators reduce the chance that larger and better established firms will undersell them. Yet markets without barriers to entry usually offer little protection from imitators. And even a firm whose costs of production are as low as any potential competitor's must contend with the fact that the R&D costs of imitators and the risks they assume stand a good chance of being lower than the innovator's original costs.

Because R&D is a fixed cost the innovating firm can compensate for higher R&D costs to the extent that its volume of sales is greater than competitors'. This puts a premium on the innovator's gaining the largest market share in the long run as well as the short-term monopoly that an innovator can usually count on. For either of these, in the markets to which they have access, small, new innovators must bank on the advantages that accrue to them by virtue of being first movers. First mover advantages are most obvious when the innovator carves out a new market that is free of incumbents, but they are not necessarily negligible when the innovation improves upon a product in an existing market. There are at least seven potential sources of advantage to a first mover.

1. Once an innovation is on the market, the fact that imitators must invest time, in addition to resources, to develop a replica delays

the arrival of competition. If potential imitators have already begun development of a similar product before the innovation appears, the lag may not be long.

2.   Once the replica is developed, the time it takes competitors to mobilize resources and arrange for production and marketing of it further postpones the arrival of competition. For any given lag, the innovator's share of the surplus depends on the proportion of the market that it can mobilize the resources to serve during the interval.

3.   If production of the innovation requires a specialized resource that is limited in supply, the first mover may have an opportunity to monopolize the supply or secure it at a lower price than can followers.

4.   A first mover may be able to protect his innovation from imitation through patents or trade secrets.

5.   If the production process is characterized by a steep learning curve, the first mover will, for a time at least, enjoy lower unit costs than followers.

6.   When the market for a new product is so limited that one small firm of optimal scale can serve all of the market (a natural monopoly), the "percentage economy of scale" barrier may protect the first mover from competition.

7.   A first mover may enjoy a subjective product differentiation advantage, especially in the marketing of "experience" goods: products whose characteristics are difficult for customers to evaluate other than through purchase and use.[33] Once customers have invested in experimenting with such a product and are satisfied, followers can attract them only by charging a lower price or incurring higher selling costs, with the consequence that the first mover can sustain a price greater than average cost without losing his initial customers. The greater the risk of experimenting with a product relative to its cost and the less frequently individual customers purchase the product, the greater the barrier. As the market for the new product grows, competitors have a chance to tie up new customers in the same way, but its head start may permit the first mover to retain a larger market share than any one of them in the long run.

Although first-mover advantages are potentially significant, in many of the markets in which small, new enterprises can innovate they will, on balance, be quite insubstantial, allowing the innovator to appropriate only a very small proportion of the surplus from an innovation. Under such circumstances, an adequate return on investment depends on a high value of the exogenous opportunity for innovation.

GROWTH, TECHNOLOGICAL CHANGE, AND NEW MARKETS

All of the markets examined here underwent rapid growth and technological change. Moreover, they were all new at the point that their story is taken up, and not infrequently small, new innovators created entirely new markets. How do these factors bear on the ability of such firms to overcome or surmount potential barriers to entry?

Some studies suggest that industry growth can be adverse to the entry of new firms, but in the present instance this was not the case.[34] The inability of established companies to keep pace with a rapid growth in demand for their products can make room for small new firms to enter by supplying excess demand. Moreover, when technology advances very rapidly, no product remains state of the art for long and many products are obsolete by the time they are on the market. Before a firm updates its technology, competitors have a chance to gain temporary advantages by leapfrogging ahead with more current models, and obsolescence can force some incumbents out of the market. Small firms often respond faster than others to new technological opportunities because of their more flexible organizational structures, smaller investments in established technology, and focus on a single component of a system rather than an entire system or full line of products.

Rapidly changing technology provides opportunities for new firms to innovate in virgin territory, creating markets that are free of large, well-established competitors by offering new products that are not substitutes for existing products but, rather, perform functions that were not previously possible or economically feasible and that appeal to customers who are not served by established producers. A market without incumbents is not necessarily free of barriers, however. It differs from an established one chiefly in that the competition has not yet arrived. Competition is waiting in the wings, nevertheless, and a new firm contemplating entry must weigh its threat or risk failure at the hands of competitors after it enters. How does the newness of a market affect the conditions of entry?

A new market does not confront the first mover, new or established, with the percentage economies of scale barrier, but that is not, in any event, a deterrent to small, new firms except when demand is very limited. It is, rather, scale economies combined with the absolute capital cost barrier that deters small, new firms. A firm that is first into a market may operate profitably at less than MOS in the short run, but if its average cost is significantly above the MOS level it will soon have to increase scale or invite competition from firms that can. Similarly, if established firms from other markets can transfer advantages to the new market, the first mover's advantage may be short-lived. A new market affords a firm breathing space, however, to accumulate profits that can be invested in greater scale or to demonstrate promise that attracts more capital or permits the firm to be sold at a profit to one that can support greater scale.

New markets also offer greater opportunities to exploit first-mover advantages and, finally, established firms typically respond more slowly to opportunities in newly created markets than to opportunities closer to home. We will observe that they rarely chose to exercise their potential advantages in markets that were created by new firms. Instead, first movers in such markets were generally followed by other new firms.

NOTES

1. In a recent survey by Levin and his associates of a large percentage of all U.S. firms that engage in significant R&D, patents were rated the least effective mechanism of appropriation. Secrecy was rated somewhat more effective. See Richard C. Levin, Alvin K. Klevorick, Richard R. Nelson, and Sidney G. Winter, "Survey Research on R&D Appropriability and Technological Opportunity, Part I: Appropriability," unpublished manuscript, Yale University, New Haven, Conn., July 1984.
2. Howard H. Hines, "Effectiveness of Entry by Already Established Firms," *Quarterly Journal of Economics* (February 1957):132–50. R.E. Caves and M.E. Porter, "From Entry Barriers to Mobility Barriers," *Quarterly Journal of Economics* (May 1977):241–42.
3. Bain measured the advantage of incumbents in a given market over potential competitors according to the percentage by which incumbents can, as a consequence of that advantage, persistently maintain the price of their products above the competitive level without attracting new firms into the industry. The "competitive price level" is equal to the minimum attainable average cost of production, distribution, and

selling, allowing for a normal return on investment. See pages 5 and 6 of Bain, *Barriers to New Competition* (Cambridge, Mass.: Harvard University Press, 1956).

4. George J. Stigler, *The Organization of Industry* (Homewood, Ill.: Irwin, 1968). William J. Baumol, John C. Panzar, and Robert D. Willig, *Contestable Markets and the Theory of Industry Structure* (New York: Harcourt Brace Jovanovich, 1982), ch. 10.

5. Baumol, Panzar, and Willig, *Contestable Markets and the Theory of Industry Structure*, p. 282. Stigler, *Organization of Industry*. A barrier reduces the sum of consumers' and producers' surplus whereas, the above argue, fixed costs and scale economies need not do so. The distinction between long-run fixed costs and sunk costs is critical in Baumol's case. The former can be reduced only by ceasing production altogether, whereas the latter cannot be eliminated even with total cessation of production except in the long run. Costs that are fixed but not sunk present incumbents and new entrants with the same opportunity costs and do not meet Baumol's criterion for an entry barrier. Although high fixed, as distinct from sunk, costs can set the stage for a natural monopoly, entry can be deterred only by charging the competitive price.

6. Aubrey Silberston, "Economies of Scale in Theory and in Practice," *Economic Journal* (Supplement, March 1972):369–91.

7. Bain, *Barriers to New Competition*, p. 55.

8. F.M. Scherer, Alan Beckenstein, Erich Kaufer, Dennis R. Murphy, and Francine Bougeon-Massen, *The Economics of Multi-Plant Operations: An International Comparison Study* (Cambridge, Mass.: Harvard University Press, 1975).

9. Stigler, *Organization of Industry*, p. 223.

10. Scherer et al., *Economics of Multi-Plant Operations*.

11. Silberston, "Economies of Scale in Theory and Practice."

12. Ibid.

13. Richard R. Nelson, "The Simple Economics of Basic Scientific Research," *Journal of Political Economy* 67 (1959):297–306.

14. Franklin M. Fisher and Peter Temin, "Returns to Scale in R&D: What Does the Schumpeterian Hypothesis Show?" *Journal of Political Economy* (January–February 1973):56–70.

15. Morton I. Kamien and Nancy L. Schwartz, *Market Structure and Innovation* (Cambridge, England: Cambridge University Press, 1982).

16. Richard R. Nelson, "Competition, Innovation, Productivity Growth, and Public Policy," in *Towards an Explanation of Economic Growth: Symposium 1980,* ed. Herbert Giersch (Tubingen: Mohn, 1981).

17. Jacob Schmookler, *Patents, Invention and Economic Change* (Cambridge, Mass.: Harvard University Press, 1972).

18. Caves and Porter, "From Entry Barriers to Mobility Barriers."

19. E.A.G. Robinson, *The Structure of Competitive Industry* (Chicago: University of Chicago Press, revised 1958), p. 76.

20. S.H. Archer and L.G. Faerber, "Firm Size and Cost of Internally Secured Capital," *Journal of Finance* (March 1966):69–83.

21. Glen R. Miller, "Long Term Small Business Financing from the Underwriter's Point of View," *Journal of Finance* (May 1961):280–90.

22. Some economists, such as Baumol, classify the higher profits that result from numbers 1 and 3 as economic rents that do not result in a misallocation of resources; but, once again, the issue relates to the social welfare implications rather than to the ability of any particular class of firm to enter.

23. Hines, "Effectiveness of Entry by Already Established Firms."

24. The return to experience is sometimes regarded as an economic rent, in which case experience is not strictly speaking a barrier to entry. It nevertheless can effectively deter entry of new firms.

25. Howard Demsetz, "Barriers to Entry," *American Economic Review* (March 1982):47–57.

26. Pearson et al. report that managerial incompetence is considered to be the primary cause of failure among new and small businesses. [Hunt Pearson, Charles M. Williams, and Gordon Donaldson, *Basic Business Finance*, 4th ed. (Homewood, Ill.: Irwin, 1971).]

27. Funding limits are less strict when the capital is invested in assets whose value can be recovered if the enterprise fails rather than in R&D or other intangibles. We are reminded here of the distinction that Baumol makes between fixed and sunk costs. When capital is invested in resources such as rolling stock or aircraft that can be transferred to another firm or industry relatively costlessly, recovery of capital is far more certain than when it is invested in the development of a new product.

28. Scherer et al., *Economics of Multi-Plant Operations.*

29. E.H. Chamberlin, who first focused attention on the phenomenon in his *Theory of Monopolistic Competition* in 1933, treated product differentiation that cannot be duplicated by other firms at the same cost as a special case, the only one leading to monopoly profits [8th ed. (Cambridge, Mass.: Harvard University Press, 1962), pp. 112, 113]. In his more general case, competition among product differentiating firms results in prices greater than minimum average cost but not monopoly profits. It is only in the first sense that it is an entry barrier.

30. Stigler (*Organization of Industry*) added that other natural or legal obstacles to perfect imitation (such as franchises) can also lead to a sloping demand curve for the product of an incumbent. In order to meet his definition of a barrier to entry, product differentiation must impose higher costs on potential entrants than on incumbents at any scale of operation, while Bain's definition allows that economies of scale in

advertising or other product differentiating measures can also lead to barriers. Although the effect of scale economies on market performance may be in dispute, as we saw above, their deterrence to entry of new firms is not. For our purposes it does not matter whether a new firm is deterred by high costs of imitation at any scale or by the fact that it cannot enter at a sufficient scale to avoid higher costs than established firms.

31. Richard Schmalensee, "Product Differentiation Advantages of Pioneering Brands," *American Economic Review* (June 1982):349–65.

32. By way of testing the Schumpeterian hypothesis, economists in recent years have analyzed formally the effect that an increase in the number of firms that invest in R&D for an innovation would have on any one firm's expectation of being the first to develop the innovation and, in turn, on the total amount of R&D that will be undertaken by all firms in the industry. See F.M. Scherer, "Research and Development Resource Allocation under Rivalry," *Quarterly Journal of Economics* (August 1967):359–94; Glen C. Loury, "Market Structure and Innovation," *Quarterly Journal of Economics* (August 1979):395–410; and Morton I. Kamien and Nancy L. Schwartz, "The Degree of Rivalry for Maximum Innovative Activity," *Quarterly Journal of Economics* (May 1976):245–60.

The issue is, Does the greater number of firms that make up competitive markets lead to an increase in the amount of R&D that will be undertaken? The assumption that underlies these models is that the first to succeed can monopolize the innovation through patents or other means and capture all of the stream of rewards that is available from it. But a prior question that needs to be raised is whether it is reasonable to assume that the first to succeed can monopolize the innovation.

33. Schmalensee, "Product Differentiation Advantages of Pioneering Brands."

34. In an investigation of 50 industries in the fifties and sixties, Gorecki concluded that while industry growth was the main determinant of entry, it did not help new firms overcome entry barriers. Sylos-Labini observed that when a market grows rapidly, entrants who can exploit economies of scale are able to be accommodated and small firms may be driven out. [Paul K. Gorecki, "The Determinants of Entry of New and Diversifying Enterprises," *Applied Economics* (June 1975):139–47; and Paolo Sylos-Labini, *Oligopoly and Technological Progress* (Cambridge, Mass.: Harvard University Press, 1962).]

3 MAINFRAME COMPUTERS: THE FIRST TWO DECADES

The history of innovation during the first 20 years of the electronic computer industry was basically the story of large computers called mainframes. Minicomputers made their appearance around 1960 but it was not until after the middle of that decade that their market exploded, and microcomputers did not arrive on the scene until the late seventies. The study begins, therefore, with the birth of the mainframe computer in the forties, followed by the inception and early growth of the commercial market for the general purpose mainframe from 1951 to 1965. Chapter 4 explores developments in the market as a whole, and the mainframe industry in particular, from the mid-sixties to the early eighties.

The structural characteristics of the computer industry were markedly different during each of the three periods. During the first period the commercial market had not emerged and innovation depended mainly on nonprofit research institutions, usually with government sponsorship. The commercial market evolved in the early fifties and quickly came to be dominated by a single firm, IBM, with a handful of rivals. Until the middle of the sixties, the computer industry was occupied almost entirely by large, established companies, with a few important exceptions. It follows that most of the major innovations until that time were contributed by older firms, and it has not been necessary to document them in detail to demonstrate that fact for the purposes of this study. Beginning in the middle of the 1960s, events reshaped the structure of the computer market as a whole to provide opportunities for new enterprises, many of which entered with innovative products.

THE PRECOMMERCIAL ERA: MID-1940s TO EARLY 1950s

The early development of the electronic computer, spanning the period from about 1940 to the early 1950s, was almost entirely in the hands of university research laboratories under contract to government agencies. One exception was IBM's support for the Mark I computer at Harvard's Computation Laboratory. The government's early interest in computing was stimulated by opportunities for wartime applications and Census Bureau needs. Seven or eight entries into the computer field during this period are generally recognized as innovative landmarks.[1]

Landmark Innovations

Harvard's Automatic Sequence-Controlled Calculator (Mark I), was the earliest machine actually to be built that exploited the principles of the analytic engine conceived by Charles Babbage over a hundred years earlier. Completed in 1944 under the direction of Harvard University's Howard Aiken, it was the outcome of a joint project between Harvard and IBM that had begun in 1939. The Mark I was the largest electromechanical calculator ever constructed. Programs were stored on paper tape, making it necessary to feed instructions into it one at a time as on punched cards, but it was 100 times faster than the desk calculators of that day. It was also huge, weighing 5 tons, and it consumed enormous amounts of energy. Subsequent models were developed at Aiken's laboratory and delivered to the U.S. Navy and Air Force.

The Electronic Numerical Integrator and Calculator (ENIAC), built at the University of Pennsylvania's Moore School of Electrical Engineering under the supervision of J. Presper Eckert and John W. Mauchly, was the first fully electronic digital computer to be put into operation.[2] It was several hundred times faster than electromechanical and relay type machines like the Mark I. Delivered to the Ballistic Research Laboratories at Aberdeen, Maryland in 1946, it was used for 10 years thereafter.

There emerged another claimant to the title of inventor of the electronic computer, however. His name was John Vincent Atanasoff, and in 1973 a federal judge adjudicating a patent infringement case against Honeywell brought by Sperry Rand, which then controlled the ENIAC patents, ruled (whether rightly or not has been disputed by some experts) that the "subject matter" of the ENIAC was derived from a machine first built by Atanasoff at the University of Iowa several years before ENIAC.

The Servomechanism Laboratory at the Massachusetts Institute of Technology began work on Whirlwind I, under Jay Forrester's direction, in 1947. It was developed for the U.S. Navy and Air Force to operate as an aircraft stability and control mechanism.[3] The project, which was not completed until 1955, employed dozens of highly skilled engineers and drew upon technical expertise that was not available at the time in commercial laboratories. Whirlwind was probably the first computer designed with eventual real-time applications in mind.[4] (A computer is said to operate in "real time" if it can receive a signal from a source, carry out the necessary processing of that signal, and return the results to the source in time for the source to modify its behavior in accordance with those results.) But by far its most important contribution was the coincident concurrent magnetic core memory, which was in use by the mid-1950s. With much greater capacity and speed than magnetic drums and superior reliability compared with the electrostatic Williams tube memories, it became the major form of computer main memory until replaced by the faster and less expensive semiconductor memories in the late 1970s. One historian of computers wrote that "development of reliable, high speed ferrite core memories that could be mass produced was probably the most important innovation that made stored-program computers a practical commercial reality."[5] Although MIT eventually was awarded major patent rights, the invention was the product of many minds, including engineers at RCA and IBM as well as An Wang, founder of Wang Laboratories, and its commercial feasibility depended on the development of core processing and mass production techniques, in which IBM led the way.[6]

In 1949 the Electronic Delay Storage Automatic Calculator (EDSAC) became the first general purpose stored-program computer. It was started in 1944 at the Mathematical Laboratory of the University of Cambridge in England by Maurice Wilkes, who had spent the previous summer at the University of Pennsylvania's Moore School. The concept of the stored program was first published by John von Neumann of the Princeton

Institute for Advanced Study in a draft proposal for the Electronic Discrete Variable Computer (EDVAC), a stored-program computer developed at the University of Pennsylvania which was a significant improvement over ENIAC in terms of cost and performance. Progress on EDVAC was delayed when Eckert and Mauchly pulled out of the project to form their own company in 1946,[7] and the Standard Eastern Automatic Computer (SEAC), built by the National Bureau of Standards, became the first stored-program computer running in the United States. Placed in operation in 1950, it was used into the early 1960s. Storing the program in the machine vastly increased processing power and made the computer a valuable tool for commercial applications. Until that time instructions had been fed into the machine at the speed of paper tape or punched cards. Now they could be transferred from memory to the calculator at the speed of electronic pulses.

At about the same time, the University of Manchester in England was building computers, and the Williams tube memory developed there became the first practical electrostatic storage system, providing the fastest memory available at the time. The 1949 Manchester computer contained the first index registers as well as other important new features.[8]

At the Institute for Advanced Studies at Princeton, the IAS computer, started by von Neumann in 1946 and completed in 1952, was particularly influential for the series of reports published by the project. RCA was a codeveloper.[9] The IAS computer had a random access electrostatic storage system and parallel binary arithmetic, which made it faster than the preceding delay line computers with sequential memories and serial arithmetic.[10]

The First Commercial Efforts

Throughout the precommercial era a number of other nonprofit organizations in the United States and Europe were developing and designing stored-program computers, and a few large commercial firms, in addition to those already mentioned, showed interest in computer research. AT&T, as well as IBM, produced a number of special purpose computers and other companies developed technological expertise in the field.[11] None, however, was prepared to take the leap into commercial production. There prevailed, indeed, a profound skepticism concerning the market for such machines, and their cost of several hundred thousand dollars (well over $1 million in 1980s dollars) did nothing to enhance their prospects. It remained for a handful of individuals to take the plunge. The first of these were Eckert and Mauchly, the pioneers who had developed the first electronic digital computer, ENIAC, at the Moore School. They were almost alone at that time in believing that the computer could be successfully commercialized.[12] Others, including Thomas J. Watson Sr. of IBM, recognized only their capabilities for scientific computation.

In 1946 Eckert and Mauchly left their work on EDVAC at the Moore School to found a company, eventually to become Eckert-Mauchly Computer Corporation, with the aim of producing a general purpose computer for the commercial market. This enterprise was to lead to the marketing of the world's first commercial computer in 1951, UNIVAC I (Universal Automatic Computer), after the company had been acquired by Remington Rand. A direct descendent of ENIAC and EDVAC, it was delivered first to the U.S. Bureau of the Census and was "probably the best large scale computer in use for data processing for the next 5 years," according to Rosen.[13]

Eckert-Mauchly and UNIVAC I.   The struggles and setbacks of Eckert and Mauchly in trying to launch their new product testify to the obstacles that can stand in the way of a new enterprise intent on introducing a commercial product that creates an entirely new industry. Although Eckert and Mauchly were widely recognized for their contributions to the development of the computer, serious doubts about the financial viability of their firm and their ability to deliver on schedule and within budget plagued them from the founding of the firm until it was sold to Remington Rand to avoid bankruptcy in 1950.

The company was founded on the strength of an offer from the National Bureau of Standards to award it a series of grants amounting to $270,000, beginning with a $75,000 payment in 1946 to construct scale models of two mercury delay tubes for use in a future computer. Since the grant would not support the firm for long, Eckert and Mauchly immediately sought contracts in the commercial market. The Prudential Life Insurance Company and A.C. Nielson, a market research firm, each expressed interest in acquiring a computer but in the end were willing to purchase only piecemeal. Prudential offered to buy the company's new input/output device which used metal tape that could be driven past read/write heads at speeds far in excess of punched card potential. Nielson, doubtful of the partners' ability to come through, settled finally on a modest monthly subsidy to support development work.[14]

Northrop Aircraft helped to stave off the new firm's bankruptcy in 1947 with a $100,000 contract to build a special purpose computer system, but with 40 people on the payroll and preoccupation with producing a marketable general purpose computer, this infusion of cash did not go far. Help was sought unavailingly from American Research and Development, the Boston investment firm that subsequently floated Digital Equipment Corporation (DEC). Delivery postponements and cost overruns as well as cash flow problems were sources of concern to potential investors as well as customers. In 1948 a manufacturer of parimutuel betting machines, American Totalisator, became Eckert and Mauchly's chief financial supporter by lending them $400,000 to be paid back over time in shares amounting to no more than 40 percent of outstanding stock. But in late 1949 the owner of Totalisator was killed in an airplane crash, leaving the partners once again in search of continuing support. By that time the company's cash crunch was crippling relations with suppliers and continued work on UNIVAC was seriously endangered. At least $1 million in cash advances was needed for its completion. Thus, in January 1950, Eckert and Mauchly agreed to allow the Remington Rand Corporation, a major office equipment supplier, to take over a majority stock interest in the company in return for settlement of its indebtedness to Totalisator and a small amount of cash for the two partners.[15] The newly acquired company was allowed to operate as the independent Univac Division of the parent company and in June 1951, UNIVAC I, the first stored-program computer to be sold commercially, was delivered to the U.S. Bureau of the Census.[16] One of its most impressive achievements was the buffered magnetic tape system that could read forward and backward at speeds comparable to some that were still available in the late sixties, making it possible to store information being transferred from the tape to main memory until it was needed, at which point it could be read at high speed into the computer.

ERA and the UNIVAC 1100 Series.   At about the time that Eckert and Mauchly were starting their company, one other group of entrepreneurs was eyeing the computer market. William Norris (later to found Control Data Corporation) and Howard Engstrom, both engineers with the Office of Naval Cryptography during World War II, decided, together with an investment banker, to form a company to continue work on secret computer projects under contract to the navy. They named their company Engineering Research Associates (ERA). The Atlas (later to become the 1101), a large-scale, general purpose computer which ERA delivered to the navy in 1950, was possibly the first computer to employ magnetic drum storage, a concept that had been developed in 1946 at Princeton's Institute for Advanced Study. Harvard and Manchester University, along with ERA, made the concept practical.[17] It was followed by another magnetic drum computer, the 1102, and later the 1103 (called Atlas II at the time), a very powerful scientific computer. These machines became the basis for the UNIVAC 1100 series after ERA, too, sold out to Remington Rand.

By 1952, ERA employed 500 people and its unique relationship with the National Security Agency made it the dominant supplier for defense agencies, but it lacked the capital and marketing skills to compete aggressively in the commercial market.[18] For example, it offered its machines for sale without an operating system or a programming manual and with only a typewriter for input/output.[19] The firm needed $5–10 million in capital for further growth if it was to enter the commercial market seriously. Eckert-Mauchly's record of declining profits did not make it easier for ERA to find backers, and in May 1952 it followed in Eckert-Mauchly's footsteps, in return for $1.7 million from Remington Rand. It operated RR's Minneapolis computer division independently of the Eckert-Mauchly operation. Although neither of these two enterprises achieved commercial success, they must be credited with developing the first marketable commercial machines.

The Dearth of Commercial Enterprises.   The dearth of commercial enterprises before 1952 can be explained by the lack of foreseeable opportunities for profitable investment. Katz and Phillips point to three characteristics of the industry that were responsible. First was the prevailing view that there was no commercial demand for computers. Thomas J. Watson, Sr., argued that IBM's one-of-a-kind Selective Sequence Electronic Calculator (SSEC), a successor to Harvard's Mark I, "could solve all of the important scientific problems in the world involving scientific calculations,"[20] and the data processing potential for computers was simply not foreseen, in spite of the fact that in the late 1940s IBM had produced an electronic calculating punch machine, which could accept programs but not store them. Second, no general purpose machines of advanced design were yet in operation. The technology was still highly experimental and the main emphasis of research was on technological advance rather than on producing machines at a price that would create a market. Finally, the technologies were diverse and changing very rapidly. No "mainstream" technology had emerged to point the direction of the future.

Under these circumstances, the government, with its interest in military applications and without the budget constraints of the commercial market, was virtually the only source of financial support. Moreover, university laboratories were where the scientific and theoretical expertise was. A number of companies had produced one-of-a-kind machines, experimentally or for the U.S. government, and at least two dozen others had acquired technological grounding in the field,[21] but none was prepared to take the first step into commercialization.

The only individuals to be undaunted by the murkiness of the market founded new enterprises in an attempt to enter into commercial production more than five years ahead of the going concerns that were obvious candidates for the role. In retrospect, it is clear that the entrepreneurs were correct in their judgment that a commercial market existed for the computer technologies that were available at the time. But most of their successors took a very long time to become profitable and some of their computers were commercial failures, including IBM's 709, Burroughs's 220, and Sperry Rand's 1105, all of which were 10 to 20 times faster than UNIVAC I.[22] In the end, Remington Rand, the first large firm to commit itself to the commercial market, was the beneficiary of the foresight of the founders of Eckert-Mauchly and ERA. Its management, too, must be credited with an uncommon perceptiveness and willingness to risk capital in order to back its convictions. Nevertheless, its Univac Division did not make a profit for over 10 years.

The founders of the two new enterprises were products of noncommercial research laboratories and brought with them know-how and technology ready for transfer, setting the pattern for many of the firms that were to be founded in their wake. The counterpart of this transfer was Remington Rand's acquistion of the new technology through the purchase of two new enterprises, a precedent that also had many followers during the next three decades.

THE COMMERCIAL MARKET TAKES SHAPE

Remington Rand's acquisition of Eckert-Mauchly and ERA introduced the second stage in the development of the electronic computer industry, during which it was to be occupied almost entirely by large, established companies, competing for shares of the general purpose mainframe industry, and very early dominated by IBM. This stage was to last until the mid-1960s. (In the remainder of this chapter the reader may wish to refer to Table 3–1, which gives the dates on which computers discussed were first introduced.)

Table 3–1.   Dates of Introduction of Computers, 1951–65

Year	Company	Computer
1951	Remington Rand	UNIVAC I
1953	Electronic Data	Datatron
	IBM	701
1954	IBM	650
	Remington Rand	1103A
1956	IBM	704
	IBM	705
1957	Sperry Rand	UNIVAC II
	IBM	608
1958	IBM	709
	Sperry Rand	1105
1959	Sperry Rand	LARC
	IBM	7090
1960	Control Data	1604
	Digital Equipment	PDP-1
	IBM	Stretch
	IBM	1401
	Philco	S-2000
	Honeywell	HIS-800
1961	Burroughs	BGH-200
1962	Sperry Rand	UNIVAC III
	Scientific Data	910
1963	Burroughs	B-5000
	Burroughs	B-6500
	Control Data	6600
1964	Scientific Data	92
	Control Data	3600
	Honeywell	H-200
1965	RCA	Spectra-70
	IBM	System 360/24, 30, 40, 50, 65
	Digital Equipment	PDP-8

Source: See text of Chapter 3.

But before the industry settled into its mold, a brief flurry of entry by new enterprises occurred in the early 1950s, spurred by the development of practical magnetic drum storage systems (at Manchester University, Harvard, and ERA) which could provide large amounts of medium-speed storage at a very low price per bit compared with mercury delay line or electrostatic or magnetic core main memory. According to Rosen, the magnetic drum made it possible to build relatively inexpensive computers which, though not comparable in speed or capacity to the very large, expensive ones, provided computational and data processing capabilities that were not otherwise available to many users. Rosen goes on to say that it was "almost too easy" to design and build a prototype magnetic drum computer, and between 1950 and 1957 many new firms did. It was not so easy "to develop production facilities, marketable products and support."[23]

New Firms and Magnetic Drum Computers

Among the new magnetic drum computer manufacturers was Computer Research Corporation, which produced a compact binary computer and soon merged with National Cash Register Corporation (NCR), which marketed the product with only marginal success. Electronic Computer Corporation was founded by a former scientist from the Moore School and built a small computer for the Ballistic Research Laboratories. It was absorbed by the Underwood Corporation, which produced subsequent models of the computer before withdrawing entirely from the market. A more successful new entrant was a division that Computer Engineering spun off as Electronic Data Corporation. Its product, Datatron, was slightly larger and more powerful than the two mentioned above and contained some innovative features, and it was also more successful. Datatron was the first production line computer to have an index register (which had been developed at the University of Manchester) and automatic relocation subroutines in hardware, which were to become standard on scientific machines.[24] In 1956 the company was absorbed by Burroughs and its machine became the basis for the Burroughs 200, whose success assured Burroughs an important place in the computer industry.[25]

Small companies had the low end of the market virtually to themselves until 1954 when the IBM 650 came along. It had a number of advantages, including a speed three times its competitors', along with certain drawbacks; for example, it was designed initially only for card handling. But IBM's position in the punched card field gave it a tremendous advantage and, so far as we know, none of the new firms survived under its own steam. Nevertheless, they provided the major office machine manufacturers with the basis from which to launch their own entry into the computer market. Only Datatron is remembered for its innovativeness.

Remington Rand and IBM

When Remington Rand (RR) entered the computer business in 1951 with Eckert and Mauchly's UNIVAC I, the first general purpose computer (that is, not one-of-a-kind), it started the commercial computer industry. Early models were sold to government agencies until 1954 when General Electric became the first commercial customer, after which demand picked up. Forty-six machines were eventually sold to government and commercial users.[26] In 1954 the 1103, a much improved version of ERA's 1101 scientific computer and the first commercial computer to use magnetic core storage came out of Remington Rand's Minneapolis branch. Two hundred times faster than the 1101 and 50 times faster than UNIVAC I, it was essentially the Atlas II, which ERA had built earlier for the military.

Remington Rand had been in the tabulating machine business since 1927, but it manufactured a full line of office equipment and tabulating machines were not its major product. IBM held 90 percent of that market compared with RR's 10 percent. Nevertheless, while RR was preparing to deliver UNIVAC I and the 1100 series, IBM was a sleeping giant, unimpressed by the opportunities for commercial exploitation of computers and facing opposition from its tabulating machine chieftains. Company officials maintained that magnetic tape was unreliable, untested, and risky and that there was a commercial need for no more than a handful of large computers.[27] It took the delivery of UNIVAC I to the Census Bureau to awaken IBM to the computer's threat to its traditional turf.

IBM had, however, actively pursued research and development of large, scientific computers. Following its collaboration with Harvard in building the ASCC, it had developed the SSEC, a much faster and more reliable machine, which employed an electronic memory together with a larger mechanical relay memory and automated certain instructions for the first time. This one-of-a-kind machine, first publicly demonstrated in January 1948, was, according to Pugh, the first stored-program computer.[28] Two years later, in response to the Korean War, IBM began work on the Defense Calculator, later called the 701, a large-scale scientific, magnetic drum computer whose architecture was similar to Princeton's IAS. When it was delivered in 1953 it was less flexible than UNIVAC I, but it had a number of advantages such as plastic tape and a new vacuum column tape drive (the 726) that provided significant advances in speed and reliability of recording. It was the first computer packaged in modules so that it could be moved in an elevator and did not have to be constructed on the spot.[29] RR's 1103 (ERA's Atlas II), delivered the next year, performed calculations at about the same speed as the 701, but its input/output was slower.[30]

After delivery of the 701, IBM's computer activities followed three branches until they merged 10 years later with the 360 family of computers: 1) continued development of large-scale scientific computers, 2) development of large-scale computers for data processing, and 3) development of medium-scale business computers, beginning with the 650, for its massive tabulating machine customer base. By the end of the decade it had a near monopoly in all three areas.

Scientific Computers.   When IBM's 704 replacement for the 701 was delivered in 1956, its great advance over the 701 was the magnetic core memory whose speed and capacity permitted the adoption of floating point arithmetic, three index registers, and the FORTRAN programming language, which IBM had developed. Two years earlier UNIVAC's 1103A had actually been the first commercial machine to use core memory, however. The 704 achieved a near monopoly of the large-scale scientific market. Some regarded the 1103 series, which was its only competitor, as superior, but Univac managed to gain few installations. IBM's 700 series culminated in the 709 in 1958, which was obsolete by the time it was introduced since transistors had by then become economical for computers. It gave way the next year to the transistorized 7090, which remained for at least a decade the most popular large scientific computer on the market. Univac's 1105, a buffered version of the 1103, met the same fate as the 709.

Large-Scale Data Processing Computers.   By the time the 701 was delivered in 1953, IBM had seen the handwriting on the wall and announced the character-oriented 702 for commercial data processing. But before its scheduled delivery in 1955 it was apparent that it was inferior to UNIVAC I, so IBM withdrew it and announced the 705, which it delivered a year later. The 705 replaced the electrostatic memory with the faster and more reliable magnetic core. It was almost two years before Sperry Rand (formerly Remington Rand) delivered UNIVAC II, with its magnetic core memory, for the data processing market. Although it was in some respects superior to the 705, Sperry Rand's delay in delivery gave IBM a lead in the large-scale commercial market that no manufacturer has ever successfully challenged.

Medium-Scale Business Computers. IBM's magnetic drum 650, delivered in 1954, was originally designed for the small-scale scientific market but turned out to be a huge success in business applications as well.[31] It appealed to IBM's massive accounting machine customer base. Although relatively slow, it was more reliable, simpler to maintain, smaller, and less expensive than the more powerful IBM and Univac machines. Its major competitors were the small magnetic drum companies described earlier, which were absorbed by other office machine manufacturers. IBM's overwhelming success in spite of the ease of new entry into that sector of the market must be attributed in no small part to the fact that it held 90 percent of the tabulating machine business to begin with. Its customers had large quantities of information coded on punched cards and formalized procedures for processing it. With its extensive contacts and reputation for service it was well placed to convince them that the 650 was a fast and versatile replacement for their existing equipment, and the software and first class service it provided eased the transition.

In 1960 the 650 was succeeded by the 1401, the enormous success of which (10,000 installations by 1962)[32] once again surprised IBM. It was a small, low-cost stored-program computer designed to handle the work of accounting machines and it transformed the market for accounting machines into a market for small computers. The 1401 was not the most advanced machine in its class, but it came with the 1403 printer whose speed and quality was way ahead of any other equipment and is credited by some with the 1401's huge success.[33]

The Shape of the Market

By 1956 the computer was here to stay and IBM, after its lethargic start, had overtaken the early lead of Remington Rand, by then Sperry Rand

(RR having merged with the Sperry Corporation to help shore up its finances), to account for 85 percent of the value of new systems sold in that year, compared with less than 10 percent for Sperry Rand.[34] Burroughs, the Radio Corporation of America (RCA), and National Cash Register (NCR) shared most of the remainder. In the early fifties, at least a dozen well-established companies were involved to some degree in computers, almost all from the office machine or electronics industries,[35] but they did not all survive into the sixties. Many did not make the major investment that was necessary. Although its lead has been slightly eroded, IBM has never lost the dominance of the mainframe industry that it established within three years of entry into the commercial market. Thereafter it was difficult for firms with even the strongest financial backing to bite off a piece of that market and virtually impossible for small, new enterprises. The only successful new companies during that period, as we shall see, entered by creating new markets for themselves.

By the mid-1960s eight mainframe computer manufacturers accounted for over 98 percent of all installations: IBM, with 74 percent, and the so-called seven dwarfs with the remainder. They included Sperry Rand Univac, the new CDC, Burroughs, Honeywell, RCA, NCR, and GE, in order of market shares. RCA and GE were to leave the market in the early seventies. Philco had already tested the waters and withdrawn (but later reentered).

All of the office machine companies other than IBM achieved their positions in the computer industry by acquiring new computer companies: RR acquired ERA and Eckert-Mauchly, NCR the Computer Research Corporation, and Burroughs bought Computer Engineering. Later another successful start-up, Scientific Data Systems (SDS), was acquired by Xerox before the latter left the computer business. RCA, GE, and Philco were all associated with the electronics industry to begin with; the first two had been involved in work on related problems for the military in the 1940s and early 1950s. Honeywell teamed up with the electronics company, Raytheon, to form a computer division and later purchased Raytheon's share. Thus, only IBM seems to have combined a strong internal capability in both office machines and marketing with experience in computer development when the commercial era opened.

How Sperry Rand Lost Its Lead.   Why was Sperry Rand, with its head start (as Remington Rand) unable to maintain its lead? The two computer firms it acquired brought the company some of the most distiguished talent in the field along with two advanced products ready to be launched as the first in their respective markets. In 1951 it had no competitors. How did the company manage to snatch defeat from the jaws of victory?

The Univac Division of Sperry Rand has rarely been faulted for the quality of its products, yet between 1956 and 1967 it lost $250 million.[36] IBM's advantageous position in the tabulating market provides only part of the answer, albeit an important part. Although Remmington Rand had been in the tabulating business since 1927, tabulating equipment was regarded by the top management as its least important product. The company had the shrewdness to purchase two outstanding computer companies, but it never managed to get them to work together. Matters of style and personality interferred, and in 1957 William Norris left the Minneapolis branch of Univac to form CDC, taking some top members of the team with him. It seems to be generally agreed, however, that the critical factor in the company's failure to keep pace with IBM was its poor sales effort.[37] Eckert and Mauchly's orientation was scientific rather than business. Sales managers were not familiar with the equipment they were selling and there was little rapport between the sales force and the Ph.D.'s in Eckert and Mauchly's shop. In addition, it had recently emerged from financial difficulties and felt constrained to sell, rather than lease, its equipment. The early UNIVAC systems were incompletely supplied with peripheral equipment.[38] Punch-to-tape conversion equipment, originally developed for the Census Bureau's UNIVAC I, handled only 90-column cards whereas the IBM punched card installations that normally supported UNIVAC I commercial equipment used 80 columns. Lastly, the company simply did not commit enough resources to development to maintain its early technological lead.[39]

But the adequacy of the company's marketing effort must be evaluated with respect to the competition, and in IBM it confronted a master of marketing techniques with a worldwide sales force dedicated to identifying customers' needs and designing packages to meet them. Watson's philosophy had always been that IBM was in the business of supplying the customer with a service and he carried this over into computers, providing the education, consulting, and software that customers required in order to exploit the new technology.

Once IBM had established its position in the large systems industry, competitors contended mainly with each other for the remaining share of the market. Once potential buyers had become a part of IBM's customer base, it seemed to be almost impossible to dislodge them.

New Enterprises: Successful Strategies for Innovation

No new enterprise succeeded in penetrating the barriers that protected the market for the large general purpose mainframe systems during this period, but three new companies were conspicuously successful in circumventing those barriers by introducing products that created new markets or attracted new customers into the market. They were Control Data Corporation (CDC), Scientific Data System (SDS), and Digital Equipment Corporation (DEC). DEC's computers were what have come to be known as minicomputers (treated at greater length in Chapter 5).

Control Data Corporation. CDC was started in 1957 when William C. Norris, one of the original founders of ERA, left Remington Rand's Univac Division five years after its acquisition of ERA. Among the members of Univac's Minneapolis contingent who accompanied him was Seymour Cray, who was to become the designer of a series of spectacularly successful supercomputers for CDC and later to form his own company. The group had designed transistorized military computers at Univac. Norris's track record allowed them to finance themselves by a public offering that was taken up immediately, mostly by friends and former colleagues at Univac.[40]

The firm's original strategy was to build a large scientific computer with "a lot more bang for the buck," according to Norris. "This we achieved by very high performance hardware with a relatively small amount of software and with the customer doing most of the work."[41] Its sophisticated customers did not require heavy support, they could design their own software and were willing to purchase, rather than lease, the equipment. The company quickly developed a one-tenth scale model of a transistorized computer, after which it received government funding for R&D and production.[42] In 1960 it delivered the CDC 1604. Although it was not as fast as IBM's 7090 or Philco's 2000, transistorized machines that were delivered about the same time, it was considerably less expensive and its success made CDC profitable immediately, an extraordinary record in the mainframe industry.[43] Cray went on to design the 6600, delivered to the Atomic Energy Commission's (AEC) Livermore Laboratory at the end of 1963, which made CDC's reputation as the leading producer of supercomputers. It was 20 times as fast as the 1604 and more than 3 times as fast as the high speed, transistorized Sretch computer which IBM had delivered to Los Alamos in 1960.

IBM reacted to CDC's powerful new machine by announcing a very fast series 90 in its 360 line, but by 1967 it had not been able to deliver while 63 of CDC's 6600s were successfully debugged and in place. The series 90 offering was subsequently withdrawn, but the announcement had cost CDC revenues. Typically when IBM announced a new computer some customers would hold off on orders for competing computers. Furthermore, CDC was obliged to escalate specifications in order to meet promised performance characteristics of the series 90, delaying deliveries and increasing costs. In 1968 Norris filed suit against IBM for a range of alleged monopolistic practices, including the marketing of "paper machines and phantom computers".[44] A month later the U.S. Department of Justice filed against IBM as well and in 1973 an out-of-court settlement favorable to CDC was agreed to.[45]

CDC produced faster and improved versions of the 1604 (the 3600) and the 6600 (the 6800) and in 1968 it delivered the 7600, which executed between 20 and 25 million words per second. No other machine compared in speed. This time IBM countered with its System/360 model 195 but it was never as popular as CDC's 7600.[46]

CDC's products did not compete head on with IBM's but its less expensive machines threatened a corner of IBM's market and its more powerful machines captured a new market that IBM evidently coveted if for no other reason than to demonstrate its superior capability. CDC's success was probably due in large part to the extraordinary talent of Seymour Cray and to Norris's leadership. Norris attributed it to "our willingness to take risks" and "total commitment of the company to development of a new product."[47] Although companies other than IBM also tried (Univac's LARC was one example) none seemed to be able to produce computers of comparable quality and power at corresponding prices.

In the late 1970s, CDC was to be the third vendor to enter the plug-compatible mainframe market,[48] and by 1982, it had the third largest computer related sales of any U.S. firm, behind IBM and DEC.[49] It continued to produce innovative supercomputers, as we will see in Chapter 4, and Norris headed the company until 1986. By then it had become the biggest purveyor of computer services and second only to IBM in sales of peripherals.

Scientific Data Systems.   Another successful new entrant into the computer industry during this period was SDS, founded in 1962 by Max Pavlevsky, who had designed computers for Packard-Bell and Bendix. He put a million dollars of capital from a San Francisco venture capital company together with about $80,000 of his own to produce a premium grade scientific computer that he offered to sophisticated customers with very little in the way of support. The SDS 910 was a high-performance computer designed for real-time applications, a market which, according to Pavlevsky, "essentially no one had attended to."[50] It was the first nonmilitary computer equipped entirely with silicon, rather than germanium, transistors.[51] Peripherals were very primitive and software in the beginning consisted only of an operating system. It took less than a year for Pavlevsky and his dozen or so employees to get the first computer out onto the market, where it sold for under $100,000. It went to the Apollo space program in particular and also to AEC laboratories, oil companies, hospitals, and other research-oriented institutions. Later SDS expanded to serve a wider range of customers and applications and to produce its own peripherals. The company was primarily a design and assembly operation, purchasing parts from original equipment manufacturers (OEMs) or other manufacturers.[52] SDS was profitable at once and subsequently brought out other new machines, including the SDS 92 in 1964, which was the first computer to use monolithic integrated circuits.[53] In 1969 it merged with Xerox to become XDS, but, with the cutback in the space program and a sagging scientific market, the operation lost money and in 1975 Xerox left the computer business.

Digital Equipment Corporation.   In 1957, the same year that Norris founded CDC, Kenneth Olsen started the Digital Equipment Corporation (DEC), a company that was to "create" the market for minicomputers in the 1960s. Kenneth Olsen, along with his associate Harlan Anderson, came out of MIT's Lincoln Laboratory and its predecessor laboratories where Olsen had worked on Whirlwind and later the TX-O, one of the first transistorized computers. Whirlwind established the feasibility of operating in a real-time environment and the TX-O was its lineal descendent. Olsen's experience at MIT gave him the idea and the model for the PDP-1, which became the first commercially available interactive computer when it was introduced in 1960, selling for just $120,000. DEC got its start with $70,000 in capital from American Research and Development, a Boston venture capital firm, and began by building circuit modules for testing equipment. The PDP-1 was followed by the PDP-4 and PDP-5, and in 1965 the PDP-8, a real-time, interactive computer that DEC was able to sell for only $18,000 by virtue of mass production techniques that made assembly possible by semiskilled

workers rather than engineers. It was this machine that laun
boom in minicomputers. Today minicomputers come in all ¡
prices, competing with mainframes at the upper end and m
puters at the lower end. But in the 1960s they were a breed apart, used
at first for laboratory instrumentation and for monitoring and control
of industrial processes. Later they moved into business data processing
and paved the way for distributed processing.

Like CDC and SDS, DEC's machines were designed for "smart"
customers and the company did not supply a battery of services or software, nor did it lease its equipment. Systems houses and OEMs, who
packaged the CPU with peripherals and often added their own software to meet customers' special needs, were the most important outlet
and relieved the company of the need for an extensive marketing and
servicing network or software support and peripherals capability. DEC
continued to turn out more advanced machines, expanding into the
"supermini" market in the 1970s, and became the second largest computer manufacturer in the world. It was still under Olsen's leadership
in 1986. Many other new enterprises followed DEC into the minicomputer market during the sixties and seventies.

Elements of a Successful Strategy for New Enterprises.   All three of these
new companies managed in similar ways to skirt the industry's main
entry barriers: high initial capital costs, customer dependence on the
established reputation of a supplier, and the superior position of
established firms vis-à-vis their locked-in customers. The first was
avoided by starting up with very low cost machines that were marketed
with little or no software and stripped down peripherals or none at all.
R&D costs were minimized by the relative simplicity of their initial of-
ferings and, in the case of DEC at least, by drawing on research that
the founder engaged in for previous employers. None of the three assumed the capital cost of leasing equipment to customers, and SDS and
CDS obtained government financing for their first machines. Large software and other support costs were avoided by targeting sophisticated
customers in the scientific rather than the commercial market. These
customers could, moreover, evaluate the quality of the product without
leaning on the reputation of an established supplier. Computers had
come a long way in terms of market acceptance by the late 1950s.

Finally, the three avoided head-on competition with IBM or any other
major firm for its established base of customers by supplying equipment for as yet untapped markets. Nevertheless, CDC's 6600 and later its

7600 captured new customers that IBM would like to have had and caused IBM to respond by trying to produce competing machines. IBM was unable, however, to produce supercomputers of corresponding quality in the same price range. Part of CDC's success may thus be attributable to the unique technical ability of its personnel, an absolute cost advantage that favored a new firm in this case.

INNOVATIONS AND INNOVATORS: EARLY 1950s TO MID-1960s

The early commercial period saw the computer advance from a huge vacuum tube machine to the second generation transistorized computer and the beginning of the third generation, which employed integrated circuits. Progress in semiconductor technology, which was mainly responsible for the spectacular increases in performance and reductions in price and size of computers, were accounted for by firms outside of the computer industry on the whole, although RCA, Philco, and GE made computers and also contributed to advances in semiconductor technology, and IBM eventually became a leader in that technology for its captive market (see Chapter 8). Other giant steps in the progress of computer hardware and software during this era went a long way toward defining the basic structure of the computer as it is used today. They included advances in data storage, most notably the magnetic core memory and magnetic disk storage, high-level programming languages, measures to facilitate more efficient use of the central processor, such as multiprogramming, multiprocessing, and time sharing (which did not become commercially viable until the seventies), and on-line systems. IBM's 1403 line printer, which accompanied its 1401 computer, was a vast improvement over its predecessors, and the development of its 360 family of computers, which were compatible in terms of both software and hardware moving up the line was a momentous achievement. It would not have been possible but for the use of microprogramming, which substituted programmed instructions in the computer's read-only memory for hard-wired instructions (see Chapter 4).

Because new enterprises were excluded by market barriers from entry into all but a few small sectors of the computer industry at the time, their innovative contributions were limited, but they were not altogether lacking. Most notably, CDC engineered the first supercomputer and, at the other extreme, DEC introduced real-time, interactive computers and started the boom in low-cost minicomputers. Small, new firms typically led the way in adopting advances in solid state technology, with SDS fielding the first nonmilitary computer to use silicon chips and later the first to be equipped with integrated circuits. Later Data General would be responsible for the adoption of medium-scale integration (SMI) and semiconductor memory for its minicomputers. (Chapter 5) Far less risk is involved in introducing new components when the machine is small, relatively simple, and sold as a discrete unit rather than part of a large system in an extensive line of compatible machines. IBM testified that it takes four years to develop a large scientific computer compared with two years on the average for a small mainframe.[54] Since components must be frozen into design relatively early, technology lags further behind the longer the development stage of the computer. Moreover, failure of a new component exacts a greater cost the greater the number of models into which it is simultaneously introduced. IBM was unwilling to risk the use of integrated circuits when it first developed the 360 family even though other machines on the market had already adopted them.

MARKET ANALYSIS

Although it was perhaps not inevitable that the computer industry should become as concentrated in the hands of a dominant firm as it did during its first decade, the nature of the industry virtually guaranteed that a few large, established firms would share the market for the general purpose mainframe, albeit with a considerable amount of rivalry. All three of the traditional barriers to entry discussed in Chapter 2 operated in one way or another to prevent all but a handful of new enterprises from entering the computer industry successfully during this period: economies of scale combined with absolute cost barriers, and product differentiation advantages of established firms. We examine each of them separately and then consider the influence of U.S. government activities on the entry of new enterprises.

Economies of Scale

Except in very small markets, scale economies deter entry by small, new firms through the "absolute capital cost effect," rather than the "percentage effect" (see Chapter 2). The former is a consequence of the large amount of capital that is required to achieve sufficient scale to compete effectively, combined with the small, new firm's disadvantage in the capital market. Scale economies are not conspicuous in the manufacturing of computers, which can be conducted fairly labor intensively by assembling components. The production of some components is more susceptible to scale economies, but components are generally available from independent vendors who are in a position to exploit such economies. As time went on, however, manufacturing became a declining proportion of the total cost of computers and the fixed cost of software development an increasingly large proportion. R&D, from the beginning, was a large fixed cost.

Empirical data on which to base estimates of scale economies in the computer industry, as in most others, are difficult to come by. Engineering data are usually proprietary and not generally assembled in the form needed for making an accurate evaluation. In the early 1970s Gerald Brock attempted to make a very rough estimate of returns to scale in mainframe production. Based on an IBM study of the manufacturing costs of different numbers of Pisces (370/168) computers which was undertaken in connection with Telex versus IBM in 1972, he concluded that in the CPU manufacturing phase, a firm with 10 percent of total output would find its average costs 5 to 15 percent higher than a firm with 100 percent of the market.[55] But the fact that, unlike most computer manufacturers, IBM makes most of its components would tend to exaggerate this advantage. Marketing, which is conducted by personal sales representatives, also offers some modest opportunities for cost reductions as the number of customers increases, and cost reductions are somewhat greater in the maintenance of installed equipment because, in order to respond rapidly to calls for unscheduled repairs, service personnel must be located within easy reach of installations. The greater the number of installations, the fewer the personnel required per installation.

The major source of scale economies in Brock's study was found to be in the development of systems' software (operating systems, compilers), where the marginal cost of applying knowledge to additional production is close to zero as the fixed cost is spread over increasing numbers of computers. Economies of scale in producing applications software are less important because software must be tailored to the demands of individual customers. The fraction of the cost of a system that is attributable to its software has increased steadily since the beginning of the second generation. It rose from 15 percent in the mid-1950s to 50 percent 10 years later and to 80 percent by 1979.[56] A small firm, however, may be able to substitute hardware for software, thereby increasing average costs for large production runs but reducing them at low levels of production.

Brock figured, very roughly, that a firm with a 10 percent market share could find itself with average costs about 10 percent higher overall than a firm with 100 percent of the market. This admittedly crude estimate would surely vary over time and from one sector of the mainframe industry to another, but it suggests that a firm competing head on with IBM would have to be prepared to sell below cost if IBM charged only enough to cover its long-run average cost. However, the size of the market share of IBM or any other firm that produces a diversified line of computer equipment is likely to overstate its scale advantage relative to smaller, more specialized firms because economies of scope will rarely be as great as economies of scale.

Brock did not, however, explicitly take into account increasing returns to R&D other than software development. R&D costs of a large mainframe system have consistently run into millions and even hundreds of millions of dollars spread over several years at high risk. Irrespective of whether the R&D process itself is subject to significant returns to scale (see Chapter 2), it is a fixed cost of production that can be extremely high, and unit cost falls indefinitely as it is spread over increasing output of the final product. A high threshold R&D cost is necessary in this industry not only for the development of new products but for the continuing research that is mandatory if a firm is to keep abreast of technology in an industry whose product life cycle is only about five years.[57] Because this high threshold of "defensive" expenditures is independent of the level of sales, it can eat seriously into profits for a small-scale firm. Stoneman concluded in a study of the U.K. computer industry that, whereas scale economies in computer manufacturing are negligible, when returns to R&D are taken into account they are not insignificant.[58] His conclusion held whether scale referred to increasing units of the same computer or the production of increasingly powerful computers.

The influence of these scale economies on the overall production function depends on the amount that a firm must invest in R&D to compete in the industry. That amount varies with the size and complexity of the computer, the uniqueness of the technology being developed, the extent to which the technology can be borrowed from other sources, and its rate of change. It is evident that in order to compete with IBM and other established firms, the investment was very great. IBM maintained a worldwide research establishment that employed 15,000 in the early 1960s. It invested $25 million in the Stretch computer (half supplied by the AEC) and $500 million in development of the 360 series, not counting the $4.5 billion in capital invested in plant, equipment, and in machines out on lease.[59] (IBM's System 360 was the largest development project for an industrial firm on record at the time.) GE invested $160 million to develop time sharing before exiting from the computer market. RCA spent $15 million in the early sixties to develop the Spectra 70, which turned out to be a commercial failure. Small new firms are doubly deterred by high threshold R&D costs because, even could they raise the capital for it, unit costs would exceed those of large firms unless they invested also in correspondingly large-scale production.

The standardization of processor logic and programming across IBM's 360 family of computers afforded economies of scope, as well, in the manufacture of multiple systems. IBM testified that economies occurred in training of field personnel, development of software, and in installation and maintenance procedures, and in manufacturing because parts were shared among different machines.[60] Economies of scope are also available in the application of R&D output across product lines as we observe below in IBM's commercial exploitation of the high-speed memory and semiconductor circuits that were developed for the Stretch computer.

Absolute Cost Barriers

The absolute cost barrier that was singularly effective in deterring entry of small new companies into the mainframe industry was their handicap in raising capital, most importantly the ceiling on the amount of capital that was available for a given length of time. There is no persuasive evidence that new firms were as a group disadvantaged in acquiring strategic resources or other factors of production, or in the prices that they paid for them, the only critical resource being specialized personnel, in the hiring of which small new firms may actually have had an advantage. IBM's inability to produce supercomputers that could compete with the 6600 that Seymour Cray designed for CDC could be attributed to CDC's cornering of a "strategic" human resource. Access to critical technology could potentially have given an advantage to established firms but, for reasons discussed later, it was not likely to have been very important.

Capital Costs. The handicap that small, new firms almost universally must bear in acquiring capital mattered because the minimum amount of capital required for entry into general purpose mainframes was, and remains, extremely high and the recovery period in the beginning was very long. All who survived the industry's first 15 years were well-established firms with accumulated reserves or current revenues from sales of other products to draw upon as well as track records to reassure investors. Not until the late 1960s did the capital market become enamored of new electronics firms, and the love affair waxed and waned. Even had investor confidence materialized sooner, a new company could not have hoped for funding at any price in the quantities that were invested by IBM, Sperry Rand, RCA, GE, and others in bringing large systems to the market. The sums were great and recovery was long delayed. Of IBM's competitors who survived into the seventies, Sperry Rand's Univac Division was the first to enter and the first to show a profit, but not until 15 years later in 1966. National Cash Register (NCR) was the last to break even, in 1973.[61] The high risk that a product would become obsolete before its capital costs were recovered was manifest by the failure of commercial models like IBM's 709, Univac's 1105, and Burroughs's 220, all first generation computers that outperformed their predecessors but did not have respectable careers.[62]

The extremely large capital costs of entry resulted from a combination of the substantial total value of output that needed to be supported and the large threshold investment in R&D (including software development) that was necessary for any level of output. The latter was not only the chief source of scale economies, but it was responsible as well for the relatively high capital cost of achieving any scale. In other respects, production could be conducted competitively in a relatively labor intensive manner.

A high unit value of mainframe systems and the presence of economies of scope combined with economies of scale to account for the very substantial minimum value of total output that was needed to be competitive. Mainframes cost between several hundred thousand and several million dollars to build, and they were marketed with peripheral equipment and operating systems as well as the software, consulting, and other services that were bundled into the package. Marketing and maintenance costs per unit of output were also relatively high. Economies of scope in R&D, maintenance, and in the production of components, as well as in marketing to customers who employed a range of computers and looked to the vendor for upward migration of their systems, provided advantages to a company like IBM that could supply a broad menu of products, especially with the arrival of its System 360.

Given the value of total output, the amount of long-term capital required varies with the advantages of capital intensity in the manufacturing process, of vertical integration, and of investment in intangibles such as R&D and advertising. Except for R&D, none of these advantages was very strong in the computer industry.

The manufacture of electronic capital goods did not, during this period, offer significant opportunities for reducing costs by employing capital intensively. Freeman found that in 1965 typical installations in the electronics capital goods industries consisted of "ordinary work benches or 'lazy susans', with test gear and inspection machines as the most expensive items."[63] According to the U.S. Census Bureau, the value of assets per employee in the electronic computer and equipment industry in 1967 was $7,000, compared with an average of over $11,000 for manufacturing as a whole.[64] (The industry was not defined by the Census prior to 1967.) The ratio of total assets to value of shipments was less than half as great in computers as in all manufacturing.

Vertical integration may have offered some advantages to computer manufacturers during this period, judging from the fact that IBM integrated backward into semiconductor chips and core memories. According to Pugh, IBM had developed a capability in transistors as early as 1955 but customarily turned design and manufacturing over to specialized vendors like Texas Instruments for volume production in order to capitalize on their greater experience and lower profit margins.[65] With development of the System 360 computers Pugh reports, IBM management concluded that in-house production of components would provide advantages in control over costs and over proprietary technologies, and at that stage it set up a formal components division that subsequently produced all of the semiconductor devices for its mainframes. Similarly, for the 360 IBM developed a showpiece of automated production for core memories, from the ferrite cores to the complete memory unit. Large volumes of reliable, low-cost components were critical to the success of the 360 system and one way to guarantee the supply was to integrate. Nevertheless, the other mainframe vendors obtained their components from independent vendors in a thriving market. Not until the 1970s did compelling reasons to integrate upstream emerge with the increasing complexity of the interrelationships between large-scale integrated circuits and systems design.

Components production is intrinsically more capital intensive than building computers, and IBM chose to make it more so by investing in automated facilities for producing both semiconductors and core memories. But there is no evidence that automated plants were more cost effective than hand wiring performed by low-cost workers overseas, the option chosen by most manufacturers of solid state devices during the 1960s. And, according to Pugh, IBM found that it was no more costly to have magnetic core planes wired by hand in the Orient than to produce them in their automated plants in the United States.

The need for operating capital was under particular pressure from the practice of leasing mainframes to customers which prevailed from the beginning. Leases were usually geared to recover the sales price in 48 months and, according to IBM, companies have, on the average, more than recovered costs.[66] But leasing defers revenues, thereby increasing capital requirements during periods of growth. Rapidly growing companies that lease their products need continual infusions of new capital. Moreover, as Brock points out,[67] leasing decreases a firm's profits as they appear in financial statements since current accounting practices charge most costs other than hardware manufacturing to expenses in the year incurred while revenues are deferred. As a result, a firm is likely to show a loss in its income statement for machines that it places on lease in that year, making it more difficult to raise capital to cover the negative cash flow.

Access to Technology. Access to critical production technology can potentially be restricted by patents, secrecy, or knowledge that is best acquired through experience. Most technological advances in computers have been in product design rather than in production techniques and in neither case were patents effective barriers to imitation. Nevertheless, experience in large-scale production and marketing of computers can no doubt afford learning economies. IBM's experience with mass producing the 650, the first large-scale production of a computer, reportedly gave it an advantage over newcomers. Its earlier experience in providing service and support to users of its tabulating machines was an advantage when it entered the computer industry. Univac's loss of its early market lead is generally attributed to lack of such expertise, as well as some lack of marketing effort.

When technology changes rapidly, up-to-the-minute technical expertise and know-how is absolutely critical, especially to success in innovating, but expertise has been liberally transferred from one laboratory or firm to another throughout the history of the industry by transfers of personnel. The successful founders of the three new firms described earlier brought with them skills and experience and sometimes actual concepts or prototypes for new products along with a team of engineers from former employers. Numerous examples of new firms hiring specialists from IBM's staff appear in subsequent chapters.

As important as experience can be the advantage of a going organization. IBM's worldwide sales and engineering field forces and the research organization that had served its office equipment business gave it a head start in the computer business. Others that entered the market from office machines or electrical equipment shared this advantage over many potential competitors and certainly over new firms. Freeman observed that firms that succeeded in the electronic capital goods industries "combined a well-organized research, development and test program with good production planning and efficient marketing and technical service."[68] None of these can be brought into being overnight.

Product Differentiation

There are two main sources of product differentiation in the mainframe industry: physical differences in product design that are proprietary, and customer dependence on the reputation of the manufacturer combined with opportunities for personal contacts between producer representatives and customers in marketing and providing support. Both afforded a special advantage to the dominant firm in the industry.

Physical Product Differentiation.   Computers and computer systems of different suppliers (and often of the same supplier) vary in physical design characteristics that determine their performance. No two suppliers provide identical equipment or configurations of equipment and different characteristics are preferred by different customers. But physical differences in products impose entry barriers only when they cannot be imitated by potential competitors at the same cost. Either patents or trade secrets covering product design can potentially prevent such imitation.

Patents.   Patents have not been very successful in deterring imitators in the market for computers.[69] A 1981 statistical analysis of R&D and patents covering a sample of over 2,500 American manufacturing firms found that the computer industry (SIC 3570 and 3573) does not use patents extensively to protect the output of research departments, in spite of the fact that the industry is the most R&D intensive one in the sample.[70] One reason for shunning patent procedures has been the very rapid rate of technological change. It takes several years to obtain a patent and by the time it is awarded the product may be obsolete. Until the early 1980s, it was not possible to patent systems software, the source of many advances in computer design. In addition, because of the complexity of the systems and the number of different components involved, the product cannot be manufactured without the right to use hundreds of patented items. As a consequence, firms cross license extensively, using patents to improve the terms of licensing rather than as a source of income or a barrier to imitation.

IBM's willingness to cross license may have been encouraged by its dominant position in the industry, a position that resulted in its intense scrutiny by the Justice Department. But the Justice Department also played a more direct role in facilitating the exchange of patents. In 1952 it charged IBM with monopolizing the tabulating machine industry in a suit that culminated in a 1956 consent decree in which IBM agreed to grant licenses on all tabulating and EDP patents it had applied for before 1961 and to charge no more than reasonable royalties.

The industry was not free from hard fought rivalry over patent rights, but no single incumbent successfully barred competitors from the use of an important technology. Two major patent disputes punctuated the early commercial period. In 1947 Eckert and Mauchley applied for a patent on the ENIAC which covered very broad claims to fundamental computer technology.[71] The patent was not granted until 1964. At that time, in response to a demand for royalties from Sperry Rand (which held the patent), Honeywell claimed that the patent was invalid because the technology had been in use for more than a year before the patent had been applied for. In the early 1970s the suit was settled in Honeywell's favor, leaving the technology free of patent restrictions.

Conflicting claims to patents covering some of the fundamental concepts underlying the core memory were also litigated. The most heated and prolonged dispute was between RCA and MIT, representing a dozen or so claims to contributions by Jay Forrester.[72] In the end, MIT won a major share of its claims and IBM negotiated a one-time payment of $13 million for the use of the contributions, which amounted, according to computer historian Pugh, to the largest such fee ever recorded at that time. Ultimately it proved to be a trivial price per unit installed. An Wang, who founded Wang Laboratories in the 1950s, won

15 of 16 disputed claims in a case covering his development of a shift-register in 1948 using magnetic cores. In addition to developments by Forrester, Wang, J.A. Rajcham at RCA, and others, many further innovations were required to make the magnetic core memory a practical reality, relating to the processing of ferrite cores, noise reduction, support circuits, wiring and packaging, and manufacturing and test techniques.[73] In this and other cases, the number of patents necessary to produce even a single major component of a processor far exceeded what any one producer could hope to control.

Trade Secrets.   The physical attribute of computers that most seriously deterred new entry was the need for compatibility between the software and the hardware of the major components of a system. Until IBM's 360 family of computers came along in 1965, even different models of any one manufacturer were not compatible—characteristics such as instruction and character codes, word length, and controller interfaces differed among machines. Unless the customer's new equipment is compatible with installed equipment, the customer must develop new programs.

Mainframe customers typically have a heavy investment in applications software that is committed to specific systems. In the information processing industries it may be several times as great as the investment in computers. Conversion was especially costly before high-level computer languages were developed in the 1960s. Moreover, operators are trained to work on a specific vendor's equipment, and with incompatible equipment new operating procedures may have to be established at the same time that data bases must be recoded and reorganized. The greater the differences in the equipment of different vendors and the larger the customer's investment in software, data bases, and personnel training, the more costly the switch to a new brand. Because customers were thus locked into their original equipment, a vendor seeking to gain market share had either to target customers new to the industry or to introduce a machine that was, or could be made to be, compatible with another vendor's installed equipment.

IBM's customers, because of its market share, were the obvious target for the second strategy, but because of the proprietary nature of its circuitry, development of compatible equipment could not commence until after the IBM machine was first delivered to the market. The capital cost barrier alone was sufficient to prevent small, new enterprises from entering the mainframe market by producing IBM-compatible processors during this early period, but RCA and Honeywell each tried with varying degrees of success.[74] At this time it took many months after IBM delivery to produce a compatible machine, and, moreover, a loss in memory capacity was an inevitable price. Not until well into the seventies did flexible modular design techniques such as microcoding and plug-in architecture make more rapid response possible.[75] Before that the incentive was almost overwhelming for a customer to stick with the vendor it started with and the same remains largely the case today, although a market for IBM-compatible mainframes did develop in the seventies.

Subjective Product Differentiation.   Strong customer preferences associated with the image and reputation of a particular firm, most notably IBM, have been manifested throughout the history of the industry. They derive from the nature of the product, the impressive record of performance with which IBM entered the market, and its ability to maintain its image over time. When a firm's reputation has been acquired over many years it cannot be emulated by a new firm in the short run, if at all.

Several characteristics of mainframe computers contribute to the strong customer dependence on the name and reputation of the supplier. In addition to the very complex and sophisticated technology of the mainframe, the fact that it is marketed as a component of a complete system, bundled with a variety of services that include maintenance, education, and software support, makes comparisons between brands a matter of considerable uncertainty. Indeed, precise cost/performance evaluations are virtually impossible. Each different vendor's package is likely to outrank others' in some respects and important tradeoffs are involved that are difficult to measure. The only way for a customer to accurately compare performance of large systems is to run them with his specific applications, but this requires reworking his software for the different systems being considered. Moreover, new computers are frequently ordered before they are available for testing. Although less direct methods of assessing performance are available, they leave much to be desired in terms of accuracy. In addition, the reliability of performance of promised services and delivery schedules, and availability of future enhancements involve further tradeoffs and uncertainty. Among other things, the customer wants assurance that the vendor will be in business in the future. Together, these factors combine to create strong pressures for a customer to choose a vendor with a proven reputation initially and to stick with that vendor in replacing and expanding the system. Mainframe systems are a classic case of an experience good.

These attributes of the product gave a powerful advantage to a firm with IBM's established reputation and customer service network in the tabulating machine business during the infancy of the computer industry, and from the beginning its sales and service representatives exploited long-standing relationships with customers who were candidates to replace their older mechanical equipment with computers. The rudimentary software, educational services, and maintenance that were bundled into the system package helped to promote relationships with the customers who would become candidates for expansion and replacement equipment as computer technology progressed. The reputation it had built and the large share of the market it occupied almost from the beginning made IBM a safe bet for purchasing agents at a time when any new purchase of equipment entailed considerable risk.

The Role of Government

The federal government in its triple-barreled role of customer, supporter of R&D, and regulator had an important effect on the direction and speed of developments in the computer industry. It is not always easy, however, to discern its influence on the structure of the market and on the ability of new or small enterprises to innovate.

Government Procurement and R&D Support.   The federal government was the main supporter of research and development in the computer industry until the commercial market began to develop in the early 1950s. Thereafter, it continued to be the mainstay of support for R&D relating to very powerful systems. Federal agencies like the Defense Department, NASA, AEC, and the Bureau of the Census were also the leading customers for computers during the industry's formative years, and remain the leading customers for the most powerful computers to this day. Half of IBM's computer sales during the fifties were to the federal government. Because government R&D support was generally directed toward delivery of a computer with specific performance characteristics, its consequences cannot easily be disentangled from those of government procurement. Government contracts for R&D and for procurement of new products not only provided financial support to the computer industry, but a significant spillover of new technology that benefited the entire industry. But the spillover was likely to be of most immediate benefit to the contractor.

The Livermore Atomic Research Computer (LARC) and Stretch computers, contracted to Sperry Rand's Univac Division and IBM, respectively, in 1956 through the AEC, were probably the two most impressive government-sponsored computer projects of this era awarded to commercial enterprises. Each company counted on emerging with a marketable product that would help to recoup some of the cost of development and each failed in this aspiration. Yet both projects provided a major stimulus to the computer industry, and Stretch led directly to IBM's 7090, delivered in 1959 to become the most successful large-scale computer that any company had marketed by the end of the seventies.[76] The LARC and Stretch programs were targeted to produce very fast machines and handle very large arrays of data, employing the core memory and replacing vacuum tubes with transistors for the first time in large machines. IBM aimed to produce a machine 100 times as fast as its 704 but in the end achieved less than one-half of its goal. Both LARC and Stretch were delivered significantly behind schedule. Nevertheless, each project was responsible for the development of important advances in computer architecture. Stretch, for example, employed the first addressing system and organization of data into bytes and bits, as well as a powerful interrupt-control system that made multiprocessing possible.[78]

Stretch cost $25 million to develop, of which half was IBM's own money which it hoped to recover through government contracts and sales of engineering models. But in order to avoid a loss it had to benefit from technologies that it developed.[78] The disappointing speed of Stretch forced IBM to cut its price in half, leaving no margin for profit, and the machine was withdrawn from the market soon after delivery in 1961. But its work on Stretch gave IBM a jump on its competitors in producing the 7090, a transistorized version of the 709 which cost about one-third as much as Stretch and could do considerably more work.[79] The transistorized version of its 705 business-oriented machine, the 7080, also employed the high-speed memory that had been designed for Stretch, and the 1401 used semiconductor circuits developed for Stretch. Thus, in the long run, IBM gained important benefits from the contract.

Another spillover from government contracts is the training and experience employees of the contractor receive in the development of advanced technologies. While many engineers may eventually carry their experience with them to other companies, the initial benefits accrue to the contractor.

The extent to which government contracts influence the ability specifically of new or small enterprises to compete is a function of the inherent nature of government demand and the way in which it chooses to make it effective. The fact that government agencies typically demand large, complex systems with a strong preference for compatibility among the systems that they purchase would be expected intrinsically to bias their purchases in favor of large systems manufacturers. The procurement practices themselves may be either more or less favorable to small new businesses than those that are followed in the civilian market. The question is whether the presence of the government as a dominant customer makes it harder or easier for new firms to enter and innovate in the computer market than it would be in the absence of the government buyer. The evidence as it concerns computers alone is not conclusive. However, it suggests that the government has not hindered new entry but, on the contrary, may have encouraged it.

Since 1971 most government computers have been purchased through a competitive bidding process.[80] Earlier, Federal Supply Schedule (FSS) contracts seem to have been more prevalent. FSS contracts are negotiated with individual contractors and permit extensions to previous contracts to be made without competitive bidding. FSS contracts would, thus, appear to give an advantage to established government suppliers. Competitive bidding also entails high overhead costs and awards are not always free from political influence. The need to adhere to government regulations regarding accounting, reporting, and recordkeeping imposes additional overhead costs. Overhead costs generate economies of scale that place small firms at a disadvantage. On the other hand, there are economies of scale in selling in many commercial markets, as well; risk can be averted through government cost reimbursement contracts and capital outlays are minimized through progress payments which the government makes in the course of the contract. Moreover, there are strong political pressures on the government to give small business a fair share of its market.

Gansler, in a study of the U.S. defense industry, concludes that there are serious barriers to entry of small firms into the defense market. In addition to the factors mentioned above, he points to the heavy reliance on prior technological experience in selecting contractors and to the fact that invitations to bid are frequently issued only to so-called qualified sources, namely those with plant and equipment already in place to handle the contract. The Department of Defense prefers to reduce its administrative load by contracting in large dollar amounts, and finally, the department demands a high level of technical performance whereas, he argues, small firms traditionally have been better at designing low cost products.[81]

Systematic evidence on the share of new or small companies in government procurement of computers does not exist, as far as we can tell. There is evidence, however, that the government has been especially supportive of young firms in the development of new products. Utterback and Murray, in a study of the effect of Defense Department activities on the "Civilian Electronics Industry" in the United States, come to a conclusion opposite to Gansler's, namely that as a first user of new products, willing to experiment with radical innovations, to pay the high expenses involved in initial production runs, and to support new and untried suppliers, the government has played an important role in stimulating the early introduction and success of new technology, especially in the face of defensive efforts by established suppliers to push the old technology (such as vacuum tubes) to higher levels of performance.[82]

Utterback and Murray appear to base their conclusions mainly on impressions from the semiconductor field rather than electronics generally, but the conclusions are consistent with the evidence gathered from the examination of innovators in the present study. The only two innovative new companies that successfully broke into the general purpose mainframe market before the mid-1960s, Control Data Corporation and Scientific Data Systems, developed their products for the U.S. government: CDC's 1604 received government R&D as well as manufacturing support and the 6600, which made CDC's reputation as the leading supplier of supercomputers, was first delivered to AEC's Livermore Laboratory in 1963. SDS launched its business by selling to the Apollo space program and AEC labs, as well as to other research oriented institutions. In the 1970s, Cray Research leased its first computer to Los Alamos. In their study of high-technology companies that spun off from MIT laboratories and departments during the 1960s in the Route 128 region of Massachusetts, Roberts and Wainer found that a high proportion got their start by selling to the U.S. government.[83]

The third innovative young company discussed in this chapter, DEC, in contrast, did not rely directly on government contracts for developing its minicomputers, although many were sold to government agencies and to customers who were under contract to government agencies. But, it should not be overlooked that the very first minicomputers that DEC turned out were based on government-supported projects that DEC's founder Ken Olsen had helped to develop at MIT laboratories. This suggests another way that the government's support of R&D assisted new firms in getting started. Olsen was not alone in commercially exploiting firsthand experience with a new technology that had been gained in a government-sponsored laboratory.

From the early sixties on, the importance of commercial computer markets and access to them by new enterprises grew while the dominion of the U.S. government in the market declined.

Standards.   A second way in which the federal government exercises its market power to influence the structure of the computer industry is through its ability to set standards. Standards are one method of assuring compatibility among computers, peripherals, programs, and data by forcing all manufacturers to follow the same conventions in establishing interfaces. To the extent that standards are effective, the advantages of product differentiation among established companies are reduced.

For a decade or more no standards existed to guide the computer industry's development of digital coding systems, program languages, or peripherals interfaces. Subsequent efforts to set industrywide standards, largely through the efforts of the American National Standards Institute (ANSI), depended on voluntary compliance. As might be expected, standardization was of interest to firms trying to penetrate the market share of a large company, not to the firm that claimed that share. Thus, IBM was not likely to adhere to voluntary industry standards. Because of the volume of its purchases, the U.S. government was, however, in a position to impose standards to bring about uniformity in the equipment of different vendors and, according to Brock, most progress that has been made in this direction has occurred as a result of such pressure.[84] In 1965 the National Bureau of Standards was given the job of developing standards for all computers used within the government. Not until 1969, however, was the first official standard promulgated. It attempted to establish a uniform code for assigning binary number to characters and symbols (the American Standard Code for Information Interchange, ASCII) for government-used computers. But strong pressure from IBM succeeded in significantly watering down its application within the government.

Antitrust Regulation.   A form of government regulation that has profoundly affected the computer industry is enforcement of the antitrust laws. As early as 1952, before IBM's first commercial computer was on the market, the Justice Department filed suit against the firm for monopolizing the tabulating machine industry, and the 1956 consent decree that settled the suit held a number of important implications for the pattern of development that the computer industry was to follow. For example, it required IBM to permit customers to purchase rather than lease its machines and to offer and price services separately, which permitted the emergence, eventually, of independent firms set up to lease and service IBM equipment. But the provision that required IBM to license any applicant to use patents awarded to it before 1961 for tabulating machinery and electronic data processing machines at reasonable royalty fees set the stage for the liberal licensing policy that has prevailed in the industry ever since. In the same year another consent decree that brought to a close a Justice Department suit against AT&T had even more profound implications for the development of the computer industry. AT&T, which had invented the transistor in 1947 at its Bell Laboratories, was precluded from selling it outside of the government market. Historically, the giant communications company's manufacturing arm, Western Electric, had been restrained from selling equipment in the open market. Had AT&T been allowed to compete in the computer market or to dominate the component field, the computer market might have taken on quite a different configuration than it actually did. The ability of new computer firms to obtain semiconductor devices in a competitive market was critical to entry. In Europe and Japan, where component markets are dominated by equipment manufacturers, new computer companies have not emerged in large numbers, although other deterrents are partially responsible. The trend in the late seventies toward acquisition of independent semiconductor houses by large equipment manufacturers may signal the appearance of new barriers to entry into the computer market.

In 1969 a second suit was filed by the Justice Department charging IBM with monopolizing the general purpose computer industry. After dragging on for well over a decade, the suit was dismissed in 1982. But, as we shall see in the following chapter, there is some reason to believe that that suit and the mere threat of antitrust actions earlier prevented IBM from competing as vigorously as it might otherwise have done in some sectors of the market, including those that were open to new entrants such as peripherals and small computers. It is evident from findings in various antitrust suits that the giant company was sensitive to the possible implications of increasing its market share beyond certain limits.[86]

Summary

The main deterrents to entry of newly founded firms into the general purpose mainframe industry during its first decade and a half were 1) factors that generated very high initial capital requirements, in light of the disadvantage typically faced by new enterprises in raising capital; 2) the importance of an established reputation in building customers' confidence, and 3) the high cost to the customer of shifting from one line of equipment to another that operated with incompatible software, which locked the customer into equipment of its original supplier. The influence of the federal government on entry of new firms was mixed but, on balance was probably a favorable one.

Notes

1. Barbara Goody Katz and Almarin Phillips, "The Computer Industry," in *Government and Technological Change: A Cross-Industry Analysis*, ed. Richard R. Nelson (New York: Pergamon, 1982); Saul Rosen, "Electronic Computers: A Historical Survey," American Computer Manufacturers, *Computing Survey* (January 1969): 7–36; and G.W.A. Dummer, *Electronic Innovations and Discoveries*, 2d ed. (New York: Pergamon Press, 1978).
2. Katz and Phillips, "The Computer Industry"; and Rosen, "Electronic Computers."
3. R. Moureau, *The Computer Comes of Age: The People, The Hardware, The Software* (Cambridge, Mass.: MIT Press, 1984).
4. Rosen, "Electronic Computers."
5. Emerson Pugh, *Memories That Shaped an Industry* (Cambridge, Mass.: MIT Press, 1984), Preface.
6. Ibid., p. 237.
7. Rosen, "Electronic Computers"; and Dummer, *Electronic Innovations and Discoveries*.
8. Rosen, "Electronic Computers."
9. Pugh, *Memories That Shaped an Industry*.
10. Rosen, "Electronic Computers."
11. Katz and Phillips, "The Computer Industry."
12. Gerald W. Brock, *The U.S. Computer Industry: A Study of Market Power* (Cambridge, Mass.: Ballinger, 1975).
13. Rosen, "Electronic Computers."
14. Harold Wulforst, *Breakthrough to the Computer Age* (New York: Scribner, 1982).

15. Ibid.
16. Rosen, "Electronic Computers."
17. Ibid.
18. Pugh, "Memories That Shaped an Industry."
19. Erwin Tomash and Arnold A Cohen, "The Birth of an ERA: Engineering Research Associates, Inc. 1946–1955," *Annals of the History of Computing* 1, no. 2 (October 1979): 83–101.
20. Cuthbert Hurd, "Direct Testimony," Defendent's Exhibit 8951, *U.S. v. IBM*, 69 Cir. 200 (SDNY), pp. 9–10, cited in Katz and Phillips, "The Computer Industry."
21. Ibid.
22. Ibid.
23. Rosen, "Electronic Computers," p. 13.
24. Ibid.
25. Moreau, *The Computer Comes of Age.*
26. Pugh, "Memories That Shaped an Industry."
27. Katz and Phillips, "The Computer Industry."
28. Pugh, "Memories That Shaped an Industry."
29. IBM, "Historical Narrative Statement of Richard B. Mancke, Franklin M. Fisher, and James W. McKie," *United States of America v. International Business Machines*, Doc. 69 CIV. (DNE) U.S. District Court, Southern District, New York, pp. 36–38.
30. Pugh, "Memories That Shaped an Industry."
31. IBM, "Historical Narrative Statement."
32. Pugh, "Memories That Shaped an Industry."
33. IBM, "Historical Narrative Statement."
34. Brock, *The U.S. Computer Industry.*
35. IBM, "Historical Narrative Statement."
36. Katherine Davis Fishman, *The Computer Establishment* (New York: Harper & Row, 1981).
37. Rosen, "Electronic Computers"; Tomash and Cohen, "Birth of an ERA"; and Fishman, *The Computer Establishment.*
38. Rosen, "Electronic Computers."
39. Brock, *The U.S. Computer Industry.*
40. Fishman, *The Computer Establishment.*
41. IBM, "Historical Narrative Statement," p. 244.
42. Katz and Phillips, "The Computer Industry."
43. Rosen, "Electronic Computers."
44. Fishman, *The Computer Establishment.*
45. Brock, *The U.S. Computer Industry.*
46. The Editors of Electronics, *An Age of Innovation: The World of Electronics: 1930–2000* (New York: McGraw-Hill, 1981).
47. IBM, "Historical Narrative Statement," p. 250.

48. Mary Bartholomew and Elinor Gebredmedhin, "The PCM Vendors," *Datamation*, February 1979, p. 104.

49. "The Datamation 100," *Datamation*, June 1982, p. 114.

50. IBM, "Historical Narrative Statement," p. 694.

51. Brock, *The U.S. Computer Industry*.

52. IBM, "Historical Narrative Statement," p. 696.

53. The Editors of Electronics, *Age of Innovation*.

54. IBM, "Historical Narrative Statement."

55. Brock (*The U.S. Computer Industry*) cautioned that the IBM data were difficult to interpret because of a lack of detailed information on the assumptions behind them and on how overhead was calculated.

56. Moreau, *The Computer Comes of Age*.

57. Christopher Freeman, "Research and Development in Electronic Capital Goods," *National Institute Economic Review* 33 (1965):40–97.

58. Paul Stoneman, *Technological Diffusion and the Computer Revolution: The UK Experience* (London: Cambridge University Press, 1976).

59. Christopher Freeman, *The Economics of Industrial Innovation* (Cambridge, Mass.: MIT Press, 1982).

60. IBM, "Historical Narrative Statement," pp. 200–300.

61. Fishman, *The Computer Establishment*.

62. Katz and Phillips, "The Computer Industry."

63. Freeman, "Research and Development in Electronic Capital Goods," p. 51.

64. U.S. Bureau of the Census, *Census of Manufacturers, 1967*, Table 1a.

65. Pugh, *Memories That Shaped an Industry*.

66. IBM, "Historical Narrative Statement," p. 168.

67. Brock, *The U.S. Computer Industry*.

68. Freeman, "Research and Development in Electronic Capital Goods," p. 62.

69. Ibid.; Daniel Shimshoni, "Aspects of Scientific Entrepreneurship," unpublished Ph.D. thesis, Harvard University, Cambridge, Mass., May 1966; and James M. Utterback and Albert E. Murray, "The Influence of Defense Procurement and Sponsorship of Research and Development on the Development of the Civilian Electronics Industry," Center for Policy Alternatives, Massachsuetts Institute of Technology, Cambridge, Mass., June 30, 1977.

70. John Bound, Clint Cummins, Zvi Grilliches, Bronwyn H. Hall, and Adam Jaffe, "Who Does R&D and Who Patents?" in *R&D, Patents, and Productivity*, ed. Zvi Grilliches (Chicago: University of Chicago Press, 1984).

71. Brock, *The U.S. Computer Industry*.

72. This dispute resulted in some tense moments in the early 1960s for IBM, which was counting on implementing the core memory in its

comprehensive 360 series. IBM had hedged by entering into a cross-licensing agreement with RCA in 1957, which enabled each party to "practice patent methods and processes of the other party in the manufacture and use of Data Processing Machines and Systems," including RCA patents pertaining to the core memory (Pugh, *Memories That Shaped an Industry*). But it had no such agreement with MIT.

73. Pugh, *Memories That Shaped an Industry*.
74. In 1964 Honeywell's H 200 replacement for the IBM 1401 was equipped with a program called the Liberator that could convert 1401 programs. It turned out to be fairly successful because it was technologically superior and IBM's 360/30 successor was not compatible with the 1401. The Spectra that RCA delivered the next year, which could run on 360 programs, did not, however, make much of a dent in IBM's market in spite of its lower price and more advanced circuitry. (See Brock *The U.S. Computer Industry*.
75. Scott Schmedal, "Taking on the Industry Giant," *Harvard Business Review* (March/April 1980):82.
76. Rosen, "Electronic Computers."
77. Moreau, *The Computer Comes of Age*.
78. Pugh, *Memories That Shaped an Industry*.
79. Rosen, "Electronic Computers."
80. Brock, *The U.S. Computer Industry*.
81. Jacques S. Gansler, *The Defense Industry* (Cambridge, Mass.: MIT Press, 1981).
82. Utterback and Murray, "Influence of Defense Procurement."
83. Edward B. Roberts and H.A. Wainer, "New Enterprises Along Route 128," *Science Journal* (December 1968):79–83.
84. Brock, *The U.S. Computer Industry*.
85. Ibid.

4 MAINFRAMES AND THE COMPUTER INDUSTRY: 1965 AND AFTER

This chapter examines the evolution of the computer industry after 1965, focusing on developments that influenced the ability of new firms to enter and innovate. The analysis of the mainframe sector begun in Chapter 3 continues and at the same time the stage is set for the story of minicomputers and peripheral equipment in the three chapters that follow.

THE CHANGING MARKET

Toward the middle of the 1960s, a metamorphosis of the computer industry began that was to vastly expand opportunities for new entrants. Some of the barriers to entry of new firms that had marked the earlier decades commenced to crumble and, at the same time, new markets opened whose barriers were less formidable. A consequence of these developments was the entry into the computer industry of hundreds of new enterprises and older ones as well. Nevertheless, to keep the trend in perspective, note that by the late 1970s IBM still accounted for half of the entire U.S. computer industry's revenues and the next six companies (which included the relative newcomers DEC and CDC) accounted for another 30 percent, leaving only 20 percent to all other enterprises, new and old.[1]

Two sets of developments loosened IBM's grip on the market as a whole during this period. The first was the steep decline in the cost of achieving a given level of performance, which, together with their expanding capabilities, put computers within the reach of previously untapped classes of users and created opportunities for entirely new applications outside of the traditional market. Accompanying the decline in costs were lower capital requirements for entry into the emerging sectors of the computer industry. The second set of developments consisted of institutional and technological changes that made it easier to produce computers and peripherals that were compatible with IBM processors. The first of these developments stimulated the creation of new markets outside of IBM's traditional customer base and the second made it possible for independent companies to attract some customers away from that base.

The main forces driving down costs were the growing amount of circuitry that could be packed onto the silicon chips that began to replace transistors in the 1960s, and the increasing modularity of equipment. Between 1960 and 1980 the number of circuits per chip doubled every year, while the price of an integrated circuit fell from about $50.00 when ICs first appeared in 1960 to $1.00 a decade later. (Large-scale integrated circuits, LSIs, and very-large-scale integrated circuits, VLSIs, which arrived in the 1970s, cost considerably more, of course.) Economies achieved in the production of components were passed on to large and small computer manufacturers alike in the merchant market. A crucial factor in permitting small, new computer firms to exploit the solid state revolution was the existence of a well-developed supply of semiconductors for the merchant market in the United States, in contrast to the situation in Europe and Japan, where semiconductors were supplied almost entirely by captive producers.

Computer systems became increasingly modular with the emergence of microprogramming, which began to replace hard-wired instructions in the computer's control unit around the middle of the 1960s as the high-speed magnetic core memory reduced the time involved in reading programmed instructions from the memory sufficently to make the process worthwhile.[2] Microprogramming, invented by Maurice Wilkes in 1951, stores programs for complex operations in the computer's memory and gives users a certain amount of freedom to design their own machines. Later, with the arrival of the general purpose microprocessor in the 1970s, specialized microcoding became less expensive than specialized electronics, with the result that computer systems became clusters of modules, each performing a specific system function. Markets developed for suppliers of many different kinds of modules, each containing a microprocessor and its microcode supporting the controlled device. No longer did a computer manufacturer have to develop and produce a complete system.

Microprogramming also made it possible to program a computer to perform the machine language operations of a competitor's machine, the first successful example of which had been the Honeywell 200, introduced in 1964 as a compatible replacement for IBM's 1401 mainframe. It also permitted IBM to develop the 360 family of computers that were compatible throughout moving up the line.

As a consequence of these developments, near the middle of the 1960s the computer industry began to branch out in two directions from the central artery of general purpose mainframes, while the latter continued, for the most part, to be supplied by a handful of established firms. The first branch led to the marketing by independent companies of peripheral equipment, and later central processors, that were compatible with IBM processors, and the second towards smaller and less expensive computers.

IBM COMPATIBILITY

Plug-Compatible Peripherals

The production of peripheral equipment that was compatible with IBM processors and could be easily attached to them (plug-compatible peripherals) began around 1965 following IBM's delivery of the first entire family of computers to be both hardware- and software-compatible, moving up the line from the least to the most powerful model. Before the System 360, IBM offered 15 different processors, included in 7 different lines of second generation (transistorized) computer systems, all dissimilar in architecture and programming. Input/output equipment was developed almost uniquely for each processor in order to optimize performance but, at the same time, it limited flexibility and attachment possibilities. The same was true of competing manufacturers' systems.[3] With the System 360, IBM developed a simple architecture for all of its computers and adopted standard interfaces so that the same peripherals could operate with any of the family of processors. This permitted a wide range of system configurations and made it possible for customers to upgrade modularly. Standard instruction codes and formats provided programming compatibility which permitted upgrading without software conversion. The achievement was a momentous one. Later, other companies moved in the same direction, but it was 10 years or more before any achieved compatibility throughout a broad range of systems.

The market consequences of the 360's modular compatibility were of two opposing sorts. First, it raised the capital cost of entry to suppliers of competing processors. The advantages to the buyer of owning a system that could be upgraded without new software, and the economies realized by the supplier in producing and servicing such systems were significant, but the capital costs of developing them were very substantial. (We saw in Chapter 3 that IBM invested a half billion dollars in development costs alone for the 360). On the other hand, by creating defacto standardization, the 360 opened up a market for independent suppliers of IBM-compatible peripherals. A plug-compatible peripheral can replace a unit supplied by the mainframe manufacturer simply by unplugging the old peripheral and plugging in the new one. But a peripheral manufacturer cannot be sure of achieving compatibility with the appropriate controller until it obtains the detailed device-to-controller interface specifications, and this cannot be done (legally) until the mainframe reaches the market. Advances in microprogramming shortened the time it took to bring a compatible peripheral to the market and the 360 family of computers vastly expanded the potential market for such peripherals.

A number of independent companies had manufacturered peripherals for sale to various other mainframe manufacturers since the early 1960s, but IBM had traditionally made its own. When, to compete in the IBM replacement market, it was necessary to design a separate peripheral for each of IBM's central processing units, the venture was evidently not attractive to independents. But once a single peripheral could be offered as a replacement throughout the entire 360 family, the market became more enticing, just so long as IBM held the prices of its peripherals high enough. Until the early seventies it did under its so-called price umbrella, and independents who had formerly sold only to computer vendors or original equipment manufacturers (OEMs) now turned to the end-user market. (OEMs assemble the major components of a system for sale to final consumers, after adding software.)

The peripherals market was one that new firms could penetrate. Considerably less capital was required to manufacture and market peripheral equipment than to deploy a mainframe system, and for customers the purchase of a printer or a disk drive from an untested vendor entailed much less risk than the purchase of an entire system. Peripherals were, by comparison, inexpensive and simple, and their performance could be more easily evaluated relative to competing brands on the basis of a test run. Moreover, since PCs are compatible with the customer's existing hardware, software conversion problems are not involved. Nevertheless, customers' concern, in the beginning at least, about the consequences of deploying a mixed system had to be overcome or compensated by charging a lower price.

The first to succeed in the market for IBM-compatible peripherals was a new company called Mohawk Data Sciences, founded in 1964. Mohawk invented the Keyed Data Recorder, the earliest device to transcribe data from a keyboard directly onto standard magnetic tape mounted on a tape drive. As a replacement for the keypunch, it was fast and cheap and reduced the number of operators required, and one reel of tape could store data that would require 36,000 IBM cards.[4] Although the device sold slowly at first, by 1966 Mohawk had installed 15,000 units. It did not actually plug into an IBM system; instead it worked independently, side by side with it. Fishman suggests that it was no accident that the product of the first company to enter the plug-compatible market did not plug into the system.[5] Its separateness helped to allay customers' fears that the equipment of an upstart firm might bring down the entire system, and it certainly eliminated possible disputes over which vendor's equipment was at fault in the case of a breakdown. Even though Mohawk's device did not plug in, it demonstrated for the first time that a small company could market a product to replace part of an IBM system.

Mohawk was founded by a group that left Sperry Rand's Univac Division after the latter dropped its effort to develop the same device,[6] and it went on to become a major supplier of data entry equipment and distributed data processing terminals. In 1967 and 1968 several other companies introduced similar machines, among them IBM, signaling the end of its singleminded commitment to punched cards.[7]

Plug-compatible peripherals first appeared in 1967 when Potter Instrument offered a replacement for the IBM 729 and 2401 tape drives, which it marketed through Management Assistance Incorporated (MAI). At about the same time (some sources say earlier) a small firm called Telex came out with a plug-compatible tape drive priced to undersell IBM's drive and still make a considerable profit, although the product did not represent any kind of an innovation. In April 1973 IBM won a countersuit filed in response to a complaint brought by Telex. In the countersuit Telex was found guilty of "infringing IBM's copyrighted manuals and illegally inducing former employees to reveal IBM trade secrets."[8] Telex had recruited IBM employees with specific knowledge about products it intended to copy. The suit highlights the problem of plug-compatible manufacturers (PCMs) in gaining access to specifications of the competing equipment they were to replace, which meant waiting until the IBM model was on the market before "reverse engineering" could begin. The delay, of course, reduced the life cycle of the independents' peripherals. As a part of the Telex decision in 1973, IBM was required thereafter to disclose its peripheral interface specifications as soon as the product was announced or went into production.[9]

In 1968 Memorex, a seven-year-old peripherals vendor, became the first to offer a plug-compatible disk drive. It had, according to IBM testimony, hired 600 IBM employees between 1967 and 1970.[10] According to the same testimony, by 1969 all major peripherals vendors offered IBM 2311 and 2314 type disk drives. The early PCMs struck where IBM was vulnerable on both price and technology,[11] and they targeted the largest markets, where each installation averaged several disk and tape drives.

Other peripherals manufacturers turned to the plug-compatible market in the late 1960s, moved in part by the fact that mainframe suppliers other than IBM were starting to make their own peripherals, as peripherals became an increasing proportion of a system's total cost. Also, the recession that began around 1969 may have made IBM customers more cost conscious. Although the independents' peripherals were often slightly ahead of IBM's due to the technological leapfrogging that characterizes sustained periods of rapid advance in technology, their main advantage was price. The PCM market for disks, tapes, memories, and input-output equipment attracted hundreds of companies for a while, including already established OEM suppliers (suppliers to original equipment manufacturers who assemble systems for sale to customers) such as Potter and Memorex as well as many newcomers.

Until the early 1970s IBM's "price umbrella" permitted firms operating on a much smaller scale to undersell it and still make an attractive profit and, indeed, provided the one reason for the existence of the PCMs.[12] Development costs were relatively low since independents could rely on reverse engineering. By the early 1970s, independents had gained 10 to 13 percent of IBM's disk and tape customer base and their share was expected to grow. IBM, which seemed to be willing to tolerate a share of about 10 percent but no more,[13] struck back with selective price cuts and with its Fixed Term Lease Plan. The FTP offered customers an 8 percent price reduction on the first year's lease and a 16 percent discount on the second year of the lease, with stiff cancellation penalties, whereas, previously, leases had been on a month-to-month basis. Other price and product actions aimed to drive the PCMs out of the market followed, many of which are described in internal IBM documents filed in the Telex case.[14]

By the late seventies, all but a handful of U.S. PCMs had left the peripherals market or merged with other companies. The remainder held between one-third and one-quarter of the IBM peripherals market.[15] They were chiefly CDC, Memorex, and Storage Technology (which was to file for bankruptcy in 1985), all founded in the early sixties. But numerous peripherals manufacturers still catered to the booming minicomputer and later the microcomputer market. Plug-compatible peripherals manufacturers were not, on the whole, conspicuous for their innovations. With the exception of Mohawk, they tended to be followers, keeping pace with IBM technology or a little ahead as the trend toward progressively better and less expensive equipment continued and IBM was slow to update its technology. (We will, however, see in Chapter 7 that STC and CDC introduced advances in disk drive technology.) It was common to obtain know-how by hiring former IBM employees (the founders of STC and Memorex were former IBM engineers). Capital requirements were relatively low in this market where the product was only a single component of a system and IBM provided the basic technology. The market was there and PCMs had only to detach the customers from IBM. They could succeed with some customers by underselling the giant so long as it failed to follow a limit pricing strategy. IBM was discouraged from following that strategy by the fear and actuality of antitrust actions; but it was also more profitable for the company to maintain its price umbrella so long as it could eliminate competition when the going got tough. The evidence suggests that, on the whole, it could.

Plug-Compatible Mainframes

The mainframe industry seemed to have settled into a groove of maturity by the beginning of the seventies, with each of the major manufacturers concentrating on upgrading for its own captive users rather than capturing new markets. Then, in fall 1975, the first IBM-compatible mainframe was introduced by Gene M. Amdahl. Plug-compatible processors use the same programs, operating instructions, and peripheral equipment as IBM machines.[16] Amdahl had left IBM in 1970 after designing three of the company's most powerful computers (starting with the 704), managing the development of the architecture for the revolutionary 360 family and later supervising an advanced, large-scale computer design project. When IBM decided to abandon that project, Amdahl decided to found the Amdahl Corporation to continue it on his own.[17] His first mainframe contained a number of innovative features and, more important, it started a trend toward the manufacture of replacements for IBM CPUs by independent companies which gave them, for the first time, a toehold in IBM's established mainframe market.

Amdahl's machine had the first 80-pin logic package (state-of-the-art packaging was 48 pins). It was the first to use individualized convection patterns to make unique components, and it introduced the concept of separate logic paths for diagnostics to allow remote diagnosis.[18] Besides these and other innovative features, Amdahl offered IBM customers something that IBM did not: a compatible upgrade from the top of the IBM line. The Amdahl machine also had a performance/price advantage of 50 percent over IBM's highest grade equipment.

IBM had abandoned the advanced design project that Amdahl directed when it concluded that the new computer would not make a profit under the pricing strategy for its 370 series. (The 370 had by 1970 become the main line of IBM computers, succeeding the 360.) According to Amdahl, the price, which was based on the new machine's performance relative to other IBM 370 machines, would have put it out of reach of so many potential customers that revenues would not cover its development costs. Since his was an independent enterprise, not bound by that pricing policy, Amdahl was convinced he could produce the machines at a profit, and he proved to be correct.[19] Like the three new entrants in the earlier stage of mainframe development (DEC, CDC, SDS), Amdahl was able to dispense with a large marketing organization since he targeted a relatively small group of highly sophisticated customers, and, like the others, he began with a purchase-only policy. Also, in common with some of his predecessors, Amdahl had made considerable progress in the development of his product before he left his former employer. (He reported that when he departed he had not solved the problem of large-scale integration that underlay the new machine but believed he understood the nature of the problem.) Moreover, his development costs were only 15 to 20 percent of IBM's because IBM manufactured all of its own components and had to support their production with R&D, whereas he concentrated on making logic chips and purchased memory and other components in the commercial market. Because his machine was compatible with IBM's, Amdahl did not have to invest in software development. Finally, following in the footsteps of his three predecessors, he avoided competition with any of IBM's existing machines. His, like CDC's 6600, was an upgrade, with the advantage that IBM customers could migrate to it without software conversion.

In spite of lower capital requirements, Amdahl needed to raise $40 to $50 million in a market where venture capitalists were convinced that it was impossible to compete with IBM. The going was not easy. He obtained $2 million in first-stage capital from a venture capital company and, after completing the circuit design, was able to attract funds from two foreign computer companies and some American investors through joint ventures. Japan's largest computer company, Fujitsu, in 1972 set Amdahl on its course by putting up $35 million in equity, loans, and inventory financing to form a joint venture. It was enough to see Amdahl's first machine onto the market.[20] The company continued to offer mainframes more powerful than IBM's and by using software that corresponded to IBM's advanced function microcode, kept up with changes in IBM circuitry. IBM caught up by the end of the seventies and in 1980 Gene Amdahl left the firm he had founded.

IBM was, however, slow in responding to the more powerful performance offered by Amdahl. It was three years before it bounced back with the 3303, the first of a new series, which had a price/performance ratio better by a factor of two than its 370 predecessor and outperformed the Amdahl machine.[21] Delivery delays however, left room for plug-compatible processors in the late seventies. Near the end of the decade National Advanced Systems (National Semiconductor) came out with a machine that was competitive with Amdahl's and IBM's most powerful models. Fujitsu and Hitachi, active contenders in the PCM market abroad, supplied American PCMs with hardware.

In the latter half of the 1970s there was a surge of interest in plug-compatible processors, once users had demonstrated their receptivity to Amdahl's machine. The rapid decline in component prices, along with the continuing evolution of microprogramming and other flexible modular design techniques, permitted increasingly rapid response to IBM design changes. At the same time, the rising cost of software rendered changes in architecture less and less attractive to customers because of high conversion costs and IBM was encouraged to slow its rate of change in processor design.

IBM's pricing behavior in the early 1970s was also a factor in the entry of PCMs into the processor market. Stiff competition from peripherals manufacturers led IBM to shift its profits to processors in order to lower margins on peripherals while maintaining overall profitability, on the theory that demand for processors was relatively inelastic because of more limited competition. Thus, in spite of the fact that costs of electronic components had fallen steadily, IBM processor prices rose sharply until 1976. In that year Itel, a large CPM peripherals vendor, introduced the Itel As/5, manufactured by National Semiconductor, the first plug-compatible replacement for an IBM CPU. (Amdahl's computer had been a step up from any of IBM's models.) From that year on, IBM processor prices slid downward. But the price umbrella still permitted PCMs something like a 10 percent margin until after the conclusion of the government's antitrust suit against IBM in the early 1980s.[22] By the end of the decade it was possible to enter the low end of the plug-compatible processor business with as little as $5 million and one firm managed with only $2 million. Low-end plug-compatible CPUs were packaged and priced like minicomputers with very little effort toward product differentiation. The leading PCMs, however, were not new companies, but came typically, like Itel and CDC, from other branches of the industry.[23] The PC processor vendors never achieved more than a tiny fraction of the mainframe market, and by the early eighties almost all had left it, except for Fujitsu and Hitachi and their affiliates, which included Amdahl and National Semiconductor. Except for Amdahl, none of the plug-compatible machines is recorded in the annals of important innovations, although some were active in upgrading technology.

MINICOMPUTERS AND MICROCOMPUTERS

The arrival of the low-cost minicomputer with DEC's $18,000 PDP-8 in 1965 heralded the opening of an entirely new market for computers in which the traditional mainframe suppliers, for the most part, were to take a back seat. A decade later "super minicomputers" came into competition with mainframes, but the traditional minicomputer was not a replacement for the mainframe; in many applications it complemented it. The distinctive feature of the minicomputer at the outset was its ability to operate in a real-time and interactive mode. Thus, it was introduced originally as a dedicated machine for laboratory instrumentation or industrial control purposes where it did not compete with mainframes. Later, distributed processing, networking, and small business applications came to claim a larger share of minicomputer applications. Their low price and real-time capabilities paved the way for acceptance in settings and applications that were previously unimagined.

Many of the factors that helped to lower the capital costs of entry for PCMs were at work in the minicomputer industry, and they are discussed in Chapter 5, but, because minicomputer manufacturers did not compete for customers of mainframe vendors, they did not have to hurdle barriers to entry presented by the dominant firm in that market. By the early 1970s about 50 firms were supplying minicomputers, composed of a mixture of old and new enterprises, with the latter dominating the market. Only one of them, Honeywell, supplied mainframes as well.

An inevitable complement to the minicomputer was a miniperipherals industry. The cost of standard peripherals often exceeded the cost of the processor and a new peripherals industry was spawned to serve the minicomputer and later the microcomputer customer. No single firm dominated the minicomputer market the way IBM dominated mainframes and CPU suppliers were content to let the independent suppliers of peripherals do the innovating. Although DEC is the largest single supplier of miniperipherals, it does not attempt to set standards. OEMs are major distributors of minicomputer systems and they, rather than the customer, select the peripherals to be packaged with the system. Unlike mainframe peripherals, there was no end-user market for minicomputer peripherals in the 1970s. The trend among miniperipherals suppliers has been toward increasing diversification, but each peripheral tends to have a dominant supplier within a price class.

The invention of the microprocessor at Intel in 1972 set the stage for still another wave of computers even smaller and cheaper than minicomputers, namely the microcomputer, or personal computer, which came along in the late seventies. The costs of starting up in this industry were even lower than in minicomputers and at the outset the established suppliers of mainframes and minicomputers posed no threat to new entrants. The earliest entrants were new to the field and they were followed by hundreds of small competitors. But the pioneer, Apple Computer, maintained a dominant position by virtue of the enormous volume of applications software that was available through independent vendors that interfaced with its system alone.

By the early 1980s the doors were closing on the small microcomputer entrepreneur with the entry of IBM into the market and strong price competition from the Far East. IBM's entry created, however, a new market for independent suppliers of parts and peripherals for small machines because, in a major departure from precedent, it farmed out production and assembly of its personal computers to manufacturers of nonproprietary parts, most of them relatively small companies.

MAINFRAMES

Testifying in the 1970s for the government in *United States v. IBM*, F.G. Withington, a respected analyst of the computer industry, pronounced that "technological innovation in the general purpose computer business (is) at least as rapid today as at any period in the past and more rapid than in some periods."[24] Processor speed continued to grow and the cost per 100,000 multiplications and per million bytes of memory moved steadily down. Other advances included increased ease of programming and of error detection, reliability, ability to perform diverse functions, serviceability, and the advantages of modularity and compatibility across a single vendor's family of computers.

While the computer industry as a whole was branching in two directions that were more inviting to new entrants than traditional mainframes, the mainframe industry proceeded along its earlier course. Except in the PCM market, the barriers to entry were more firmly established than ever. By the 1970s, according to testimony on behalf of IBM in the Justice Department's antitrust suit, it would take $200 million to $300 million to develop a general purpose mainframe system and set up a nationwide marketing and servicing organization.[25] Government witnesses claimed the amount was still higher, and Brock estimated that initial capital requirements were over a billion dollars.[26] In the early eighties IBM still claimed 60 to 70 percent of mainframe revenues. Burroughs, Honeywell, Sperry, NCR, and CDC were next in line, RCA and GE having dropped out in the early seventies. (In 1986 the merger of Burroughs and Sperry put them in second place.)

The only notably innovative general purpose mainframes (aside from Amdahl's plug-compatible machine) that were produced by new or relatively new companies during this period were in the supercomputer class, and the persons chiefly responsible had been closely associated with each other since the infancy of the commercial computer industry. They were William Norris, founder of CDC, and Seymour Cray, chief architect at CDC until he left to found Cray Research in 1972.[27] In 1971, CDC delivered its Star 100 ("Star" stood for String Array Processor), the first computer capable of 100 million instructions per second. Utilizing many advanced features, including distributed processing, virtual addressing, and recent advances in monolithic memory, it represented an evolution of CDC 6600 ideas. The Star 100 and Texas Instruments' Advanced Scientific Computer (ASC) were the first large-scale computers to concentrate on efficient pipeline array processing and take advantage of the parallelism available when processing vectors or numerical arrays.[28] But TI subsequently left the mainframe industry and CDC's Star 100 was plagued with problems.[29]

Only four of the Star 100s and seven of the ASCs were installed before what was referred to as the first generation of supercomputers gave way to the second generation when Cray Reasearch delivered the Cray-1 in 1976. It was optimized for speed and arranged in a semicircle to minimize the length of connections.[30] The Cray-1 was described as a "new architecture . . . with evolutionary similarities to the CDC 6600 and 7600."[31] It extended their pipeline concepts and added vector processing, but its most important improvement over the first generation was its scalar processor for nonvector operations. It was still the world's fastest scalar computer in 1983.

Cray followed in the footsteps of other successful new computer firms to circumvent entry barriers. First, it avoided competition with IBM, CDC or any other computer manufacturer, by building a machine that was considerably more powerful than any other. The Cray-1 made possible entirely new operations rather than replacing existing machines. Second, the initial capital required was low. Seymour Cray's unique reputation permitted him to raise $2.5 million through a private stock offering at once and again two years later, to be used mainly for research and engineering development and the purchase of components.[32] Although Cray computers sold for $10 million, only one or two a year were produced and the company could start out with only 30 employees. (By 1985 there were 1,500 employees and annual R&D costs had risen to $75 million.) Customers were sophisticated research organizations that provided their own applications software and required minimal marketing expenditures ($450,000 during the first three years). The first computer was leased to Los Alamos in 1976 and thereafter equipment was sold. Although the cost of servicing is relatively high, it is not subject to economies of scale because each customer installation employs a permanent maintenance crew. Cray determinedly continued to specialize in a narrow line of supercomputers, resisting pressure to move down the line or diversify into peripherals or services.

Elsewhere in the mainframe industry technology continued to advance. With the 4300 series in the late seventies, IBM achieved what has been described as "its first really new computer hardware technology since the introduction of the System 360/85," 11 years earlier.[33] It resulted from IBM's new highly automated design process, which married computer manufacturing with semiconductor manufacturing to increase performance and reliability and eliminate waste in the use of standard LSI chips.

Burroughs continued to be first in the market with new technology,[34] introducing the first intelligent terminal with its TC 500 forms-handling machine and later the B1700, which eliminated the need for a compilation stage, executing program languages directly out of control memory. One small mainframe company that made a name for itself by innovating early in this period was Standard Computer Corporation, which introduced loadable microprogramming with its IC6000 series in 1969.[35]

It is generally agreed that the most sweeping advances in performance of mainframes and all other computers were propelled by the spectacular progress in the semiconductor industry. In 1966 Scientific Data Systems was the first to incorporate integrated circuits in a commercial computer, launching the third generation. Later, Data General, a new minicomputer firm, pioneered with medium-scale integration and subsequently became the first to use semiconductor memory in a commercial computer. In 1971, IBM's 370 computers became the first large-scale commercial systems to adopt monolithic semiconductor main memory. A small firm, Advanced Memory Systems, had three months earlier marketed a semiconductor add-on memory.[36] Later, in its 4331 and 4341, IBM was ahead of the pack in incorporating a 64K (that is, with the capacity to store 64,000 binary digits—or bits—of information) memory chip. Unlike its competitors, IBM made most of its own semiconductor devices and beat the Japanese in the race to produce the first 64K dynamic RAM chip (see Chapter 8), but it encountered difficulties in performance and IBM was forced to turn to outside suppliers.

MARKET ANALYSIS

Nothing occurred during this period to fundamentally alter the structure of the mainframe market, where the seeds of the industry had first taken root. Old line firms remained entrenched. The prominent newcomers, Cray and Amdahl, following in the footsteps of CDC, carved out niches at the very-high-performance end of the market, which IBM and its competitors did not serve, while other new firms flooded into new markets at the opposite end of the spectrum. Only the PCMs competed head on with IBM, and their success, such as it was, was mainly confined to the peripherals market by the end of the seventies.

Newly founded companies followed one of two strategies. Either they produced products that did not compete with existing products (and in some cases, like Mohawk and Amdahl, complemented them), or they marketed products that IBM allowed to compete under its "price umbrella." Because it was easier than before to achieve compatibility with another vendors' products, customers were less firmly locked into their installed equipment. Plug-compatible peripherals vendors could not avoid product differentiation barriers but instead surmounted them by underselling IBM so long as it maintained higher than normal profit margins. Had it chosen to follow a limit pricing strategy, IBM could no doubt have prevented entry.

New firms nevertheless faced the usual handicap in assembling capital. In spite of the fact that a venture capital market had developed by the late sixties and small, new electronics firms, as a group, were beginning to acquire an aura of success, the amount of capital that most new companies could assemble remained small. They were obliged to find markets and strategies whose threshold capital requirements were correspondingly limited.

NOTES

1. F.G. Withington, "Transformation of the Information Industries," *Datamation*, November 15, 1978, p. 8. See table 1, p.11.
2. R. Moreau, *The Computer Comes of Age: The People, The Hardware, The Software* (Cambridge, Mass.: MIT Press, 1984), p. 107.
3. IBM, "Historical Narrative Statement of Richard B. Mancke, Franklin M. Fisher, and James W. McKie," *United States of America v.*

International Business Machines, Doc. 69 (IV) CIV. (DNE), U.S. District Court, Southern District, New York, pp. 271 ff.

4. Katherine Davis Fishman, *The Computer Establishment* (New York: Harper & Row, 1981).

5. Ibid.

6. International Data Corporation, *Data Capture Equipment*, July 24, 1970.

7. International Data Corporation, *EDP Newsletter*, April 25, 1968.

8. Gerald W. Brock, *The U.S. Computer Industry: A Study of Market Power* (Cambridge, Mass.: Ballinger, 1975).

9. International Data Corporation, *EDP Newsletter*, September 24, 1973; and Brock, *The Computer Industry*.

10. IBM, "Historical Narrative Statement."

11. Datapro Research Corporation, *Datapro 70*, March 1984.

12. Philip H. Dorn, "The Mixed Blessings of Mixed Installations, *Datamation*, April 1972, p. 61; and International Data Corporation, *EDP Newsletter*, June 3, 1971.

13. International Data Corporation, *EDP Newsletter*, June 3, 1971.

14. See Brock, *The U.S. Computer Industry*. One example was moving the controller for the 3300 disk drive into the 370's central processor. IBM claimed that the shift from the disk drive to the CPU was motivated by efficiency considerations. [See Franklin M. Fisher, John J. McGowen, and Joen E. Greenwood, *Folded, Spindled, and Mutilated* (Cambridge, Mass.: MIT Press, 1983).] Whatever the reason, one consequence was to restrict the ability of PCM disks to attach to the 370 CPU.

15. Mary Bartholomew and Elinor Gebredmedhin, "The PCM Vendors," *Datamation*, February 1979, p. 104.

16. Laurence Solomon, "IBM Versus the PCM's," *Datamation*, February 1979, p. 100.

17. Scott Schmedel, "Taking on the Industry Giants," *Harvard Business Review* (April/May 1970):82.

18. Bartholomew and Gebredmedhin, "The PCM Vendors."

19. Schmedel, "Taking on the Industry Giants."

20. Gene M. Amdahl, "The Early Chapters of the PCM Story," *Datamation*, February 1979, p. 113.

21. Stephen J. Ippolito, "Measure for Countermeasure," *Datamation*, February 1970, p. 120.

22. It is widely believed that under the threat of that suit, IBM avoided actions that might have increased its market share. Its more aggressive behavior after the cloud of the suit was lifted helped to drive Magnuson, one of the four remaining PCMs, into Chapter XI proceedings in 1983.

23. CDC, the third company to enter the PCM market, after Itel, was not only a leading supplier of supercomputers and PCM peripheral equipment

but operated an extensive EDP service network as well. Its plug-compatible CPU, the Omega Series, was developed by IPL Systems in Waltham, Massachusetts, a spin-off from Cambridge Memories. CDC purchased IPL's marketing rights in 1974 and funded further development.

24. Fisher, McGowan, and Greenwood, *Folded, Spindled, and Mutilated*, p. 173.

25. Ibid.

26. Brock, *The U.S. Computer Industry*, p. 57.

27. Recall from Chapter 3 that Norris had also founded ERA which, along with Eckert-Mauchly in the late 1940s, was one of only two companies to take the plunge into the commercial computer market. After joining Remington Rand in 1952, Norris left that company's Univac Division, along with Cray, to found CDC in 1957. At CDC Cray designed the CDC 6600, the most powerful computer of its day, and the still more powerful 7600 in 1968, which was far ahead of any of its competitors in computing speed.

28. Edward W. Kozdrowicki, "Supercomputers for the Eighties," *Digital Design*, May 1983, p. 94.

29. *Business Week*, October 29, 1979, p. 156.

30. The Editors of Electronics, *An Age of Innovation: The World of Electronics, 1930–2000* (New York: McGraw-Hill, 1981), p. 8.

31. Kozdrowicki, "Supercomputers for the Eighties."

32. Telephone conversation in 1984 with John Carlson, chief financial officer and executive vice president, Cray Research, Inc.

33. David Stein, "Price/Performance, Semiconductors and the Future," *Datamation*, November 25, 1979, p. 41.

34. International Data Corporation, *EDP Newsletter*, December 9, 1975.

35. It permitted the operator to load a special set of cards that set instructions in micromemory in order that different emulators could be loaded into the same machine ("IBM Follows a Tiny Leader," *Datamation*, August 1968, p. 89). IBM soon added the technology to its 360/25 (Dorn, "The Mixed Blessings of Mixed Installations").

36. Dorn, "The Mixed Blessings of Mixed Installations."

5 MINICOMPUTERS

INDUSTRY OVERVIEW

In 1965 the minicomputer industry took off. Although similar machines had been produced earlier, that was the year that Digital Equipment Corporation (DEC) of Maynard, Massachusetts launched its PDP-8 (Programmed Digital Processor Model 8), a stripped-down model selling for $18,000. It was a high-speed computer, built for real-time, interactive operations, designed to be used on a dedicated basis, and its modularity permitted it to be easily interfaced with other equipment. The PDP-8 had only a 12-bit word length (compared with 32 or 36 for most mainframes at the time).[1] DEC was founded by Kenneth Olsen and Harlan Anderson after they left MIT's Lincoln Laboratory where Olsen had worked on Whirlwind and its descendent the TX-0, the precursor of the minicomputer. Before the PDP-8, DEC had built the PDP-1, with an 18-bit word length and the best performance/cost ratio of any real-time computer of its day.[2] Other companies, too, offered 24-bit machines, but it was soon recognized that for interactive or other dedicated tasks a computer with a smaller word length would reduce the cost while retaining the ability to perform a wide range of functions. The PDP-5, a second generation minicomputer, was in effect a brilliant compromise, delivered in 1963. Two years later, through very careful engineering of modules, DEC was able to mass produce the

PDP-8 for a price that broke the $20,000 barrier for the first time. Its 4K memory became standard, and it was four times faster and a third less expensive than the PDP-5.[3] The PDP-8 essentially defined what was to become the traditional minicomputer and created the market for such machines.

The Shaping of the Industry

Minicomputers did not, at the outset, compete in any way with mainframes. Being small and cheap, they could undertake real-time functions that could not be performed economically or at all on the larger machines. The minicomputer was every bit as powerful as many more expensive counterparts for most applications, but because of its small size and modularity, it was regarded as a tool for problem solving and often as a component of a larger system. At first minicomputers were employed almost entirely in scientific research and industrial process control. By the 1980s these applications still constituted half of the market but about a quarter of all minicomputers were used in the rapidly growing commercial and automatic transactions sector and the remainder in either problem solving and computation or system support functions. Early minicomputers had to be programmed in assembly language or even machine language, but their sophisticated users could be counted on to do the programming. Soon a group of independent firms emerged whose role was to combine proprietary software with hardware to create minicomputer packages for special applications. These were the original equipment manufacturers (OEMs) or systems houses. To this day they remain the most important group of customers for minicomputer manufacturers. The growth of OEM sales was strongly influenced by the very highly specialized nature of minicomputer applications, each requiring its own systems configuration and software. To facilitate specialization, microprogramming is typically provided as an "open box" with which users or OEMs can adapt the computer to the customer's needs, an option that mainframe manufacturers do not generally offer. Microprogramming permits instruction codes to be stored in the memory rather than hard wired into the computer, and with programmable read-only memory instructions can be rewritten to suit the user's need.

As it gradually became evident that minicomputers could also be used as general purpose problem-solving machines to supplement the increasingly powerful mainframes, minicomputer manufacturers began to supply systems software to facilitate applications programming in higher level languages. DEC's PDP-11, announced in 1971, had only a paper tape assembler (which operated on the same principle as punched cards) and very little software, while the PDP-11/70 top-of-the-line computer announced in 1975 was supported with sophisticated systems software on which the company spent as much as on the hardware.[4] The number and variety of applications programs offered by third parties expanded greatly for both batch type and interactive applications.

In the early seventies, successively more powerful and less expensive new minicomputers were introduced by a growing number of vendors— about 50 in all by then. The price of the PDP-8 fell to $2,000 and the speed and memory capacity of new machines doubled within a few years. By 1974 the 16-bit minicomputer was replacing the 12-bit as a standard and was available with 4K memory for $20,000.[5]

Minicomputers expanded into business functions where they were used as general purpose machines, as the central element in intelligent terminals, and as processors in special applications, such as word processing, data collection, retail accounting systems and many others.[6] A distinctive characteristic of the minicomputer continued to be the highly specialized nature of the functions served by different vendors' machines and the idiosyncratic software required for each application. Almost every application was industry-unique, if not user-unique[7] and by the early seventies, individual vendors had taken on identities reflecting this specialization. Some concentrated on instrumentation, others on time sharing or on communications and real-time systems. Some dealt with OEMs and others targeted end users. Large companies like DEC supplied a wide range of processors aimed at different applications while small companies specialized.[8] For the most part, each company's computer displayed fundamental architectural distinctions, reflecting the vendor's approach to solving a particular class of problems.[9]

Early in the seventies the industry sent out shoots in two new directions that by 1977 led International Data Corporation (IDC) to divide it into three sectors: the "traditional" minicomputer, priced between $2,500 and $25,000, the "micro" minicomputer selling for under $500 in OEM quantities, and the "super" minicomputer in the $50,000 to $150,000 or over class.[10] In 1977 the total number of minicomputers shipped was divided among the three classes of computers in the following way: traditional, 60 percent; microminis, 30 percent; and superminis, 10 percent.

Classes of Minicomputers

The traditional minicomputer remains the PDP-8 and its direct descendents, which include machines with 6-bit as well as 12-bit word lengths. By the 1980s, DEC still led in this field, followed by Data General, which spun off from DEC in 1972, and Hewlett-Packard, an instruments firm that had entered the market in 1966. IBM also entered the competition in 1976 with its Series/1, whose acceptance was not enthusiastic. Industry experts have typically been reluctant to classify IBM's entries as minicomputers, mainly on the grounds that IBM's marketing strategy does not aim at the same customers as do minicomputer vendors. The Series/1, was designed primarily for use in large systems configurations that depend on an IBM mainframe.

The so-called microminicomputer was typified by DEC's LSI-11 series, introduced in 1972, which claimed half of this sector of the worldwide market in the early eighties. Another firm, Microdata, first offered the very inexpensive minicomputer, but its Microdata/1 was soon discontinued. DEC's micromini permits customers to upgrade all the way to the top-of-the-line VAX /780 without software conversion. Its chief competitors have been Data General, Texas Instruments, Computer Automation, and General Automation. DEC's inability to meet all of its demand in the late seventies opened doors to other vendors. The microminicomputer, which is sometimes sold as a board and does not necessarily follow the 4K memory standard, is distributed almost entirely through OEMs.

The superminicomputer is characterized by DEC's VAX 11/780 and the company claims about a quarter of this segment of the market. The supermini, too, was originally introduced by a smaller and newer company, Interdata. Definitions vary, but according to IDC, a superminicomputer has a 16- to 32-bit word length, main memory capacity of 128K bytes or more, a memory cycle of 1 microsecond or less, an input/output transfer rate of 2 million bytes per second or more, and must have an assembler, operating system, and at least one high-level language compiler. But perhaps the characteristic that most sharply distinguishes the supermini is its large peripherals capability along with its communications capability. Whereas traditional minicomputers are a components business, superminicomputers are a systems business. Superminicomputers are sold mainly (though not entirely) to end users, rather than to OEMs,[11] and they require lots of maintenance and software support.

The original superminicomputer had a 16-bit word length, but in 1973 Microdata introduced a 32-bit machine and others followed. By the early eighties there were over fifty 32-bit models available from 19 vendors.[12] while the 32-bit minicomputer was at first aimed at the problem-solving or computation market because of its "number crunching" ability, commercial data processing has become its major growth area.

Just as with the traditional minicomputers, many supermini vendors have carved out niches where they have virtually no competition. Large vendors like DEC, Data General, and Hewlett-Packard design for commercial applications while Interdata, Prime, and other smaller companies typically aim at the general purpose OEM market. The superminicomputer business is less price sensitive than other minicomputer sectors, in part because the CPU is a much smaller part of the total system cost. At the same time, the superminicomputer often competes with mainframes where it generally has a price advantage. Its systems capability is achieved more often through software than hardware, providing manufacturers with the ability to establish unique systems capabilities that are not easily duplicated by competitors.[13]

What is a Minicomputer?

The branching of the minicomputer industry toward more powerful, systems-oriented machines, on the one hand, and smaller and cheaper microcomputers, on the other, raised the question, what is a minicomputer? What distinguishes it from the mainframe in one direction and the personal computer in the other? Market analysts have debated the question interminably without agreeing on a clear-cut answer. The issue is complicated by the fact that there are fundamental architectural differences among the minicomputers that are available in any class. Nevertheless, until quite recently there was a fairly firm dividing line between companies deemed to operate in the minicomputer market or in one of the other markets. Probably the most widely accepted view of the minicomputer defines it in terms of a marketing philosophy rather than software or hardware specifications. Auerbach, a leading publisher of computer market information, identifies it with the philosophy of "selling the user what he needs to solve his problem," as distinct from the mainframe vendors' philosophy of selling the customer what they have in their product lines.[14] Experts have historically excluded IBM from the market on the grounds that its approach to selling was designed to extend the influence of its general purpose mainframes rather than to provide the user with tools.[15]

Another approach defines the minicomputer with reference to what it does not include, reflecting the compromises that have made it possible for minicomputers to maintain their low prices relative to other machines of comparable power. From the outset the minicomputer has been a powerful machine, capable of performing as well as its more expensive counterparts in many applications. Its low cost was achieved by eliminating characteristics that are not needed for certain applications. Originally the compromises focused on word length, programmability, and peripheral equipment, but, as time went on, it was possible to upgrade minicomputers to eliminate many of their early deficiencies without raising their cost. By the mid seventies, a fairly consistant set of traits had emerged, including relatively small size, low price, and ability to adapt to virtually any systems-related task due to their high-speed input/output (I/O) devices, their memory timing, and their direct memory access, real-time clocks, and power failure protect features.[16] At the same time, most minicomputers were ill-adapted to floating-point arithmetic operations. Finally, minicomputers are generally sold, not leased, and most can be purchased on circuit boards and through OEMs.

But the markers between minicomputers and other computers had become blurred by the end of the seventies, especially as minicomputers moved increasingly into commercial use. Superminicomputers now compete in many cases with mainframes, traditional minis with small business computers and microminicomputers with personal computers. Beginning in 1983, *Datamation*, which ranks the top 100 EDP money makers every year, concluded that superminis and mainframes like IBM's 4300 had become sufficiently competitive with each other to warrant counting mainframe vendors' sales of such equipment among minicomputer sales in their list. One result was to place IBM at the top of the list. The present analysis does not follow that classification. IBM aims at the information management sector of the market, not the traditional territory of minicomputers.

Minicomputer Companies

In sharp contrast to the mainframe industry, growth and innovation in the minicomputer industry was spurred mainly by what are defined here as new enterprises during its 20-year history, as reflected in the age of firms that are responsible for the major share of minicomputer sales. Since the early seventies, 35 to 50 firms have occupied the industry at any given time. In terms of age and status they can be divided into four groups.

First, and most important, are companies that started out with the objective of making minicomputers. Most of them continue to make only minicomputers. The company that stands out in this category is, of course, DEC, which has never accounted for less than 30 percent of total minicomputer revenues. It was the second largest computer manufacturer in the world, with revenues over $6 billion in 1985. There are three other conspicuous members of this group: Data General, which spun off from DEC in 1968, grew rapidly to claim third spot in the industry by 1977, and has been in second or third place ever since; Prime Computer, which spun off from Honeywell in 1971 and was number 4 in 1981, and Tandem, which spun off from Hewlett-Packard in 1974 and was number 8 in 1981. Many other leading contenders qualify as new, including General Automation, and Computer Automation, founded in 1966–67. This entire group has claimed well over 50 percent of the market all along and, according to *Datamation*, held about 65 percent in 1982 (before IBM was included in its list).[17] In addition, many successful new entrants were acquired by established companies to gain footholds in the industry, notably Microdata, founded in the late sixties and bought by McDonnell-Douglas, and Computer Control Corporation, founded in the early sixties and acquired by Honeywell.

The second group consists of firms of roughly World War II vintage, which entered the minicomputer business from closely related industries. Most prominent is Hewlett-Packard, founded in 1938 to manufacture scientific instruments. Throughout most of the seventies and the early eighties it held second or third place in the minicomputer industry. Three other instrument makers of about the same vintage were at various times prominent minicomputer manufacturers: Varian, Gould, and Perkin-Elmer. Wang Laboratories, founded by An Wang after leaving Harvard University's computer laboratory in 1951, is generally credited with the success of the word processor and became one of the top ten minicomputer vendors. Texas Instruments, a small geological survey company that became a major innovator and the market leader in semiconductors, also entered the minicomputer industry.

The third group of enterprises consists of the leading American mainframe vendors. The major contender historically has been Honeywell, which bought out a small innovative minicomputer company in the late sixties to provide support for its systems operations and had managed to stay among the top five minicomputer money makers by the early eighties. Control Data (CDC) and Sperry Univac had negligible market shares, and IBM's role in the industry is, as we saw, ambiguous. Both IBM and Honeywell marketed minicomputers to support their large systems.

The small share of the market that remains, goes to older companies that entered from noncomputer fields, such as McDonnell-Douglas and Raytheon, established aircraft and electronics companies, respectively. Established companies, new and old, that moved into minicomputers came mainly from fields of potential minicomputer applications like instruments and aircraft, and one from mainframes. Only Texas Instruments integrated forward into the industry. With a few exceptions (most notably IBM and Hewlett-Packard), they entered by acquiring relatively new minicomputer manufacturers, a pattern that we saw earlier in the mainframe industry when Remington Rand, Burroughs, and NCR each got its start through acquisition.

INNOVATIONS AND INNOVATORS

Rapid advances in performance and sophistication during the minicomputer's first decade were due as much to the ingenuity of component manufacturers as to computer designers. Limitations of early machines, such as memory speed, were overcome by the introduction of semiconductor memories and their rapidly falling prices during the seventies (see Chapter 8). The need for extensive and complex overhead such as buffers, multiphase clocks, and refresh amplifiers, was almost eliminated by semiconductor manufacturers, which incorporated most of these functions into the monolithic chip, while low-cost read-only memories (ROMs) and programmable read-only memories (p/ROMs) made it possible to greatly enhance the flexibility of microprogramming in order to optimize computer operations for individual applications.[18]

Minicomputer manufacturers have generally been ahead of mainframe vendors in adopting advances in solid state technology, in part because the size and complexity of their systems allowed for a shorter development period, and in part because their adoption was often of greater value in the production of low-cost machines. Replacement of the core memory by the much less expensive semi-conductor memory was of particular significance to minicomputers.

Because minicomputers have historically been distinguished by the large variety of different applications for which they are designed and the uniqueness of different vendors' approaches, there has been a continuous development of novel concepts that cannot be ranked in terms of overall importance. The attempt to identify innovations in the industry has chiefly turned up first usage of a variety of concepts or ⁻echnologies of the sort that can be fairly easily demarcated or quantified. To use such measures as a basis for classifying innovators in any industry involves a risk that some companies whose innovations were qualitative in nature will be left out of the count and that others who simply finished the race a jump ahead of a competitors will be given more credit than is their due. I feel confident that these dangers are unlikely in the case of minicomputers to misrepresent the relative roles of new compared with older groups of firms since the evidence points overwhelmingly to the importance of new companies in shaping the industry's direction and growth.

It is widely held, of course, that DEC pioneered the minicomputer and started the boom in the industry with its PDP-8 in 1965. Prior to the PDP-8, DEC had built the first computer designed specifically for time sharing, the PDP-6, and also the lowest cost system for remote access immediate response (RAIR) operations.[19] Nevertheless, there are experts who regard the founder of another small company, Gardner Hendrie of Computer Control Corporation (CCC), as the father of the minicomputer. A small manufacturer of computer modules, CCC came out with its first production computer in 1963 and followed up with fast, low-cost processors for scientific and special systems. It was ahead of DEC in sales by 1965 ($25 million compared with $15 million). The company offered a 16-bit minicomputer that was not only one of the very first but which has been described as offering just the right mix of capacity and economy to make the minicomputer take off.[20] But in 1966 CCC was bought out by Honeywell, which directed the efforts of its new acquisition toward support of Honeywell systems. Later Hendrie was laid off and by 1975, when DEC's sales had climbed to $500 million, Honeywell's minicomputer revenues were $90 million. Nevertheless, Honeywell remained consistently among the top five revenue earners in the minicomputer industry.

In 1968 a group of engineers left DEC to form Data General. The spin-off managed to become profitable within two years and has typically competed head on with DEC. Some describe the firm as merely following in DEC's footsteps. However that may be, the company produced a barrage of "firsts" in its formative years. It started out with the Nova, which sold for only $8,000 in spite of being equipped with many large computer features previously unavailable on minicomputers.[21] A year later the company introduced the first commercial computer in any size class to use medium-scale integration (MSI). In 1970 it brought out the Super Nova, which was 5 to 15 times faster than the Nova, and a later model of the same machine in 1971 became the first computer in any class to use semiconductor memory.[22]

Meanwhile, DEC's PDP-11, introduced in 1970, was based on an innovative architecture centered on a single, bidirectional bus. All processing, memory, and I/O elements were connected to the bus, allowing the computer to be modularly configured for a user's specific needs.

We saw that Interdata, founded in 1966, offered the first superminicomputer a few years later and Microdata delivered the first 32-bit supermini, which expanded the amount of memory that could be addressed directly and permitted a more sophisticated instructions set that greatly simplified programming. DEC was next with a 32-bit machine and other minicomputer vendors later followed. Data General's 32-bit machine was not introduced until 1980. Interdata's machines were also the first minicomputers to allow direct addressing to all main memory and to provide multiple (16) general purpose registers.[23] Microdata introduced the first microminicomputer, but its model was not a success. After the mid-1970s, advances in minicomputer technology became increasingly dependent on software, and hardware developments were directed mainly at the superminicomputer sector.

In 1974 James G. Treybig left his position as marketing manager for Hewlett-Packard to found Tandem Computers, which *Computerworld* described in 1983 as "probably the greatest success story in recent history in the computer industry." Tandem developed a "unique new architecture" that made it possible for the first time to deliver a true fault-tolerant computer at an affordable price.[24] The machine was aimed especially at the growing on-line transactions processing market where the consequences of failure can be extremely costly. The principle on which it was designed differed from the traditional redundant backup systems previously employed in two important ways: Many single points of failure were eliminated and it was possible to remove a defective subsystem and return it to service after repairs without disrupting ongoing operations.

Tandem concentrated on a single product aimed at a clearly defined market. Its innovation was based on software, and Tandem's role in production consisted only of assembly and testing.[25] Until the early eighties it had no competitors, but subsequently a large number of companies, most of them new, were attracted into the field, each with a slightly different approach. Their machines are usually targeted at either on-line transactions or industrial processing and control.

Minicomputers are the "cutting edge" of fault-tolerant systems, which are essential to the future growth of office automation. The most successful entry in the early eighties was Stratus, founded in 1980, which managed to assemble $15 million in venture capital and begin shipments in 1982 of a machine based on a principle entirely different from Tandem's.[25] Significantly, none of the established minicomputer or mainframe companies had entered this field by 1983, with the exception of DEC who had announced what was at that time an untested software-based fault-tolerant system. One market analyst attributed their absence to the large base of installed equipment that established firms would have to replace in order to introduce fault-tolerant systems and to the enormous cost of redeveloping entire families of computers along fault-tolerant lines.[27] Fault-tolerant capability cannot as yet be achieved by an add-on, but requires a completely redesigned system. Established customers would be required to undergo costly software conversion.

Wang Laboratories, which started out in 1951 to develop specialty electronic devices and in the late sixties moved into programmable calculators, introduced a CRT-based word processor in 1976 with disk storage for 4,000 pages and a 350 word-per-minute letter-quality printer. By 1978 it was the largest worldwide supplier of such systems. In the 1980s minicomputer firms led in the delivery of office communications and networking systems.

Another minicomputer market that developed with explosive force in the late seventies is computer-aided design and manufacturing (CAD/CAM). For the most part this market is made up of either computer manufacturers like DEC, Prime, IBM, and CDC that purchase software to combine with their own machines, or newer companies that purchase computers to combine with their own software. But one firm, Computervision, founded in 1969, began by making all of its own hardware and software and in 1980 claimed 40 percent of the CAD/CAM market. (By 1985 it had run into serious financial difficulties, however.) This is a sector that is extremely demanding of software effort largely because of the graphics display that is involved.

MARKET ANALYSIS

New firms clearly dominated the minicomputer industry and led in introducing innovative concepts and adopting new technologies. The contrast with mainframes can be explained in large part by the structural characteristics of the two markets. They account for the fact that, whereas mainframes have historically been controlled by a few large, established firms, it could be said of the minicomputer industry in 1973 that "just about any financially viable and technically proficient contestant can carve out a niche."[28] They do not account, however, for the negligible entry of large, established firms from neighboring industries that simply failed to anticipate and exploit the demand in this field.

The minicomputer industry has always had its dominant firm, but that firm, DEC, has maintained only about half the market share held by IBM in mainframes. The top 6 or 8 firms claimed about 80 percent of the minicomputer market throughout the 1970s but there was turnover within that club and always an additional 30 or 40 companies actively contending in a lower tier. By the end of the industry's second decade, the structure in some subsectors had begun to resemble that of mainframes at the same time that minicomputers had come increasingly into competition with them. Even so, an enormous diversity of opportunities continued into the 1980s to provide market niches whose barriers were not too high for new enterprises to hurdle and which few, if any, mainframe companies chose to explore. With one or two exceptions, the leaders in this industry have been companies founded after the onset of the electronics revolution. The majority are less than 30 years of age, were founded for the purpose of making minicomputers and continued to specialize in that product. We consider now the reasons that barriers that effectively prevented entry by new firms into the mainframe industry were of such little consequence in minicomputers.

As in other sectors of the computer industry, a potential new entrant does not face serious absolute cost barriers in the form of restricted access to patents or know-how regarding production technology, or to strategic resources, other than capital. The manufacturer of minicomputers is straightforward and it is not subject to important learning curve economies. The chief tangible resource requirement is scientific and engineering manpower, and it would be hard to find an industry, other than semiconductors, where the mobility of personnel is greater. Nevertheless, a particular firm at a given time may be in a favored position to employ an individual with a unique talent or specialized know-how, especially if the talent resides in one of the founders of the firm.

Newly founded enterprises face the usual handicap in the capital market, however, and for this reason the relatively small amount of capital needed for entry was instrumental in opening doors to them. DEC began operations in 1957 with only $70,000 from the first venture capital company to go public in the United States, American Research and Development, and was profitable at once. Data General was launched in 1968 with $800,000[29] and was profitable within two years. During the next three years it raised an additional $20 million through public stock offerings.[30] Less than $5 million was required in the early seventies for effective entry, although continual infusions of new capital were necessary to maintain market share in an industry growing at 30 to 40 percent per year.[31] By the late seventies, entry into some sectors of the minicomputer market required substantially more capital, in particular sectors that supplied complete systems and systems support and superminicomputers. But other niches remained open for small new firms. At the opposite pole from the superminicomputer were bare bones products like Computer Automation's "Naked Mini," which received an enthusiastic reception when it was introduced in the late seventies.

Capital Requirements

The high fixed cost of R&D that characterized the mainframe industry did not confront new entrants into minicomputers and, accordingly they could operate efficiently at a relatively small scale. Opportunities for disintegrating the production process and for minimizing the scope of production and the unit value of the product contributed, as well, to extremely low threshold capital requirements for entry into most sectors of the market.

Fixed Capital Costs.
Investment in R&D.   R&D has focused on development far more than research, directed, as it generally is, toward new applications rather than advances in fundamental scientific and technological concepts. New minicomputer manufacturers were among the hundreds of small companies that rode on the backs, so to speak, of major research organizations, public and private, that paved the way for the electronics revolution and moved it along. Their new products did not require years of intensive

research or a technological breakthrough. The main cost of R&D for a new start-up was likely to be little more than the forgone earnings of its founders. The modularity of minicomputers and the availability of parts and subassemblies from outside vendors that could be assembled by hand meant that a few engineers, working in a basement or a garage, could often develop a new prototype on a shoestring.[32] Rapid advances in semiconductor components facilitated improvements in performance and cost. By the late seventies many new firms entered the industry by producing software for specialized applications that they combined with hardware purchased from other vendors.

The pace at which new firms spun off from other minicomputer vendors was matched only by the semiconductor industry (Data General from DEC, Stratus from Data General, Prime from Honeywell, Apollo from Prime, Tandem from Hewlett-Packard). There is always a high probability in a spin-off that the founders have in hand the results of a certain amount of R&D that was supported by their former employer, a tradition begun when Ken Olsen left MIT's Lincoln Laboratory.

The fixed cost of investment in the design of systems software was kept to a bare minimum in the sixties by supplying neither operating systems nor compilers. But, as commercial applications became more important in the seventies, CPUs were increasingly expected to be equipped with software that permitted them to be programmed in one or more high-level language. We observed that the software for DEC's VAX 11 cost more than the hardware.

As the industry developed, the growing complexity of the larger minicomputers and a trend toward marketing of integrated systems demanded larger research efforts in order to compete in those sectors. By the mid-1970s, DEC, following in IBM's footsteps, had developed a complete family of computers that could be upgraded from the micromini to the top of the line VAX. In the late 1970s, Data General employed two dozen engineers intensively for more than a year and a half to develop its 32-bit minicomputer merely to catch up with its chief competitor.[33]

Plant and Equipment.   The manufacturer of minicomputers does not require a significant investment in fixed plant and equipment and it has been economical to disintegrate the production process to an unusual degree. The modularity of the minicomputer's design combined with the large amount of circuitry that could be packed onto a single semiconductor chip by the time it made its entrance in the sixties permitted manufacturing to be carried out essentially by assembling purchased components. In the heart of the minicomputer industry, near Boston's Route 128, a thriving infrastructure of job shops and parts suppliers existed in the early sixties and it kept pace with growth in the computer industry.[34] This support system was crucial to new firms that were developing prototypes and starting up production, and many continued to rely on it once they were established. Prime Computer and Tandem purchased almost all of their parts off-site. Data General, on the other hand, was responsible for 85 percent of the production that went into its system in 1980.[35]

Scope of Production. New firms were able to minimize the scope as well as the scale of operations, targeting specialized groups of customers. While DEC eventually built for many markets, most companies designed for specific applications such as communications, simulation, education, upgrades or replacements for small IBM machines, and so forth. Hewlett-Packard in 1977, for example, supplied the IBM System/3 upgrade market, while Lockheed aimed at the System/3 replacement market. Some aimed at the DEC market and others specialized in CAD/CAM, fault-tolerant computers, word processors, and so forth.

Unit Value of Product. Compared with mainframes, the cost of the traditional minicomputer has always been low, starting under $20,000 in the mid 1960s and falling steadily. Its design and construction is relatively simple and it was, at first, offered on a stripped down basis. The relatively small investment in R&D, systems software and marketing, which minimized opportunities for scale economies were instrumental, as well, in keeping down unit costs. Moreover, the original customers (engineers, scientists, and OEMs) did not count on the manufacturer to supply an integrated system or to provide educational and consulting services, applications software or peripherals.

As the market branched into commercial applications, demand for software and other support services grew, and some vendors began to supply their own peripherals, as well. In 1974 DEC offered for the first time a package that included a set of hardware components in the most commonly ordered configurations, together with software, education, training, and maintenance, all at a discounted price, and a number of other vendors followed. By 1979 one market expert observed that the small second tier minicomputer companies were facing serious capital constraints in their efforts to keep up with the growth in the market as emphasis shifted away from the traditional bare bones, "black boxes," sold to OEMs, toward the end-user market, which demanded "massive" outlays for software development, customer support and field sales forces.[36]

Superminicomputers made up an increasing, though still minor, share of sales by that time. They cost more to manufacture, software availability is an important selling point, and, because they are marketed directly to customers rather than to OEMs, selling costs are higher. Few, if any, new enterprises entered the market through this door. The suppliers of superminis were no longer small new companies. At about the same time, however, the microminicomputer was introduced, which could be sold simply as a circuit board, and it helped to keep the doors open for small new firms.

Product Differentiation

Product differentiation was not a major impediment to entry of new firms into the industry. As in mainframes, patents are not very effective in preventing imitation but, unlike mainframes, the vendor's reputation was not of overwhelming importance in selling the product. When the computer industry was in its infancy, customers had good reason to look to the reputation of suppliers. The first mainframes were not only costly and unfathomably complicated, but they were novel. Moreover, the mainframe customer depended on the vendor to design the system and often applications software, to train its staff, to service the system over the lifetime of its lease, and to provide future enhancements. When the time came for the commercial computer to supplant electromechanical office machines, office equipment companies with established reputations and market contacts were strategically placed to get the job. In retrospect it is not surprising that a company with IBM's history of customer relations and its huge installed base of tabulating machines carried off the prize. The runners-up, Remington Rand, Burroughs, and NCR, also had roots in the office machine business and the names of the handful of other successful contenders in the market were household words.

By the time the minicomputer arrived the technology had lost some of its novelty, but, of much greater importance, the product was far less expensive and easier for a customer to evaluate accurately than was a mainframe system. The minicomputer was, to begin with, much simpler than most mainframes, and it was sold generally as a separate component rather than an integrated system. These characteristics, together with the fact that services were generally sold separately, rather than bundled into a single package, greatly reduced the number of tradeoffs that had to be considered by a customer and the uncertainty in choosing among vendors. Because minicomputers were usually purchased to perform a relatively small number of specialized tasks, software conversion was not a major problem. And, finally, early customers were not corporate purchasing agents but, rather, scientists and engineers who could more securely evaluate the ability of a machine to do the job they wanted done.

It should not be overlooked that those firms potentially in a position to extend the advantages of their established reputations from computers or related industries simply failed to compete, for the most part, until a decade or more after the industry evolved. Some new companies, most notably DEC, soon gained solid reputations, but the advantage was not sufficient to significantly deter new entry. DEC's inability to keep pace with demand during much of the seventies helped to ease the entry of some new firms and rapid changes in technology make it possible for new entrants to leapfrog over established vendors with more up-to-date products from time to time. An even greater inducement to entry was the vast number of specialized niches in the market that offered opportunities that did not compete with DEC head on.

In a certain sense, the minicomputer market is not one but many markets that do not directly compete with each other. Long after the industry developed, new enterprises were able to create such markets without encountering established competitors, although they often had to fend off competition from DEC, whose well-financed R&D permitted it to move into their markets once they had been tested. DEC followed the pioneers into both the micro- and the superminicomputer markets, among others.

The failure of established companies from the mainframe industry seriously to compete in this industry is a pattern observed in several other industries that were populated by small new firms. Honeywell entered by buying out a going minicomputer firm. IBM did not compete directly with minicomputer vendors until the end of the seventies. Most other established mainframe companies steered clear of the market.

As the industry evolved, several leading vendors acquired a substantial base of customers wedded to software and operating procedures that could function only with compatible equipment. By that time, however, microcoding had made it relatively easy to duplicate the interfaces of competing equipment and turn out computers that were compatible in terms of both hardware and software. Some new entrants targeted the DEC replacement market. Others continued to design computers for specialized markets that the leading minicomputer vendors were unable or unwilling to supply.

NOTES

1. Word length is the unit, defined in number of bits, in which the computer receives information. Its size limits the accuracy with which a machine can perform arithmetic operations and determines the size of the instruction sets and the size of memory that can be addressed directly.
2. It also had an ingenious high-speed channel that provided direct access to the memory, sequential access (in which items must be reached in sequence as on magnetic tape) being too slow for real-time applications. R. Moreau, *The Computer Comes of Age: The People, The Hardware, The Software* (Cambridge, Mass.: MIT Press, 1984).
3. International Data Corporation, *EDP Newsletter*, October 19, 1967.
4. Stephen E. Scrupski, "Mini Makers Confront the Giants," *Electronics*, July 24, 1973, p. 66.
5. Richard C. Friedman, "Overview of Mini Architecture," *Data Management*, February 1974, p. 12.
6. L.C. Hobbs, "Minicomputers," *Datamation*, July 1974, p. 50.
7. International Data Corporation, *Minicomputer Marketplace*, August 1973.
8. John A. Murphy, "Available Mini Mainframes," *Modern Data* August 1974, p. 46.
9. Friedman, "Overview of Mini Architecture."
10. International Data Corporation, *Minicomputer Marketplace*, February 1982.
11. Ibid.
12. Robert W. Hauserman, "Finding Balance in the Mni-Market," *Computerworld Buyer's Guide*, August 24, 1984.
13. International Data Corporation, *Minicomputer Marketplace*, February 1982.
14. "Consultants See Minicomputers as Philosophy, Not as Definition," *Computerworld*, February 23. 1976, p. 59.

15. International Data Corporation, *Minicomputer Marketplace*, February 1982.
16. "Minicomputer Makers Grapple with Product Definitions," *Computerworld*, January 12, 1976, p. 43.
17. "The Datamation Top 100," *Datamation*, June 1982, p. 115.
18. Sidney Davis, "A Fresh View of Mini & Micro Computers," *Computer Design*, May 1974, p. 67.
19. International Data Corporation, *EDP Newsletter*, August 29, 1968.
20. "Lost Opportunity," *Forbes*, September 1, 1976, p. 34.
21. The Editors of Electronics, *An Age of Innovation: The World of Computers, 1930–2000* (New York: McGraw-Hill, 1981).
22. "The Long Hairs vs. The Stuffed Shirts," *Forbes*, January 15, 1976, p. 30.
23. Murphy, "Available Mini Mainframes."
24. Omni Serlin, "Fault Tolerance, Knocking Out Downtime," *Computerworld Buyer's Guide*, October 15, 1983, p. 34.
25. Myron Magnet, "Managing by Mystique at Tandem Computers," *Fortune*, June 28, 1983, p. 84.
26. Each subsystem of its fault-tolerant computer is duplicated on separate circuit boards that continuously check with each other to make sure that they are synchronized. If not, the faulty board "pulls out" and a new board takes over until the faulty board is repaired. (Murphy, "Available Mini Mainframes.")
27. Telephone conversation with Larry Marion of *Datamation* staff, 1984.
28. International Data Corporation, *EDP Newsletter*, October 9, 1973.
29. Tracy Kidder, *The Soul of a New Machine* (Boston: Little Brown, 1981).
30. Gerald W. Brock, *The U.S. Computer Industry: A Study of Market Power* (Cambridge, Mass.: Ballinger, 1975).
31. Scrupski, "Mini Makers Confront the Giants."
32. John S. Heckman, "What Attracts Industry to New England?" Federal Reserve Bank of Boston, *Economic Indicators*, December 1978.
33. Kidder, *Soul of a New Machine*.
34. Nancy S. Dorfman, "Massachusetts' High Technology Boom in Perspective: An Investigation of its Dimensions, Causes and of the Role of New Firms," Center for Policy Alternatives, Massachusetts Institute of Technology, Cambridge, Mass., April 1982, CPA 82-2.
35. "DG's High Stakes Gamble," *Datamation*, July 1981, p. 34.
36. "Woes for the Second Tier Minis," *Business Week*, Septermber 24, 1979.

6 COMPUTER PRINTERS

The computer printer industry is in some respects the most complex sector of computer peripherals to describe. Like most peripheral equipment markets, this one tends to divide between the high price and performance equipment designed for general purpose mainframes and the medium- to low-cost equipment for minicomputers and more recently for microcomputers. But, in addition, the technologies break along three distinct lines that do not necessarily parallel those that divide the end users. Specifically, a printer may

- print either a character (serial), a complete line or a page at a time,
- use either impact or nonimpact technologies,
- print either solid font or dot matrix characters.

Moreover, within each of those seven categories, a range of technologies is applicable and usually a range of price and performance characteristics.

A computer printer is a read-only device, driven directly by a computer, that prints discrete symbols on paper. The main standards of performance that concern end-users are legibility of print, speed of printing, and reliability of equipment. In addition, the kind and cost of paper that the machine accepts, ability to make multiple copies, flexibility of character type, plotting capability, size of machine, and noisiness

123

of operation may be of serious concern. Cost is increasingly a factor as computer prices fall. Because of the wide range of performance characteristics that may matter to a user, it is not really possible to rank printers according to a consistent set of criteria.

HISTORY OF TECHNOLOGY AND INNOVATION

Technological progress was significant during the printer's first three decades, but it did not begin to match advances in other sectors of the computer industry that we have examined.[1] The speed of operation increased much more slowly than in computers or disk drives and the drop in prices was slow by comparison, due, no doubt, to the important mechanical component of printers.

The very first computers operated with printers like the Uniprinter, a device similar to an electric typewriter, driven directly from tape.[2] Then, in 1952, shortly after delivering its UNIVAC I, Remington Rand brought out the first of the high-speed impact printers, printing a line at a time of solid font (fully formed) characters, that were to support the powerful mainframe's data processing output for the next three decades. During those decades some major changes occurred in the technology and the speed improved roughly threefold.

In the early 1960s a demand for printers to support small mainframes inspired the first low-speed, low-cost line printers, and they, too, used solid-font, impact technology. More than a decade later, in 1976, the dot matrix line printer first appeared; it has since emerged as the dominant technology among medium- and low-speed line printers. At about the same time, nonimpact printers, based chiefly on photoelectronic technology, were achieving very high speeds, printing a page at a time, but their high cost and other drawbacks limited their acceptance to a small corner of the market until the early 1980s.

A demand emerged in the sixties for less expensive printers to accept output at much slower rates than line printers from minicomputers (and later microcomputers) increasingly to be operated as keyboard printers in interactive data communications applications. The response was the serial, or character, printer, which prints one character at a time at much slower speeds than the line printer. Teletype produced the leading machine in this category at the outset and later shared the market with IBM's Selectric. The first major advance occurred with the daisywheel, introduced by Diablo in the early seventies. Soon after came the first dot matrix serial printers for customers in the same market who were willing to trade off quality of print for higher speed and lower cost. Expanding small business and word processing applications caused that market to flourish as the decade moved on.

Impact Line Printers

Impact printers transfer ink to paper, either by having a character strike a ribbon against paper (like a typewriter) or a hammer strike a ribbon and, in turn, paper against a character. Their chief advantages over nonimpact printers have been their ability to produce multiple copies, their high-quality print, and use of standard quality paper. Line printers produce a line at a time, either solid font or dot matrix. Most are in the 500 to 1,000 lpm (lines per minute) range and about one-third print 1,200 to 2,000 lpm. They usually cost between $5,000 and $25,000, but the price can exceed $100,000 and they are used with correspondingly expensive computers.

The impact line printer market as a whole is made up of 25 to 30 vendors, but some of them offer the products of other manufacturers under their own labels. These machines are work horses, and reliability is of the essence; thus customers depend on the reputation of manufacturers who often provide a complete line of printers to ease in upgrading and servicing. Vendors are typically well established companies with familiar names, including IBM, which sells only to its own systems customers, and Storage Technology and Data General, along with Teletype, Xerox, and General Electric from outside the computer industry. Most manufacturers of computers and peripherals avoid the printer sector, probably because the production process is complex and its mechanical component requires different skills and knowledge than the manufacture of most electronic equipment.[3] Newcomers Dataproducts and Printronix are the leading independent manufacturers, producing for the medium- and low-speed OEM markets.

Solid Font Line Printers.   Univac's 1952 solid-font line printer achieved speeds up to 600 lpm using a rotating drum. Around the drum at each print position a complete set of characters was embossed. A hammer, placed at each print position on the line struck the appropriate character as the drum spun on its horizontal axis. In the next few years, Sperry, Potter Instruments, Shepherd, and Analex increased the speed twofold. Typical printers of this type then sold for $50,000 to $75,000.[4]

In 1959 IBM's 1403 line printer, delivered with its 1401 processor, provided an enormous improvement in print quality. It used a horizontally moving character set and chains or trains rather than a drum. Slugs carrying several complete arrays of characters were either pulled (chain) or pushed (train) around a track that passed in front of the page. Hammers behind the paper fired precisely against each character to be printed as it came into position, pressing the page against the ribbon and in turn against the character slug. Improved quality and flexibility of type faces were its main advantage over the 1403. Previously, users had accepted low print quality, waving lines, illegible carbons, and restricted page layouts. The 1403, with its interchangeable print chains worked so well for so long that it shaped users' quality standards for years to come. According to IBM, the 1403 provided a "tremendous advantage" in marketing its 1401 systems until competitors began to offer satisfactory alternatives more than a decade later.[5]

In 1964 IBM announced the 1403-NI for use with its System 360 series of computers, which operated at 1,100 lpm, almost twice the speed of its predecessor. It was particularly important for customers with business applications such as payroll, billing, accounts receivable, and inventory control. Other systems manufacturers attempted to copy the printer and some, such as RCA, simply incorporated it into their product line. In the early seventies, IBM's 3211 line printer, built for the System 370, achieved 2,000 lpm.[6]

Competition in the IBM plug-compatible market for printers emerged in 1971 when Telex offered a replacement for the 1403-NI at a slightly lower price, but it captured only a very small share of the market. Even after IBM stopped making the 1403-NI in 1970 its popularity continued to support the sales of reconditioned models at prices about 25 percent below the initial selling price, and one company, as late as 1975, produced a controller to permit the 1403 to interface with computers of other manufacturers (a plug-compatible printer in reverse).[7] Both drum and chain or train printer technologies have remained in use, but the drum was on its way out by the early eighties.

The band printer arrived in 1970 and claimed over half of the line printer market by the early eighties. With its lower cost and easily interchanged character fonts, it had a dramatic impact on the industry.[8] Print hammers behind the paper push it against a ribbon that has a continuous steel band behind it, which is etched with characters and moves horizontally. Print band prices dropped by over two-thirds in the late seventies due to increasing competition and advanced technologies such as new alloys for the band.

A one-year-old company called Data Products (later Dataproducts) brought out the first low-cost and low-speed line printer, the 3300, in 1963 and subsequently became the leading independent producer of line printers. It was founded with start-up money from the management team and from three small-business investment companies, with the objective of producing a full line of peripherals for sale to OEMs.[9] In 1969 it offered the first line printer to sell for under $6,000 and dominated the medium- and low-speed line printer markets throughout the seventies.

Dot Matrix Line Printers.   Printronix's P 300 dot matrix line printer, introduced in 1976, a year after the company was founded, was probably the most important development in impact line printer technology of the decade. The dot matrix technology, which prints between 100 and 600 lpm (compared with 1,000 to 2,000 for the solid font line printers), is geared to the minicomputer and small business market.[10] The P 300 claimed about 13 percent of the line printer market by the early eighties and was emerging as the major line printing technology in the medium- and low-speed range. It does not require drums, chains, or bands to carry the type characters. Instead, printing is done by a bank of 44 hammers that are positioned horizontally across 18 dot positions (one at every third character position). Hammers are mounted on a shuttle that sweeps horizontally across three character positions. As it sweeps, the hammers are activated electromagnetically at each position where a dot is required by the release of springs that normally hold back the hammers under pressure from a permanent magnet. Seven to nine sweeps of the shuttle are used to complete a line of characters.[11]

Because it is fundamentally simpler than solid font line printers and has few moving parts, it is more reliable and, in addition, any number of type faces can be stored and changed without the printer slowing down. Since the hammers require only about one-tenth the energy of solid font mechanisms, they are much quieter. Finally, they provide full plotting capability. The dot matrix line printer is not as fast as the high-speed solid font printers, but it costs less ($5,000 to $10,000) and produces better print quality, especially for carbons. The characters, though dot matrix, appear to be solid because of their density.

Printronix, a spin-off from the peripherals manufacturer Pertec, was founded with a million dollars of the owners' funds and proceeds from overseas licensing, and after weathering a two-year financial crisis it became profitable. Since it could not afford a sales force, it turned to outside distributors, but it also sold directly to minicomputer vendors

DEC and Prime.[12] In the early eighties, Printronix introduced the first dot matrix printer of near letter-quality and was in second place behind Dataproducts among independent printer vendors.

Impact Serial Printers

Serial impact printers produce characters one at a time, either solid font or dot matrix. In 1981 solid font impact printers made up 21 percent of the entire serial printer market and dot matrix accounted for 57 percent while nonimpact printers accounted for the rest. Serial printers are slower, cheaper, and smaller than line printers and are used to produce hard copy from relatively slow computer output generated by mini- or microcomputers. They enjoyed a huge boom with the rise of distributed processing and word processing. Solid font serial printers produce high-quality print but did not exceed 60 characters per second (cps) by the early eighties. Dot matrix serial printers are faster, less expensive, and more reliable but print quality is inferior.[13] Growth in the serial market has been fastest among lower speed printers where price is particularly important to potential customers.

In contrast to line printers, the serial market contains about 150 manufacturers, most of whom make only printers, although a few computer manufacturers are among their ranks.[14] In the serial impact field as a whole new firms are plentiful and dominate innovation.

Solid Font Serial Printers.   The earliest serial printers, like the earliest line printers, were solid font. Until the mid-1970s, Teletype, a subsidiary of AT&T, and IBM dominated this market. A large proportion of Teletype's 10 cps cylinder printers were installed in AT&T or Western Union networks.[15] IBM's Selectric, or golf ball, print mechanism, introduced in the late sixties, allowed the operator to replace type styles easily with letter-quality print at 15 cps.

In 1970, the daisywheel printer, with twice the speed of the Selectric and greater reliability, was introduced by Diablo Systems, founded the year before by a team from Singer's Friden peripherals product-development division with initial financing of $2.7 million. It was profitable a year after the product was introduced.[16] Its HiType I printer replaced many electromechanical parts with electronic elements based on medium-scale integration (MSI) logic chips. It had only a dozen or so moving parts compared with hundreds in the Selectric. Off-the-shelf integrated circuits, whose prices had fallen dramatically in the preceding decade, made it possible to sell a printer for under $1,000 that would have cost $20,000 a decade earlier. (The Selectric sold for over $1,500 in 1970.) In place of the Selectric's metal ball, the daisywheel uses a reinforced nylon disk that costs a fraction of a dollar and has a print character on each of its 96 petals and electronic servos to control character, column selection, and paper feed. Diablo had earlier developed a successful disk drive, most of whose technology was used in the new printer, enabling it to be developed in less than a year's time.

Printer customers demand reliability first of all. Teletype and IBM had previously sewed up the market by providing unrivaled service. Diablo, instead, built a printer with a low failure rate.[17] It was initially marketed for data processing applications, leaving the word processing market unattended. Qume, a spin-off from Diablo with which it had a cross-licensing agreement, emerged as the leading contender in that market and was responsible for important subsequent advances in the technology.[18] In 1980 Qume's new drive mechanism reduced the size, weight, complexity, and cost of the daisywheel and advanced speed to 45–55 cps (a few years later it was up to 75 cps). The microprocessor replaced MSI chips to permit greater flexibility of design and lower cost.

Diablo and Qume dominated the word processor printer market until falling prices of word processors and printers introduced by IBM and Wang created pressure in the OEM market to deliver lower priced printers at the end of the decade. The demand was met by two newcomers to the market, both well-established manufacturers of typewriters: Olivetti and Triumph-Adler, through its subsidiary Pertec. Both capitalized on experience and on complementarities in the production of electronic typewriters. Volume production helped Pertec cut the cost of the printer by two-thirds,[19] although it cut print speed at the same time to 20 cps. Simplified, modular construction further reduced servicing requirements and down time.[20] Japanese manufacturers soon followed into the low-cost daisywheel market, putting pressure on American producers to lower costs. In 1982 the number of firms in this market was small compared to the burgeoning dot matrix field.

Dot Matrix Serial Printers. The first dot matrix serial printer for the commercial market was introduced in the early seventies by Centronics, a company founded in 1970.[21] In 1979 Centronics still held 60 percent of the OEM market for this type of printer. Texas Instruments, its closest competitor in the OEM market, held 17 percent, according to

International Data Corporation, while DEC, with a slower and less expensive machine that came with a terminal and keyboard, was the overall market leader. By the late seventies Centronics had branched into many other sectors of the printer industry.

The dot matrix serial printer was an answer to the slow speed of solid font printers like the Teletype and Selectric, which printed characters at the rate of 10 to 15 per second, and the daisywheel, which managed 30 cps at the time. While sacrificing print quality, the first dot matrix machines achieved 100 cps and by the eighties two or three times that. In the beginning it used a head consisting of a vertical row of seven wires that could be pushed out against an inked ribbon to make dots on paper, forming characters with a 5×7 matrix of dots. The wires were fired by a microprocessor, which had only recently been invented at Intel. Subsequently, in response to word processors demands, print quality was improved by increasing the number of wires per head and the number of passes of the head at each print line, the latter ususally at a sacrifice of speed.

By the late seventies, dot matrix technology predominated among the mini- and micro-based computer systems. Its success in serial as in line printing was due to the microprocessor, which, by the early eighties, generated excellent print quality, bidirectional printing (introduced in 1976) with speeds up to 300 cps, on-the-fly selection of character sizes and types (which are stored in the read-only memory), and data buffering, which permits the printer to accept bursts of data at high speeds. The printer supported many communications protocols and could produce up to six copies at a time, although lower cost printers do not, of course, meet all of these standards.

A succession of improvements in print head and the electronics during the first decade led to increased reliability and the most dramatic price reductions of any printers. Contributing to these advances were Florida Data and Printek, both new companies, and Data Products, along with Centronics. A company founded in 1975, Sanders Technology, is credited with the first near letter-quality dot matrix serial printer, the Media 12/7, which came out in 1978.[22] Selling for around $2,500 to OEMs only, it used a microprocessor-controlled print head that made up to four horizontal passes at each line of print. By the early eighties, most printers for personal computers were dot matrix, selling in the $300 to $500 range, but inexpensive daisywheels had begun to compete with them.

In order to meet the aggressive price competition that emerged toward the end of the seventies, mass production became important and by the eighties the new entrants were well-financed Japanese firms that essentially took over the market in the under $1,000 price range. Centronics was bumped from top place in the under $500 class and other American companies retreated from the very low end of the market, where expensive tooling was now required to compete.[23] The Japanese waited for markets and standards to emerge and, by 1981, claimed over half of the low-priced printer market. The Japanese-owned Epson America, held 35 to 40 percent of it in 1983. Quality workmanship and a high degree of automation in production gave the Japanese their competitive edge. According to an Epson spokesman, high quality and volume production were the key to the success of their low-priced MX 80 (80 cps).[24] In spite of the Japanese invasion of the market, as late as 1982 there were over 70 American firms making serial dot matrix printers.[25]

Nonimpact Printers

Paralleling development of impact printers, both serial and line, have been the nonimpact character, line and page printers. Nonimpact printers generally use coated or sensitized papers that respond to thermal or electrostatic stimuli to form an image. Some use ink jet or xerography and more recently laser beams to form an image on plain paper. The latter two photoelectronic techniques can produce over 200 pages per minute. Although a variety of nonimpact technologies emerged during the sixties and seventies, they failed to find acceptance in a wide spectrum of the market until after the early eighties, largely because of their dependence on special (often costly) paper, their inability to produce duplicate copies, and in some cases technical problems that were encountered. They are, however, quieter and often more reliable than the electromechanical devices, and can be much faster.

The earliest efforts to develop nonimpact technologies were for military use. Burroughs's electrostatic Whippet was developed in 1956 for military communications and only a few were produced commercially. Its maximum speed was about 360 lpm. Dots were formed by charges emitted from wire styluses onto electrosensitive paper. Motorola, six years later, produced a low-cost dot matrix printer for the military using a spark from a stylus that destroyed the coating of specially prepared paper. Radiation Inc., founded in 1953, made a superspeed alphanumeric page printer for the Lawrence Radiation Laboratory in 1963 which achieved over 30,000 lines per minute, and others (Omnitronics, a subsidiary of Borg Warner, Hogan Faximili, a subsidiary of Telautograph, and A.B. Dick, an office machine manufacturer) marketed electrostatic printers in the early sixties, while Benson Leherer and General Dynamics used other nonimpact techniques, all but the latter for military use.

Companies in the commercial market have been, with some exceptions, well-established firms, engaged manufacturing computers, copiers, instruments, or other electronic office equipment, entering typically with new, unproven technologies like Canon USA, AM International, and Delphax, with, respectively, laser, magnetographic, and ion deposition.[26] Small, new firms have been conspicuously absent.

Nonimpact Serial Printers.   Nonimpact serial printers include ink jet, conventional thermal, thermal transfer, and electrographic, all aimed at the low to medium-speed market. In 1963 R.G. Sweet invented the ink jet printing process at Stanford University. Ink is electrostatically charged, then magnetically deflected into a character pattern on a page. A.B. Dick, an office equipment manufacturer, eventually obtained Sweet's patent rights and in 1969 marketed the technology. Several others followed with this or similar technologies and Teletype came out with its own version but none was successful during the next decade. IBM was the leading producer of ink jets in 1980 with its 6640, which printed 90 characters per second with good print quality for use mainly with IBM word processing systems. Although it was the only near letter-quality ink jet on the market, by 1984 it was out of production. Sharp, a Japanese firm, achieved higher speed with a sacrifice in quality and Diablo (Xerox) and Canon entered the colored ink jet market. Although the technology was plagued by problems of ink clogging and drying, by 1985 they seemed to have been resolved.

Thermal was relegated to portable computer service because of its objectionable paper and print quality. Because of its low cost, it experienced rapid growth in sales with the boom in low- cost computers in the late seventies, but its popularity was short-lived.[26] In 1983 thermal-transfer printers, using a completely new technology, entered the U.S. market in the form of a proven Japanese product for providing low-cost output.[27]

In 1967 Varian Associates introduced what was described as the first "true" electrostatic printer, in contrast to those that depended on electrosensitive paper. A charge was applied to the paper that was then developed. It used expensive paper and there was a delay in the appearance of the print, but it was quite, reliable, and had the best price/performance ratio at the time.[28]

Nonimpact Page Printers.   U.S. companies operating in the very high speed market in 1980 were chiefly Xerox, IBM, Hewlett-Packard, Siemens, and Delphax.[29] Most of their machines printed a page at a time. Xerox became the leader in the very-high-speed market in 1967 when it offered its Computer Forms Printer, which made it possible to substitute 8½ by 11 inch paper for the unwieldy fanfold computer printout. In 1973 its 1200 became the first xerographic page printer, using an optical character generator and a rotating drum.[30] Its big advantage over other nonimpact printers was the use of plain paper. Later, IBM's 3800 and Xerox's 9700 introduced laser page printers that use a beam of light to create latent dot images on the surface of a photographic drum or belt which are then transferred to plain or specifically coated paper by means of a dry toner. At first, both suffered from excessive down time. Hewlett-Packard and Siemens subsequently announced more compact and less expensive laser printers but few users required the 20,000 lpm that this technology provided. At $100,000 to $400,000 they could be expected to find customers only where the load was extremely heavy. General Electric, 3M, Denison, and others in the early eighties were preparing to introduce magnetic printers aimed to replace the 3800 and 9700. Like laser printers, they are an extension of the xerographic process. By 1981, no high-speed nonimpact printers were available for less then $10,000, with the exception of Delphax's ion deposition printer, introduced in that year. At the low to medium end of the page printer spectrum, the Xerox 2700 offered 12 p/m for under $30,000 and many Japanese copier manufacturers provided machines with better price/performance ratios.[31]

MARKET ANALYSIS

New firms were the early innovators in the medium- and low-cost sectors of the printer industry. They concentrated on impact, rather than nonimpact printers, including serial printers and low- and medium-speed line printers, both solid font and dot matrix. Their innovations were most notable in the development of new mechanical technologies that lent themselves to electronic control and in the substitution of electronics for mechanical components in existing technologies, resting on the microprocessor after 1972. By the 1980s U.S. companies that operated at the lowest priced end of the dot matrix serial printer market were under serious competitive pressure from the Japanese. Mass production techniques, rather than new product technologies, had become the ticket to success in that sector and few American firms appeared to be interested in trying to meet such competition.

With respect to market structure, the printer industry can be divided into three sectors: nonimpact printers as a whole, high-speed solid-font impact line printers directed toward mainframe users, and lower speed impact printers of all kinds for use with mini- and microcomputers.

The Nonimpact Market

In the nonimpact sector production and innovation have been dominated by large, established firms, most of them from computers, office machines, and instruments, but occasionally other electronics industries. Diablo, almost the only relatively new company to contribute to this field, had been absorbed by Xerox by that time. The very speculative character of research and development in this area and the large amount of high-risk capital it involves suffice to explain the absence of new enterprises.

The High-Speed Impact Printer Market

Manufacturers of high-speed line printers, led by IBM, include a few computer companies, some independent peripherals vendors, most of whom had become well established in the sixties, and a handful of other large companies. Some of these vendors simply purchase the mechanical parts and add the electronics. IBM probably deserves credit for the most influential innovation, the 1403 printer in 1959.

Entry into this sector requires substantial capital and a field sales force.[32] The machines demand constant servicing and customers want to be assured of the availability of a full line of upgrades. Much the largest group of customers for these printers has always been IBM systems users, among whom IBM has strong product differentiation advantages. These markets might have been ripe for entry by vendors of plug-compatible equipment, for reasons discussed in Chapter 4, but no competitor, large or small, was able to match the performance of IBM's 1403 series for at least a decade after its delivery. Any one of these factors would probably suffice to explain the absence of small, new enterprises in the market for high-speed, solid-font printers. But a further explanation could have been a shortage of technological opportunities for innovation. New firms often make their way into the computer market by introducing a new product or by following in the wake of another new firm that does. Solid-font line printers, resting largely on mechanical rather than electronic technologies, did not benefit from the electronic advances that drove the wheels of progress in other sectors of the computer printer market.

The Medium- and Low-Speed Printer Market

It was the medium- and low-price and performance sectors of the printer market that opened doors for new companies and which saw the most rapid succession of new products. In 1963 Dataproducts began to introduce a sequence of medium- and low-speed line printers in time for the emergence of the minicomputer, and the firm dominated that sector of the printer market throughout the seventies. Other new companies introduced markets for the dot matrix serial printer (Centronics), the dot matrix line printer (Printronix), and the daisywheel serial printer (Diablo), at the medium to low end of printing technology, and other new companies helped to move these technologies ahead.

A case study, published by the Center for Policy Alternatives at MIT, of R.C. Sanders Technology Systems' development of the high-quality, low-cost dot matrix printer sheds light on factors that made it possible for small new companies to enter that sector of the market.[33] The concept for the new microprocessor-based printer was generated by R.C. Sanders, Jr., who founded the company in 1975 and who was formerly head of Sanders Associates, a major electronics research and development firm. Design and development took approximately two years, using a staff of 13 to 15 professional engineers, programmers, and technicians. About half of the printer's parts were mechanical and, although 90 percent of them were custom made (for example, sheet metal parts), the more complex ones, such as the cooling fan, stepping motor and print head, were standard items purchased in the open market and sometimes modified thereafter. All electronic parts were also standard, including the microprocessor, the erasable, programmable read-only memory, and the power system. A major component of the system was proprietary software.

The design philosophy of replacing mechanical complexity with complex functions in the electronics simplified mechanical design and made it possible to capitalize on the economies of scale in the electronic components industry that supplied the components. It also facilitated changes in design and product improvements and the construction of an entire family of products with different capabilities and interfaces. Marketing costs were minimized by selling to OEMs. The printer at the time was Sanders' only product and it sold for $2,500 at the rate of about 100 units per month. By 1984, Sanders Technology (Santec) was reported to have patent claims on some of the most sophisticated matrix technology on the market.[34]

These sectors of the printer industry displayed many of the structural characteristics that were found in other markets in which new firms have successfully entered and innovated. We consider now the manner in which such firms, in general, either avoided or dealt with traditional entry barriers.

Product Differentiation.   Product differentiation barriers were either avoided by targeting a market that was not supplied by any established incumbent or surmounted by marketing a product that was superior in price or performance to other products on the market from the point of view at least of some customers. When Data products introduced its medium-speed, solid-font line printers, aimed at the small business, and soon after the minicomputer, markets, no comparable machine existed. DEC, unlike its counterpart in the mainframe industry, has never produced solid-font line printers. Later, the dot matrix line printers that were introduced by Printronix in the mid-1970s competed indirectly with the Dataproduct line, but they represented an entirely new technology with lower price and speed and distinct advantages in reliability and flexibility. They were more suitable for some applications than their predecessors and less suitable for others.

Diablo's daisywheel competed directly with IBM's and Teletype's character printers, but it was more than twice as fast. Diablo overcame the advantages of its competitors' established reputations for service by designing a machine whose few moving parts resulted in an extremely low failure rate. When Centronics's dot matrix serial printer was introduced, it appealed to still other customers who were willing to put up with inferior print quality in return for much higher speed and greater flexibility than the solid-font serial printers. As in the minicomputer and small disk drive markets, in which new enterprises have found notable success, there are numerous different performance characteristics of printers that are of concern to customers as well as numerous options for meeting them that must be weighed against cost considerations. As a consequence, opportunities for creating products that do not compete directly with those of other firms have proliferated.

Because of the novelty of their products, companies like Diablo and Printronix, and probably Centronix, were not constrained by patents as a barrier to entry. Indeed, Printronix exploited fees from overseas licensing to help finance its start-up. Patent disputes among newcomers were not unheard of, however. Diablo and its spin-off Qume resolved theirs through a cross-licensing agreement, and J.C. Sanders, in designing his four-pin head, was careful to avoid conflict with competing patent claims through subtle alterations such as the slant of the pin array and the paper shift mechanism.[35]

Absolute Cost Barriers.   The only absolute cost barrier that new firms confronted in this industry was the capital cost disadvantage, since the production process was relatively straightforward and did not require either expertise or proprietary production techniques that established firms controlled. The limit on the amount of capital that a small, new firm can raise was met by following strategies similar to those observed elsewhere in this study: low- to medium-cost products, produced at first on a relatively small scale, using methods that did not involve large amounts of fixed capital per dollar of output.

The cost of a printer in this class ranged from $5,000 to under $1,000, substantially less than the work-horse high-speed line printers that were designed to operate with the powerful mainframes. Cost savings were achieved by marketing through OEMs or independent distributors, eliminating the need for a personal sales force and costly contacts with end users that were required for high-speed printers. Simplification of the machine's operation usually resulted in a significant reduction of moving parts, which reduced also the need for servicing. NEC Information Systems, as an illustration, claimed in 1980 that its new 350Q printer, for the low end of the market, by reducing the number of both mechanical and electronic parts by 50 percent or more compared with its previous models eliminated the need for factory and field adjustments and for periodic preventive maintenance and lubrication of moving parts.[36]

There are evidently economies of scale to be exploited in the production of printers, however, and they are especially important to firms competing at the very low end of the market where price competition is aggressive. We saw that two large manufacturers of electronic typewriters (Olivetti and Triumph-Adler) achieved significant price cuts through high-volume production of low-speed daisywheel printers in the late 1970s.[37] At least one of these firms was able also to exploit economies of scope by using the print head that it manufactured for its typewriters. The success of Epson in capturing a major share of the dot matrix serial printer market has been credited to advanced techniques employed in large-volume production, as well as to excellent quality control, and mass produced Japanese printers took over the low-cost dot matrix market by the eighties.

But the advantages of large-scale production do not generally emerge until a product becomes standardized and competition shifts from product design to price. By that time the innovative firms have frequently, themselves, achieved a substantial size or been absorbed by larger firms. Centronics, after introducing the dot matrix serial printer in the early seventies, held 60 percent of this market in 1979 before it was edged out of its leadership position by Japanese competitors in the early eighties.

Fixed capital per dollar of output was relatively small in large part because standard electronic components and mechanical parts were readily available from independent suppliers, permitting vertical disintegration of the production process. Research and development was typically aimed at simplification and at substitution of electronic for mechanical components, a far cry from the speculative and costly R&D that underlay advances in nonimpact techniques. Diablo's daisywheel employed a technology that it had already applied to its disk drive.

As evidence of the speed with which firms brought new products to the market and their initial capital requirements: Printronix relied on a million dollars of owners' funds and was profitable within two years while Diablo developed the daisywheel printer in less than a year with under $3 million in capital and was in the black the following year.

The Absence of Competition from Computer Companies.   Except for IBM and, in the beginning, Remington Rand, computer companies were not aggressive in developing and promoting new printers at all, much less at the low end of the market. Some observers believe that they simply did not want to get involved in manufacturing an electromechanical product that was remote in concept and construction from the electronic devices that they normally produce. In a sense, there is simply no good reason for a computer company to manufacture printers except for advantages in marketing it may exploit, based on an established reputations and economies of scope. On the other hand, large, established firms, including only IBM from the computer industry, were and are at the forefront of developments in the very-high-speed nonimpact technologies, an area in which they have an advantage over small companies in mounting research and development programs and in access to certain specialized skills and technical knowledge. Because of its volume of computer sales, IBM has an incentive to develop complementary products, including printers and other peripherals, that enhance the value of its computers to customers. Unlike most computer vendors, it has been involved historically in the development of computer peripherals. It has, however, been left largely to independent companies to develop printers for smaller mainframes and minicomputers and microcomputers.

NOTES

1. "Line Printers: Band and Matrix Technologies Hold the Fort," *Mini-Micro Systems,* January 1982, p. 157; "The Impact of Nonimpact Printing," *Datamation,* September 1963, p. 24.
2. Saul Rosen, "Electronic Computers: A Historical Survey," American Computer Manufacturers, *Computing Survey* (January 1969):7–36.
3. "Line Printers"; Richard Ireland, "Print Band Technology Matures," *Mini-Micro Systems,* January 1982, p. 213; and Gerald W. Brock, *The U.S. Computer Industry: A Study of Market Power* (Cambridge, Mass.: Ballinger, 1975).
4. "Figuring the Economics of the New Page Printers," *Datamation,* May 1978, p. 171.
5. IBM, "Historical Narrative Statement of Richard B. Mancke, Franklin M. Fisher, and James W. McKie," *United States v. International Business Machines,* DOC 69 CIV. (DNE), U.S. District Court, Southern District of New York, p. 320.
6. Dataproducts, Inc., *The First 20 Years of Dataproducts,* 1982.
7. Jonathan Ayers, "Plug-Compatible Printers in Reverse," *Modern Data,* December 1975, p. 30.
8. Ireland, "Print Band Technology Matures."
9. The Editors of Electronics, *An Age of Innovation: The World of Electronics, 1930–2000* (New York: McGraw-Hill, 1981).
10. According to Moreau, IBM had introduced a dot matrix line printer as early as 1957, the 730 with a speed of 1,000 lpm, but it was delicate and expensive and did not gain acceptance. [M. Moreau, *The Computer Comes of Age: The People, The Hardware, The Software* (Cambridge, Mass.: MIT Press, 1984)].

11. "Line Printers Continue Their Impact," *Mini-Micro Systems,* January 1981, p. 61.
12. Dun's Review, March 1981, p. 44.
13. "The Impact of Nonimpact Printing," *Datamation,* September 1964, p. 24.
14. "A Look at the Japanese Printer Industry," *Mini-Micro Systems,* January 1982, p. 187.
15. David ₊H. Axner and F.H. Reagon, "Teleprinter Terminal Survey," *Datamation,* May 1978, p. 232.
16. "A Printout Unit Challenges IBM," *Business Week,* February 19, 1972.
17. Ibid.
18. "Survey of Serial Printers," *Mini-Micro Systems,* January 1981, p. 97.
19. The Editors of Electronics, *An Age of Innovation;* "Pertec Printer Undercuts Daisywheel Price 50%," *Mini-Micro Systems,* December 1980, p. 49.
20. "The Low Down on Low Cost Daisywheel Printers," *Peripheral Review,* published by Pertec Computer Corporation, Spring 1981, p. 1.
21. The Editors of Electronics, *An Age of Innovation.*
22. "The Impact of Nonimpact Printing"; R.T. Lund, M.A. Sirbu, and J.M. Utterback, "Microprocessor Applications: Cases and Observations," Center for Policy Alternatives, Massachusetts Institute of Technology, CPA-79-3, May 15, 1979.
23. "A Look at the Japanese Printer Industry"; "Japanese Infiltrate Low End of Printer Market," *Mini-Micro Systems,* May 1981, p. 27.
24. "Japanese Infiltrate Low End of Printer Market."
25. Patrick Kenealy, "Sunny Times for Serial Printers," *Mini-Micro Systems,* January 1981, p. 77.
26. "Starring the Micro and the Matrix," *Mini-Micro Systems,* January 1978, p. 71.
27. Edward Webster, "New Technology Printers Challenge Daisywheels," *Mini-Micro Systems,* January 1984.
28. "Nonimpact Printers," *Datamation,* May 1973, p. 71.
29. Jonathan W. Dower, "Challenging the Old Guard," *Computerworld Buyer's Guide,* October 1983.
30. "Figuring the Econmics of the New Page Printers."
31. Dower, "Challenging the Old Guard,"
32. "Line printers Continue Their Impact."
33. Lund, Sirbu, and Utterback, *Microprocessor Applications.*
34. Edward S. Foster, "Sanders' Print Head Could Set New Price/Performance Standard," *Mini-Micro Systems,* January 1984.
35. Ibid.
36. The Editors of Electronics, *An Age of Innovation.*
37. Ibid., "Pertec Printer Undercuts Daisywheel Price 50%."

7 MAGNETIC DISK STORAGE

In this chapter a second computer peripheral industry is examined, magnetic disk storage devices. It begins by tracing their evolution and, then, describes the major innovations and the firms that were responsible for them. In the concluding section the market forces that accounted for the performance of new firms as innovators are analyzed.

THE EVOLUTION OF MAGNETIC STORAGE DEVICES

Magnetic disks, like magnetic tapes, are a form of addressable secondary computer memory. Their main purpose is to store information (instructions and data) that is not immediately being worked on by the processor in such a way that it can be conveniently and speedily transferred to the computer's main memory when needed, while the computer's main memory stores information that can be accessed directly by the computer. Information is usually accessed in groups, or "characters," containing eight bits of data. These groups are called bytes, and the "capacity" of a memory is normally measured in terms of the number of bytes of information that it can store at any one time. The amount of time it takes to read or write a byte of information is the memory's "access" time. Because the cost per byte of storage rises steeply as access time falls, and because of the very large memory capacity that is required to process even the simplest calculations, it was early recognized that there was a need for what von Neumann called "hierarchies" of memory.[1] The "main" memory, which is the only one that communicates directly with the central processor, has the shortest cycle time and, because of its high cost, is built with the lowest capacity, while the secondary memory, with a slower cycle time, stores information that can be quickly transferred to main memory as needed. Another use for secondary storage that has evolved is to serve as an archive for information not currently in use. Both magnetic tapes and disks are used for secondary storage.

When the first digital computers arrived in the 1950s, magnetic storage devices were the natural replacement for punched cards as the principal storage medium for large data files. Compared with its predecessors, punched paper and punched tape, magnetic storage had several advantages. It was "addressable"; that is, a location could be selected in which to store a specific item of information, and it was much less bulky and more durable. Compared with electronic memories, such as magnetic drums, it was cheap per byte of information stored, it was nonvolatile and thus had broad environmental tolerances that made it versatile and hardy, and it had read, write, and erase capabilities that enabled recording media to be used over and over.

The magnetic tape drive, which records information on a spool of metal-oxide-coated tape, first achieved prominence in 1951 when Remington Rand introduced it as the peripheral storage device for the UNIVAC I system. It utilized the technology of the "Blattnerphone," a recording device used in radio broadcasting in the 1930s, and soon gained a large following. Tape drives were extremely efficient in batch and serial processing applications and, because of the low cost of storage, were heavily exploited for business data processing. They suffered the critical drawback, however, that they were not able to randomly access the data stored. To find any one file in a spool of tape, the whole series of files up to the required one had to be read. The quest for random access in peripheral memory led to the rigid and flexible disk drives, the main forms of secondary storage today.

The rigid disk drive industry took off in 1957 with IBM's 650 RAMAC (Random Access Method of Accounting and Control), the first movable-head disk drive. It used 50 rotating platters that were read from and written onto by a head similar to those found on gramophone turntables. In fact, the recording head and disk assembly looked so similar to that found in sound recording that this unit was known as a "jukebox memory." Disk technology advanced with amazing speed and the industry advanced with it, due mainly to IBM's large research effort. The disk's main advantage was that its access speed was about 200 times faster than tape, due to its random access capability.[2] Disks were much more expensive than tapes, but, as technology advanced, the price differential was eroded, and today, disks are the main on-line storage systems for computers while tapes are used chiefly as archival and back-up storage to the disk drives.

The RAMAC, coupled with IBM's 305 small business computer, laid the foundation on which developments in the industry would be based for the next 10 years. It cost IBM 3 years and $10 million to develop[3] and from its introduction, IBM dominated magnetic disk technology. It was responsible for virtually all of the fundamental advances, and more than 25 years later all major hard disk technologies in common usage were based on three IBM products that set industry standards: the 2314, dating from the mid-1960s, the 3330, from around 1970, and the Winchester, introduced in the early 1970s. "Refinements by other manufacturers have been modifications on a basic theme."[4] Independent companies (those who sell in the merchant market) have produced plug-compatible versions of IBM-type disk systems since Memorex penetrated this market in 1968, and in the late seventies independents began to make available smaller and less expensive products to serve the mini and personal computer markets. But credit for the remarkable increases in performance of disk storage systems shown in Table 7–1 goes to the company that produced the first link in the evolutionary chain.

While magnetic disk storage stands out as an irrefutable example of a major innovation for which the dominant firm in the industry can claim the credit, it evidently cannot be credited to the initiative of the firm's management. According to IBM testimony before the Hart Committee,

> The disk memory unit, the heart of today's random access computer, is not the logical outcome of a decision made by IBM management. It was developed in one of our laboratories as a bootleg project—over the stern warning from management that the project had to be dropped because of budget difficulties. A handful of men ignored the warning. They broke the rules. They risked their jobs to work on a project they believed in.[5]

As Table 7–1 shows, by 1981 areal density of disks (the number of bits per square inch) had increased 6,000 times over the original 350 system,

Table 7–1. Development of IBM Disk Drive Technologies, 1957–81

	1957	1961	1962	1963	1966	1971	1973	1976	1979	1979	1981
Year of First Shipment											
Product	350	1405	1301	1311	2314	3330	3340	3350	3310	3370	3380
Recording Density											
Areal density (Mb/in.)	0.002	0.009	0.026	0.051	0.22	0.78	1.69	3.07	3.8	7.8	>12
Linear bit density (bpi)	100	220	520	1,025	2,200	4,040	5,636	6,425	8,530	12,134	15,200
Track density (tpi)	20	40	50	**	100	192	300	478	450	635	>800
Key Geometric Parameters (microinches)											
Head-to-disk spacing	800	650	250	125	85	50	18	**	13	**	<13
Head gap length	1,000	700	500	250	105	100	60	50	40	25	**
Medium thickness	1,200	900	543	250	85	50	41	**	25	41	<25
Air Bearing & Magnetic Element											
Bearing type	hydrostatic	**	hydrodynamic	**	**	**	**	**	**	**	**
Surface contour	flat	**	cylindrical	**	**	**	taper flat	**	**	**	**
Slider material	Al	**	stainless steel	**	ceramic	**	ferrite	**	**	ceramic	**
Core material	laminated mu-metal	**	**	**	ferrite	**	**	**	**	film	**
Slider/core bond	epoxy	**	**	**	**	glass	integral	**	**	deposited	**
Disk											
Diameter (in.)	24	**	**	14	**	**	**	**	8.3	14	**
Substrate thickness (in.)	0.100	**	**	0.050	**	0.075	**	**	**	**	>0.075
RPM	1,200	1,800	1,800	1,500	2,400	3,600	2,964	3,600	3,125	2,964	3,620
Fixed/removable	fixed	**	**	removable pack	removable pack	**	module	fixed	**	**	**
Data surfaces/spindle	100	**	**	10	20	19	6	15	11	12	15

Year of First Shipment	1957	1961	1962	1963	1966	1971	1973	1976	1979	1979	1981
Actuator											
Access geometry	x-y	**	linear radial		**	**	**	rotary	linear	**	**
Heads	2 h/actuator	**	1 h/surface		**	**	2 h/surface		1 h/s	2 h/s	**
Positioning	Motor-clutch	**	hydraulic		**	voice coil motor			**	**	**
Final position	detent	**	**		**	servo surface			(+ sector)	servo surface	**
Actuators/spindle (max no.)	3	**	2	1	**	**	**	**	1	2	**
Avg. seek time (ms)	600	**	165	150	60	30	25	**	27	20	16
Read/Write Electronics											
Data rate (Kbytes/s)	8.8	17.5	68	69	312	806	885	1,198	1,031	1,859	3,000
Encoding	NRZI	**	**	**	2f	mfm	**	**	mfm	2.7	**
Detection	ampl	**	**	**	peak	delta	**	**	**	delta clip	**
Clocking	2 osc	**	clk trk	osc	vfo	**	**	**	**	**	**

**Same as preceding column.

Source: J.M. Harker, D.W. Brede, R.E. Pattison, G.R. Santana, and L.G. Taft, "A Quarter Century of Disk File Innovation," *IBM Journal of Research and Development* (September 1981): Table 1, p. 678. Copyright 1981 by International Business Machines Corporation; reprinted with permission.

and average seek time (the time it takes the head to move to the proper position on the disk) had fallen from 600 milliseconds to 16 milliseconds, while the rotational speed of the disk had tripled. Advances in disk system design progressed incrementally from year to year, but each major change emerged as a "constellation of new characteristics."[6] In a series of abrupt shifts, nearly every aspect of the system was upgraded toward higher capacity and throughput.

Flexible (floppy) disk drive technology appeared in the early seventies when IBM introduced the first such system, with disks made of mylar, as a read-only unit housed deep inside the System 370 as a program-loading device. Floppy disks later filled a gap left by rigid disks, which were too expensive for the smaller mini- and microcomputer systems that appeared in full force in the seventies. If the microprocessor made the personal computer possible, the floppy disk made it marketable by providing a small, compact, cheap, and reliable form of secondary storage. Increases in recording density and reductions in size made the technology popular also as back-up storage to the unremovable Winchester disks.

The main objectives of research in disk technology are fourfold: to increase storage capacity, reliability, and access speed, and to decrease cost per byte of storage.[7] Efforts have concentrated primarily on increasing the areal density of disks, but achievement of this objective has been less a function of the disk itself than of the read/write head; most importantly the ability to reduce its "flying" height above the platter to the absolute minimum.[8] The reason is that magnetic flux spreads with distance; therefore, the further the head flies above the magnetic surface, the larger the area that must be occupied by a single bit of information. Since the advent of the original RAMAC, the head-to-disk spacing has fallen from 800 microinches to 13 microinches.[9] Increases in areal density can also be achieved by reducing the size of the head structure since the width of the head determines the feasible track width,[10] and the maximum feasible areal density is influenced also by key mechanical components of the moving head disk system, specifically the actuator and carriage assembly that move the read/write heads from one track position to another. The more accurately they are able to position the head, the greater the permissible track density. The faster they are able to perform this function, the shorter the access time.

Beyond advances in head technology, new encoding methods and recording electronics have permitted increased areal density. As linear density and rotational speeds grew, the serial data rate on the read/write head increased from 100 kilobits per second to 24 megabits, straining the capabilities of host system data channels. Finally, developments in the disk's substrate and its magnetic coating have had an important role in increasing density.

INNOVATIONS AND INNOVATORS

Innovations in this industry can be divided into four main areas: high-performance hard disk drives developed by IBM, plug-compatible drives made predominantly by independent companies, and flexible disk drives and small Winchesters, in both of which new companies generally found their niches.

IBM

RAMAC.   IBM's first disk system, with its stack of fifty 24-inch disks, had one pair of read/write heads mounted on a pair of access arms that were moved by an electromechanical actuator to any one of the disks, positioning a head at each of its two surfaces. The disks rotated at 1,200 rpm. Because of their speed and their rigid aluminum foundation, contact between the head and the disk would destroy the storage medium. Thus, unlike the tape drive, the read/write head had to be held at a constant distance above the moving platter. It was the development at IBM of a hydrostatic air bearing that could accurately space the head close to the surface of the disk (a distance of 800 microinches) that made this first movable-head disk drive a reality.

The idea of using air as a lubricating film to allow one surface to move relative to another had been reported in the 1890s and the concept behind the design of disk drives rests on this "simple" mechanism.[11] Its use to maintain a consistent spacing between the head and the disk surface was first accomplished at IBM in 1953, employing jets of air forced out of the head by a compressor; four years later it appeared in a production version. According to IBM experts, "the ability to maintain a consistent spacing (and in subsequent generations to diminish it) has been the prime driving force for all other improvements in the recording technology."[12] When positioned at a disk, the head pair of the RAMAC could be moved in about 600 milliseconds to any one of 50 disks, each storing 50,000 characters.

The Second Generation. With a weight of 350 grams, the heads of the RAMAC drives were difficult to hold up and a motor, "the size of a washing machine" was needed to drive the air compressors that maintained the head-disk separation.[13] In 1962 IBM introduced the "second generation" of disk drives with its 1301, which replaced the externally pressurized air-bearing system with a self-acting hydrodynamic slider bearing that eliminated the need for the huge air compressors. The aerodynamic shape of the head allowed it to "fly" on the rotating film of air that adheres to the disk surface. A load was applied to the head to maintain the proper spacing.[14] Since the air compressor used to support each head could be dispensed with, it was possible to provide a separate head for each disk surface,[15] and the more limited demands on the actuator, which no longer had to move the head to different disks, permitted replacement of the mechanical actuator with a simpler hydraulic actuator, which was less cumbersome and achieved faster access times. Disk-to-disk switching was now done electronically rather than by moving the head and resulted in a reduction in the head-to-disk spacing from 800 to 250 microinches. Together with improvements in the design of the head suspension and magnetic elements, it led to an increase in areal density of more than tenfold and average seek time fell from 600 to 165 milliseconds.

It soon became evident that the needs of small systems users could not be met at an acceptable cost by the large disk files and, in 1964, IBM introduced a smaller disk file that used for the first time a removable disk assembly to allow off-line storage and back-up. The 1311 contained six interchangeable 14-inch disks (14 inches thereafter became the standard diameter) mounted in a pack, and was the first of a family of removable "disk packs."[16] The interchangeable disk pack required tight control of the absolute position and the position tolerances of the data tracks written on each pack. This raised serious problems in product engineering and production, which called for increased precision, involved a higher risk of contamination and aggravated thermal expansion problems. The 1311 also needed a simple low-cost, high-performance head actuator and carriage assembly, and for this purpose IBM developed a hydraulic actuator that exploited the smaller dimensions of the new disk file and relied on a small, commercially available gear pump to deliver the hydraulic fluid to the actuator. The basic concept of the actuator and carriage assembly were employed on successor products including the 2311 and 2314 files. IBM's introduction of the removable disk pack in its 1300 and 2300 series paved the way for plug-compatible disk drives produced by independent companies to interface with IBM processors. The first to enter this market was Memorex in 1968.

The Winchester Disk Drive.   As we see in Table 7–1, disk technology marched ahead briskly from the 1311 and 2314 systems, designed for the System/360, to the 3330, built for the System/370. But a major breakthrough occurred in 1973 with the 3340 "Winchester" disk, so-called because it contained two spindles of disks each capable of 30 megabytes of storage, suggesting an analogy with the 30-30 Winchester rifle. It came with a new, lightly loaded head that weighed only a quarter of a gram (compare this with RAMAC's 350 grams!) and permitted the head to fly less than 20 microinches above the disk surface.[17] Because the new head was much less expensive, it was decided to include two heads per surface, which cut in half the stroke length and lowered the cost of actuator and carriage.[18] A radical innovation was a lubricated surface that made it possible for the head to rest on the disk during start and stop operations, unlike earlier systems, which required that the disk be spinning before the head was loaded. But the most striking departure was the enclosure of each disk along with its own heads, spindle, carriage, and head-arm assemblies within a single airtight, shockproof module. Actually, this packaging was dictated by the fact that the lightweight slider heads depended upon the disk to support them even when stopped, thus they could not be separated from the disk. IBM decided to turn necessity into a virtue and, by permanently enclosing the head and disk, achieved significant savings through the elimination of head alignment procedures. The uncontaminated environment within the module increased reliability sufficiently that no scheduled maintenance was required for the Winchester.[19]

The IBM 3350, delivered in 1976, was an extension of the Winchester technology with more disks per drive and greater areal density, which increased the capacity per spindle by 4.5 times.[20] In 1979 a factor of two reduction in the cost per megabyte of disk storage was achieved with IBM's 3370, which used a new thin film head technology for the first time to replace the ferrite head.[21] Although the term "Winchester" was originally applied to the 3340 and extended to the 3350, it has come to be ubiquitously applied to any rigid disk drive using a sealed head/disk assembly, lubricated medium, and low-mass read/write heads that land on the surface of the disk as the drive is stopped and take off as the disk gets up to speed.[22]

Manufacturers of Plug-Compatible Disk Drives

While IBM led technology in the rigid disk market, a number of peripherals vendors, including Memorex, Control Data (CDC), and Storage Technology, raced to compete in the IBM plug-compatible market, beginning in 1968. Later, long delays in IBM's delivery of the 3350 and 3380 provided opportunities for plug-compatibles manufacturers (PCMs) to enter with improved versions of earlier IBM disks. According to an IBM source, "Independent disk-drive manufacturers have historically borrowed from IBM technology, first to produce IBM-compatible disk subsystems, and then to produce systems for use with non-IBM equipment."[23] But, also according to IBM sources, the plug-compatible products were sometimes in advance of IBM's prototypes. In a 1971 assessment of its announced products, IBM found that the Memorex, Telex, and several other versions of their 2310, 2311 and 2314 disk drives were superior to the IBM counterparts that were available at the time.[24]

Independents have sometimes used IBM technologies to develop disk drives that are architecturally unique or employ higher storage densities, often to meet special needs of customers. For example, double-density 3350s were first brought to the market by independents, and in 1979 Storage Technology (STC), a vendor of plug-compatibles that was founded in 1969 by engineers from IBM to make tape drives, introduced the first disk drive to incorporate a microprocessor in the drive itself, effectively creating an "intelligent" disk drive.[25] In 1983 STC introduced an optical storage device using laser technology, the 7600, priced at $130,000, which could hold 4 billion bytes, compared with the IBM 3380's 2.5 billion bytes.

Manufacturers of Flexible Disk Drives

Independent companies, often newly founded, also found niches in the flexible disk market and in the smaller Winchester market (considered in the next section) and were responsible for major advances in the technologies. The flexible, or "floppy," disk drive was introduced rather unobtrusively by IBM in 1971 as an 80K byte read-only microprogram loader for the 3330 big disk in the 370 system. Thus buried, it attracted little attention until the next year, when IBM started to test market a data entry terminal in Europe using the flexible disk.[27] By the third quarter of the following year three peripherals vendors, Potter, Memorex, and Century Data (later CalComp), announced "diskette" systems similar to the IBM device but with read/write capability and separated from the mainframe to become the precursors of today's floppy disk storage systems. The first floppy disks were 8 inches in diameter and beat the 8-inch Winchester disks to the market by six years.

In 1973, shortly after the three peripherals vendors announced their floppy disk drives, IBM incorporated in its 3740 series terminals a flexible disk system it called the 33 FD that had read, write, and erase capabilities. The disk revolved at a different speed and in the opposite direction from its predecessors and, along with a number of other such departures, it threatened to upset standards for the industry. By unspoken agreement, IBM's drive was accepted as the industry standard in that year. IBM-compatible floppies began to appear and new independents emerged, "staffed in large part by engineers who had left IBM and gone to Memorex or Potter, and thence to Shugart, Century, and/or Orbis".[28] There were soon more than 50 companies in the market.

In many ways floppy disk systems resemble rigid disk systems; indeed, at first glance it would seem that the only difference is in the recording medium, which is an acetate-based plastic called mylar (developed by Dupont) whereas the rigid disks use an aluminum-based medium. But there is a more fundamental difference: The head of the flexible disk drive is actually in contact with the disk when it reads and writes, unlike the rigid drives where the head must fly above it. There is, thus, no need for complicated air-pressure bearings and the drive can be housed in a much more compact unit.[29]

The major stimulus to the floppy disk industry was the burgeoning market for mini- and microcomputers, for which floppy disks serve as secondary storage. It is hard to imagine that the personal computer would have met with much success in the absence of the floppy disk for storing both data and software. The expanding use of unremovable Winchester disks also stimulated demand for floppy disks as backup. Floppy disks are reliable, cheap, small, and allow remarkable flexibility in design of the small computer system. By 1984 most had between 1 million and 2 million bytes of storage capacity. They had replaced punched cards, punched paper, tape cassettes, and cartridges; they were used in remote terminals, minicomputers, small business systems, calculators, and word processors, and they had become the medium of software publication.

The basic technology still follows the IBM 33 and 43 flexible disk drives used in IBM's 3740 data entry system in 1972, but since then it has been possible to reduce the diameter of the disk and the height of the drive, and to greatly increase storage capacity. By the mid-1980s the floppy disk market included 8-inch, 5¼-inch, and still smaller disks, like the 3½-inch, as well as full- or half-height drives with either single or doubled-sided recording, single- or double-density recording, and 48 or 96 tracks per disk. The smaller sizes were achieved without a loss in storage capacity and often with an improvement in access time.

Shugart Associates, founded by Alan Shugart after he left IBM's disk division in 1973, introduced the first 5¼-inch floppy disk drive in 1976. Its SA400 repackaged existing recording technology for personal, business, and home computer applications and became the industry standard in this class. Because of difficulty with double-sided recording, most of the so-called minifloppy disks were single-sided until 1979.

It was IBM that in 1976 introduced the first workable double-sided floppy disk. Together with double-density recording, it brought capacity to new levels and with it a sudden surge in the demand for mini- and microcomputer applications. According to Shugart executives, however,[30] the IBM disk was intended for relatively light-duty I/O or program-loading functions whereas the OEM models were intended for heavy-duty applications such as systems disks. In order to meet the latter objective, the double-sided disk head had to be redesigned, a process that Shugart says took it three years. The problem was to come up with a rugged product that would be easy to manufacture. But Tandon Magnetics, founded in 1976, anticipated Shugart with a head assembly, which it introduced in 1979, that captured most of the market. It was reliable and manufacturable in large quantities, using a fixed head on one side of the disk and a spring-loaded pivot arm on the other side.

In the early 1980s, Sony, a large Japanese electronics firm, was the first company into the market with a "microfloppy" only 3½ inches in diameter that packed almost the same capacity as its larger competitors. BASF, a major European manufacturer, pioneered in 1978 with a 5¼-inch floppy disk drive that was two-thirds the standard height. Serious technical problems had to be overcome in order to design a motor and a clutch-centering mechanism small enough to fit into the more limited quarters. BASF's product was not a huge success because it did not permit OEMs to increase the capacity of their computer systems without redesigning their housing. It was followed in 1980 by a half-height 8-inch drive which allowed two disks to fit into the space formerly occupied by one. One source credits Tandon Magnetics with the first of these "slimline" floppy disk drives,[31] and another attributes it to a

1977 start-up, Micro Peripherals.[32] By 1983 virtually all new 8-inch drives followed the new standard.[33] In 1980 several companies offered double-sided drives with twice the normal track density to provide 1M bytes of unformatted capacity and higher linear, or bit, densities were announced the next year, leading to 1.6 megabytes of storage.[34]

Three small companies that started up in 1979 and 1980 led the next advance in disk capacity. Drivetek and Amlyn raised the 5¼-inch disk capacity to 3.3M bytes (this was an attractive capacity as backup for the 10M byte Winchester available on the IBM PC because only three media changes were required.) Amlyn used a closed-loop servomechanism for positioning the head, which, by providing feedback, improved placement accuracy and made it possible to increase track density by 70 percent.[35] Drivetek's half-height drive was licensed to Kodak, which planned to use it in conjunction with a new medium produced by one of its subsidiaries (Spin Physics) which quadrupled the conventional bit densities.[36] Both Drivetek and Amlyn received major funding from Dysan, a supplier of media that was founded in 1972. The third new company, Iomega, developed the "Bernoulli box," which used a hard jacket, packaged with Winchester-like heads that floated on an air cushion to achieve 5M bytes of capacity on a 5¼-inch disk and 10M bytes on an 8-inch disk.[37]

Superdensity drives required diskettes with higher resolution coating to prevent excessive errors that result from unevenness of the disk surface and thermal distortions. By 1982 the leading manufacturers (3M, Verbatim, Hitachi, and Maxwell) were beginning to ship samples of higher quality diskettes. Media technology also held out hope for increasing capacity by using new recording techniques such as perpendicular recording, which was being explored for hard disks as well.[38] By 1984 media manufacturers like 3M were developing this technology as were some disk drive companies, including Shugart, who was working with Verbatim, a media manufacturer.

Manufacturers of Small Winchester Disk Drives

A newcomer by the name of International Memories (IMI), founded in 1977, broke IBM's hold on the Winchester disk market when it introduced the first 8-inch Winchester system: the 10M byte 7710, in 1979.[39] It used IBM 3340 technology and the entire system was the size of a floppy disk drive. IBM was second into the 8-inch market with its 3310 "Piccolo" and the race was on to supply the growing demand for reliable peripherals that were less expensive than the 14-inch Winchester but more powerful than the 8-inch floppy disk. By the following year a wide range of 8-inch Winchesters was available with capacities from 4M to 34M bytes, but the 8-inch Winchesters were difficult to manufacture, and only a few of the companies that announced them had previously manufactured the 14-inch models. Close tolerances, clean room environment, and experience were all critical. It was not until 1981 that manufacturing problems were overcome and large-volume shipments were forthcoming.[40] The new companies were often started by former IBM personnel.

By 1980, a new wave of microcomputers that required very reliable storage with low maintenance and low price tags led to a still smaller disk, the 5¼-inch Winchester, which was soon to take away more than half of the 8-inch market. It was introduced by Shugart Technology, which had been founded two years earlier by Alan Shugart and soon changed its name to Seagate Technology. Recall that Shugart was also the founder of Shugart Associates, which had pioneered with the 5¼-inch floppy disk. Seagate's new mini Winchester, the ST500, with 6M bytes of unformatted capacity, was ideal for small systems because of its flexibility and reliability.[41] The company's strategy was to match exactly the package size and DC voltages of the 5¼-inch floppy disk so that it could be used to upgrade from the floppy. Also, it wanted to ship within three months of product announcement. Thus it used standard available hardware, purchasing off-the-shelf heads, disks, and stepper motors which it assembled and tested.[42] It designed an interface similar to that available in 8-inch Winchesters to take advantage of controllers that were on the market.[43] More than 20 disk drive manufacturers had followed Seagate into the field by the next year.

The half-height Winchester drive, measuring 1.625 inches, was brought out soon after by Syquest Technology, another IBM spin-off, doubling the storage capacity obtainable within the same space.[44] In 1980 Data Peripherals marketed a removable Winchester cartridge disk drive with heads designed to stay in the drive,[45] an important advance in providing backup storage for Winchesters. Also that year Ontrax introduced its Series-8 devices, which incorporated a patented actuator that was simpler, less expensive, and more accurate than the linear/rotary actuator in standard Winchester drives. It increased disk capacity by increasing track density and reduced cost by eliminating the servohead.[46]

By 1983 two new firms, Disctron and Tulin, pushed the 10M byte limit of the 5¼-inch Winchesters to over 13M bytes.[47]

All Winchesters originally employed oxide-coated recording media and ferrite heads, rather than the more advanced thin film heads that IBM had introduced in the 3370. The capacity (generally 6M bytes) achieved on small disks by using these technologies was adequate to meet most needs at the time and greater capacity was achieved by adding more disks to the stack. But by the 1980s demand was growing for small disks with higher capacity to meet the needs of superminicomputers in multiuser and multitask environments, and the more advanced thin film recording media then becoming available held most promise for meeting this demand.[48] Thin film heads were needed, however, to exploit the thin film media, and in the early eighties a few companies started to adapt this more exacting technology to small disks. By 1981 a subsidiary of the media manufacturer Dysan, called Dastek (founded by IBM engineers), had designed and developed a thin film head for sale to Tandon,[49] and a company by the name of Magnex subsequently originated a non-IBM thin film head technology using a proprietary process.[50]

In summary, in the low-capacity Winchester sector, as in floppy disks, technological advances have mainly involved scaling down and fine tuning of the mechanical functions and electronics of basic technologies that were already in the marketplace, frequently exploiting opportunities generated by the microprocessor. The result was more compact systems with greater capacity, speed, and reliability. Companies new to the market were more often than not responsible for these innovations. Significant reductions in prices of small disks occurred in the eighties, promoted by stiff competition, partly from Japan, which led to cost-cutting measures by the volume producers, whose ranks included successful new firms and, in some sectors, established peripherals vendors like CDC. When it came to advances in recording media, larger, better established companies were usually responsible.

MARKET ANALYSIS

Suppliers of disk drives can be divided into three categories: IBM, the undisputed leader in technology as well as volume, other suppliers of high-capacity and high-performance disk drives, consisting mainly of independent companies but including also some computer manufacturers, and, finally, the several dozen suppliers of small, low-capacity disk drives, both Winchesters and floppies.

IBM

The dominance of IBM in disk drive technology rests on its willingness to commit very substantial amounts of capital to research and development of the new and untested technology beginning in the mid-1950s and to maintain that commitment over several decades, as well as to a very high degree of success in achieving its R&D goals. As the originator of the very complex and sophisticated technology, it developed a research capability that, evidently, no other firm was both willing and able to match. The especially marked tendency for new firms to depend on former IBM employees for staffing is evidence of the importance of the experience IBM gained in engineering and producing the technology.

IBM had a powerful incentive to develop secondary storage technology since the results were to greatly enhance the value of mainframe systems to customers. As the supplier of two-thirds of all mainframes, it stood to gain far more than any other firm. Competing mainframe manufacturers and independent peripherals vendors have traditionally followed IBM technology. The fact that disk drives that depart from IBM's approach have typically had difficulty finding acceptance in the large systems market may have discouraged innovation on the part of its competitors. Original concepts have sometimes found markets in the mini- or microcomputer sectors, however, encouraged by systems integrators or dealers who are willing to endorse innovative products that meet diverse needs.[51] Another possible explanation for IBM's unique position of technological leadership in this market could be an absence of potentially promising alternatives to the approach that IBM pioneered for solving the problem of secondary storage.

Other Manufacturers of High-Capacity Disk Drives

In the second category are firms that copy and sometimes improve upon IBM's disk drives for the plug-compatible market and supply OEMs with 14-inch and sometimes high-performance 8-inch Winchester drives of their own design as well. With the exception of CDC, which became a leading peripherals vendor, and more recently Amdahl, systems manufacturers generally supply only their own mainframe customers. Although a couple of dozen firms participate in this market, at different times a half dozen or so have held most of it, led by major peripherals vendors such as Storage Technology, Memorex, Telex, and CDC, all companies founded in the late fifties or in the sixties that were major peripherals vendors by the midseventies. A year after Memorex brought out the first plug-compatible disk drive in 1968, all major peripherals vendors offered replacements for IBM's 2311 and 2314 drives.[52] Some PCMs supply disk drives compatible with equipment of vendors other than IBM's, most notably DEC's.

As in other PCM markets, these firms have not, on the whole, been responsible for important advances in the technology, although some have developed architecturally unique devices or higher density drives or media, mainly for the OEM market rather than the plug-compatible market, and most often for minicomputers. CDC's 7638 disk drive had the highest transfer rate on the market when it was introduced,[53] and STC was in the forefront of optical disk technology. Several others adopted thin film recording media before IBM, and independents launched the double-density versions of IBM's 3350 Winchester. But, on the whole, success in this sector does not depend on producing innovative products but rather on producing products similar to those of the market leader to be sold with narrower profit margins. The PCMs borrowed heavily from IBM in staffing. IBM testified that Memorex hired over 600 IBM employees, including its designer of the voice coil actuator.[54]

This market is, broadly speaking, similar to those discussed in our overall view of the PCM market in Chapter 4. The principal reason for a customer to prefer a non-IBM product in the beginning was price but, increasingly, improved performance and shorter delivery schedules came to matter too.[55] IBM's price "umbrella" helped to sustain the market, but from time to time the company engaged in serious price wars.[56] Plug-compatible manufacturers tend to concentrate on older models of proven performance where IBM is vulnerable on grounds of technology as well as price and the market is large.[57] The disk market lends itself particularly well to this type of competition because old and new technologies thrive side-by-side, each having certain advantages and disadvantages that appeal to different customers.[58] PCMs also capitalize on the delays in delivery which typically accompany substantially new IBM products, by providing improved versions of older IBM disk drives. Plug-compatible disk drives on the average suffer an 18-month lag in availability from the time that the IBM product first appears on the market.[59]

Manufacturers of Small Disk Drives

In the third category are literally scores of companies that supply the market for small disk drives, more than 40 in each of the Winchester and floppy disk sectors, with some overlap. Many entered during the 1970s, after the market for small disks emerged, but some established peripherals vendors participate in this market too, mostly at the higher end, supplying 14-inch drives as well. New firms led in scaling down the size of Winchesters and flexible disks and adapting them to fit the demands and the pocketbooks of users of mini- and microcomputers and in gradually increasing their capacity and performance. For the volume leaders like Seagate and Shugart, an important objective was to simplify design in order to facilitate mass production in automated facilities. The executive vice president of Seagate explained in 1983, "What we do is to take proven technology and put it into a package that can be manufactured in high volume."[60] Simplifying often means reducing the number of critical parts and substituting microprocessors for mechanical functions.

By the mid-1980s, new firms were at the top of the markets for both 5¼-inch Winchesters and for floppy disks. Seagate (founded 1978), which had introduced the micro-Winchester in 1980, held almost half of that market. About a dozen firms made 8-inch floppies, headed by Shugart (1973) in competition with CDC, Qume, and several other leading peripherals manufacturers. Eight-inch flexible drives were giving way to the 5¼, however, and about 25 firms competed in this market, with Tandon, Micro Peripherals and Micropolis, all founded in the seventies, claiming half of it. Shugart, the originator and once the market leader, fell far behind in the eighties, although it continued to occupy the top position in 8-inch floppy disks (as well as in low-capacity 8-inch Winchesters). There was a noticeable tendency for firms to specialize in either Winchesters or floppy disks, but most offered more than one product line within a class.[61]

The contest for market shares in the standard, low-capacity disk sectors was being fought on the basis of price by the 1980s and success required volume production and automated assembly lines. By then Shugart had become a large subsidiary of Xerox and in 1983 Seagate was a $150 million a year company. Ample opportunity remained, however, for smaller firms to compete with somewhat higher performance or more specialized disk drives. New firms came to dominate these markets in the first instance by identifying and serving the needs of customers who were not being attended to by other firms, a pattern we observed earlier in minicomputers. They did not compete for the customers of large, established companies. The small disk drives in which they specialized were not simply substitutes for an existing product but, rather, by vastly extending the capabilities of small business and personal computers, they effectively created markets for disk drives that did not already exist. Potential buyers were, on the whole new customers, not former customers of IBM. Companies with solid reputations did not follow them into these sectors of the peripherals market. When IBM belatedly entered the personal computer market in the early eighties, it farmed out the manufacture of its floppy disk drives and most other components to independents, generally new companies. The 8-inch Winchesters that IBM itself produced were directed toward customers who demanded high performance, while its flexible disk drives were designed for use with its large mainframes.

As the mid-1980s approached, new firms continued to enter the low-capacity disk market and to survive in large numbers, in spite of the presence, by then, of a number of well-established, though still young, incumbents. In order to understand the survival of scores of new firms in competition with new companies that were by then firmly planted in markets where mass production now offered important cost advantages, we must look at the enormous diversity of product design and cost considerations that enter into customers' purchase decisions. These, together with the slowness of standards to develop in some sectors, promoted a huge proliferation of market niches which new firms could exploit without competing head on with better established vendors, another phenomenon that we observed in the minicomputer as well as the printer industries.

Disk drives vary with respect to storage capacity, access speed, compactness, controller interfaces, interchangeability with other vendors' recording media, reliability, durability, ruggedness, the functions performed by the controller, and still other characteristics, not least of all, price. Among most of these characteristics there are important trade-offs that make different packages more or less suitable to the needs of different customers.[62] We consider now the elements of the market that kept entry barriers low enough to be surmounted by large numbers of small new firms.

Product Differentiation.   There are, potentially, opportunities for an incumbent in these markets to gain an advantage by patenting new product designs, by exploiting a track record of reliable delivery and quality of the product, and by acquiring the clout to set standards. Although each of these served different producers from time to time, none was notably effective in deterring entry.

Patenting.   Firms that develop new disk drives or their components tend to patent them, and not infrequently license them to other vendors (for example, Tabor licensed its 3¼-inch drive to Seagate, Seagate licensed its read/write head to Shugart, Drivetek its 3.3M byte disk drive to Kodak), or they tend to enter into arrangements for joint development and marketing with other vendors. Although patents have helped to protect product designs from unlicensed imitation, as in other sectors of the computer industry they have not prevented new firms from exploiting the basic technology.

A Track Record.   A track record that reassures customers of a vendor's ability to deliver the specified quantities of disk drives on schedule is important in marketing in this rapidly growing sector, where shortages are common and it is not always a simple matter to move from prototype to volume production. The main customers are systems integrators, OEMs, and computer manufacturers, for whom the disk drive is an essential component of their final products and therefore critical in meeting their own delivery schedules. Firms without an established record of performance are generally required to find a second-source producer, a situation we will encounter again in the market for integrated circuits. Lack of a second source deterred acceptance of the new 3.3M byte disk drives introduced by Amlyn and Drivetek.[63]

But the lack of a track record has not prevented entry by new firms as evidenced by the difficulty that pioneers of popular new disk drives frequently encountered in trying to hold onto their markets. Shugart, which introduced the minifloppy, in 1976 dominated that sector only until a still newer firm, Tandon, beat it to the market with a slimline minifloppy disk drive, and by 1983 Shugart's share of the minifloppy market had fallen to under 3 percent. Seagate, who pioneered the micro-Winchester disk drive soon found more than half of it taken over by other newcomers. The explosive growth of these markets, the very large number of different products, together with opportunities for creating new ones, and the fact that no firm has been established for very long all combined to minimize the disadvantage of newness as a deterrent to entry.

Uniform Standards. The need for uniform specifications if different disks are to be interchangeable among different drives and if different disk drives are to be used with different computer systems potentially provides an advantage to a well-known supplier with the clout to make its standard stick. There is an analogy here with the problem of hardware and software compatibility, with the important difference that specifications are not protected by trade secrets. The relevant specifications cover recording and formatting of the disk, interfaces, and the physical dimensions of disks and drives. New disk drives whose specifications depart from accepted standards can have difficulty gaining acceptance unless customers are convinced that the vendor can make it stick. Standards were slow to develop in the micro- and minicomputer disk drive sectors in the absence of a dominant firm like IBM to lead the way. Drivetek and Amlyn had difficulty marketing their 3.3M byte drives because of lack of interchange capability.[64] On the other hand, when IBM introduced its Advanced Technology personal computer in 1984, with a disk having 96 tracks per inch, it was assumed that virtually every maker of desktop systems would be forced to follow suit. We saw also that IBM was able to enforce its standard of size as well as the direction and speed of rotation of the first floppy disks, which were 8 inches in diameter. But later, when it introduced its first 8-inch Winchester after International Memories it was not so successful. The diameter of its disk was 210 millimeter rather than IMI's 200 mm, and in this case IMI's standard stuck because most vendors saw the main utility for the small Winchester as an upgrade for the 200-mm floppy disk, which had previously been established.

When Shugart launched the 5¼-inch floppy disk it was already the leading supplier of 8-inch floppy disks, although only six years old. Nevertheless, the pioneers who developed the first personal computer were sufficiently concerned that its new standard would not stick that they incorporated an 8-inch drive, in spite of its higher cost.[65] When the 5¼-inch Winchester was introduced later by the fledgling Seagate, it found an instant market because it was an obvious upgrade for the 5¼-inch floppy which had by then become standard. But it was Sony, a world leader in magnetic recording techniques, that launched the nonconforming 3½-inch submini-Winchester.

Many customers crave IBM compatibility even when it is of no relevance to their use of the disk drive.[66] Such preferences can stand in the way of market acceptance of a unique new product. Thin film medium, for example, had not been adopted by IBM by 1984 and some experts traced its failure to gain widespread approval to this fact.[67] While the large systems market is slow to accept non-IBM-type products, the mini and micro markets frequently do in order to meet their diverse needs. By avoiding markets in which IBM competed, new companies, for the most part, sidestepped its advantage in setting standards. But in 1983 IBM entered the personal computer market, potentially threatening manufacturers of the low-performance disk drive. In this case, however it departed from all previous policy and purchased disk drives from independents using standard, nonproprietary designs.

Absolute Cost Barriers.

Technical Know-How.   Like other sectors of the computer industry, entry into this one is not inhibited by a scarcity of critical resources, nor have patents seriously restricted access to production process technology. But experience in producing disks and disk drives offers dividends in improving quality and production yields and cutting costs,[68] and new firms, once again, were found acquiring critical know-how by attracting personnel from the staffs of established manufacturers. In the production of all drives, a high level of manufacturing discipline is necessary,[69] and production of the recording media is, as one seasoned member of the industry put it, an "unforgiving" technology[70] where small errors can be very costly.

Without previous experience it could take a firm two years to bring an 8-inch Winchester to the market.[71] Some firms that had not previously made 14-inch Winchesters ran into trouble when they entered the 8-inch market. Nevertheless, while only three vendors shipped 8-inch Winchesters in 1979, 25 had brought them to the market two years later, hiring extensively from IBM and its spin-offs to obtain technical expertise. Pioneers of sophisticated technologies sometimes overcame production problems by merger or other ties to more experienced companies.[72]

Capital Requirements.   Starting up in the small disk sector of the industry has not called for substantial amounts of capital, and financial support has often been forthcoming from better established vendors. Seagate, had invested less than $1 million in product development and engineering and $2.6 million in equipment and improvements by the time its 5¼-inch Winchester was bringing in $10 million in revenues.[73] Tandon, founded in 1976, reported total assets of only $6 million in 1979. Syquest, the IBM spin-off that introduced the half-height Winchester, required initial funding of $2 million. Iomega, beginning in 1980, assembled $14 million in three rounds of funding to produce its inexpensive cartridge drive. In the media sector, Xidex constructed a completely automated plant to produce 100 million diskettes per year in the early eighties for only $3.5 million.

There appear to be important economies of scale in this industry. (According to one expert, they are huge.)[74] and as each new product matures and becomes standardized, volume production, using modern assembly line techniques becomes a key to successful competition, the more so the lower the cost and capabilities of the drive. Several thousand units per day are produced in some plants, and American volume producers have turned increasingly to production outside the United States in order to compete with Japanese manufacturers. Firms that enter with new products, however, do not immediately need to achieve volume production. As the industry matured, new firms were more likely to enter with drives whose capacity and performance were above the standard low-cost items for which volume production had become critical or else to design for small, specialized market niches. Large-scale production in this sector need not imply a high total value of output because of the relatively low unit cost of the product. In 1983 a double-sided, double-density floppy disk drive cost about $450 at retail and less in OEM quantities.

Capital requirements per dollar of output were relatively low, especially for firms that opted to purchase most of their components and subassemblies from other vendors. These can include read/write heads and their actuator mechanisms, the recording medium, formatter and controller, spindle assembly and motors, and microprocessor-controlled electronics. Standard components are available from a range of different vendors and more novel components are usually supplied by specialists. In developing a new product a firm can concentrate on a single component—for example, the head, actuator mechanism, or spindle assembly—without redesigning the basic technology or other major components. The capital requirements for such firms consist largely of inventories and the wages and salaries of R&D staff. Vertical integration has, however, tended to accompany expansion into volume production, and market experts believe that it is essential to success in the highly price-competitive sectors of the industry. Nevertheless Shugart designed its drives specifically to take advantage of off-the-shelf parts in order to speed their entry into production.

R&D in the small disk drive industry has generally been directed toward marginal improvements or changes in a basic technology and toward manufacturability. Because the entire industry has reaped the benefits of IBM's research effort, most new products have not required prolonged and costly research and development, although there are exceptions: Shugart spent three years trying to develop a head mechanism for the double-sided floppy disk before conceding the battle to the younger Tandon Magnetics.

One branch of the industry that invests heavily in R&D is the manufacture of recording media, where advances in thin film media, perpendicular recording, and other sophisticated techniques for increasing recording density have not yielded easy solutions. Shugart (by then a subsidiary of Xerox) spent $20 million in 1982 and again in 1983 on research into thin film technology and vertical recording. The leaders in this sector tend to be large, well-established firms, which sometimes collaborate with other companies (as Shugart did with Verbatim) or merge with smaller ones (as did Kodak with Spin Physics, Dorado with IMI, Xerox with Century Data and Shugart). Indeed, more than in other industries examined in this study, new manufacturers of disk drives have received financial support from producers of complementary products or through mergers with stronger companies. Dysan, for example, a major manufacturer of recording media helped to finance Drivetek and Amlyn, the new companies that developed high-density floppy disk drives, as well as Dastek, which developed a thin film head for use with small disks. Large orders from computer vendors have also helped to finance new firms. By far the largest volume of small disks are sold to computer manufacturers, including giants like IBM and DEC. Half of Tandon's sales were to IBM in the early eighties; Seagate received a $300 million contract from the same source and several fledgling firms were literally made by IBM's contracts for producing disk drives for its PC.

NOTES

1. R. Moreau, *The Computer Comes of Age: The People, The Hardware, The Software* (Cambridge, Mass.: MIT Press, 1984).
2. IBM, "Historical Narrative Statement of Richard E. Mancke, Franklin M. Fisher, and James W. McKie, *United States of America v.*

International Business Machines, Doc. 69 CIV. (DNE) U.S. District Court, Southern District, New York.

3. Ibid.
4. Rich Brechtlein, "Comparing Disk Technologies," *Datamation*, January 1978, p. 139.
5. D.A. Schon, Hart Committee, *Economic Concentration*, Hearings before the Sub-Committee on Anti-Trust and Monopoly of the Committee on the Judiciary, U.S. Senate, 89th Congress, Part 3, as cited in John Jewkes, David Sawers, and Richard Stillerman, *The Sources if Invention*, 2d ed. (London: MacMillan, 1969), pp. 206–207.
6. Brechtlein, "Comparing Disk Technologies."
7. Ibid.
8. J.M. Harker, D.W. Brede, R.E. Pattison, G.R. Santana, and L.G. Taft, "A Quarter Century of Disk File Innovation," *IBM Journal of Research and Development* (September 1981):677–88.
9. Ibid.
10. William L. Martin, "Putting Power in the House," *Computerworld Buyer's Guide*, October 5, 1983, p. 21.
11. Harker et al., "Disk File Innovation."
12. Ibid.
13. IBM, "Historical Narrative Statement."
14. Harker et al., "Disk File Innovation."
15. IBM, "Historical Narrative Statement."
16. Ibid.
17. Harker et al., "Disk File Innovation."
18. The iron oxide particles on the Winchester disk surface were magnetically oriented so that both the track and the bits along it were more precisely defined. Both the Winchester and the 3330, which had come out two years earlier, substituted voice coil actuators for the earlier hydraulic mechanism, but the Winchester actuator required 40 percent less power, generated less heat, and offered significant advantages in terms of size, service life, and reliability (Brechtlein, "Comparing Disk Technologies.").
19. L.D. Stevens, "The Evolution of Magnetic Storage," *IBM Journal of Research and Development* (February 4, 1980):663–74.
20. These improvements were permitted in part by the fact that, since the customer could no longer remove the data module, certain tolerances could be eliminated, leading to increased track density. A new track-following servo allowed an increase in areal density to almost five times that of the 3340 Winchester. Average seek time was reduced further by use of a new voice-coil actuator (Stevens, "Evolution of Magnetic Storage.").
21. Thin film heads are manufactured using thin film deposition and photolithographic definition of the pattern on the head, similar to the

process employed in semiconductor manufacturing (see Chapter 8). The result is high-resolution recording densities, more than twice as great as the ferrite head. In 1981, density was pushed still further with the 3380 ["A Whole New Ball Game," *Computerworld*, November 29, 1982.].

22. John Trifari, "Winchester Drives to be Focus of Attention Over Next Two Years," *Mini-Micro Systems*, February 1982, p. 135.

23. IBM, "Historical Narrative Statement."

24. Gerald W. Brock, *The U.S. Computer Industry: A Study of Market Power* (Cambridge, Mass.: Ballinger, 1975), Table 11.1, p. 204.

25. By utilizing a Motorola 6801 microprocessor, it eliminated the need for the controller, thus making the unit cheaper by anywhere from $2,000 to $10,000 and at the same time improving performance and allowing more than one disk to operate simultaneously ("Intelligent Disks Drives for the 80's," *Mini-Micro Systems*, February 1979, p. 72.).

26. Lasers traveling over the moving disk encode digital information by burning holes in the surface or creating blisters of bumps. Other optical disks on the market at the time were much less capacious and sophisticated than STC's. Its disks were not erasable, however, and in 1985 two Japanese firms, Sony and Matsushita, were reported to be close to solving that very critical problem.

27. Dan M. Bowers, "Floppy Disk Drives and Systems: Part I, Historical Perspectives," *Mini-Micro Systems*, February 1977, p. 36.

28. Ibid.

29. The floppy disk incorporates both magnetic tape and rigid disk technologies. In the drive unit, the floppy disk parallels the rigid disk, with the exceptions noted. Above all, files are randomly accessed. But the substrate of the disk is identical to that used in cassette tapes. Recording technology is therefore based on tape technology, with the significant difference that recording on floppy disks can be performed with either horizontal alignment of the magnetic field, as in tapes, or vertical. If it is vertical, there are two possible encoding techniques: frequency modulation (FM) and modified frequency modulation (MFM). The latter results in double-density recording and the former single-density.

30. Bill Klevesahl and Roger Stromsta, "The Double-Sided Floppy Is Reborn," *Mini-Micro Systems*, May 1981, p. 159.

31. Robert Abraham, "Loading Smaller Disks with More bits," *Computerworld Buyer's Guide*, October 1983, p. 27.

32. Larry Lettieri, "Half-High 8-In. Floppy Race Heats Up with Shugart Entry," *Mini-Micro Systems*, January 1982, p. 22.

33. It was achieved through miniaturization of essential parts, greater use of microprocessors and LSI circuits, and more efficient packaging techniques (Abraham, "Loading Smaller Disks with More Bits."). A major space saver in these smaller drives, both Winchesters and floppies, was

the direct drive DC spindle motors that were 60 percent smaller than their predecessors, and stepper motors 50 percent shorter. They required high-precision spindle electronics and refined motor technology (David R.Simpson, "Product Profile: Half-Height 5¼-inch Disk Drives Will Dominate Low-End Storage Market," *Mini-Micro Systems*, February 1984, p. 176.).

34. Porter, "Floppy Disk Drives."
35. The closed-loop mechanism had been introduced with IBM's 3300 drives in 1971, but low-capacity drives had generally relied on an open-loop actuator because it was cheaper and simpler. Amlyn's initial offering was not a success because it came with a full-height spindle in a market that was increasingly looking for greater compactness.
36. Robert Sehr, "Need for Winchester Backup Pushes Floppies to Higher Densities," *Mini-Micro Systems*, April 19, 1984, p. 65.
37. The medium was stabilized by Bernoulli forces (following Daniel Bernoulli's principle that the pressure of a moving fluid is inversely proportional to its speed) that created a flow of air between the rotating disk and a stable reference plate. Its capacity, performance, and price placed it in competition with small Winchester and hard-disk cartridges.
38. Perpendicular recording increases densities by orienting the magnetic fields up and down relative to the disk surface instead of parallel to the plane of the surface.
39. "8-inch Disks Come of Age," *Mini-Micro Systems*, July 1979.
40. International Data Corporation, "Winchester Backup Alternatives," Research Report.
41. Finis F. Conner, "Introducing the Micro Winchester," *Mini-Micro Systems*, April 1980.
42. Martin, "Putting Power in the House."
43. James N. Porter, "Rigid Disks: The New Small Systems Alternatives," *Mini-Micro Systems*, February 1982, p. 145.
45. Tazz Pettebone, "A Removable Lynx," *Mini-Micro Systems*, October 1980, p. 132.
46. Andrew Roman, "Winchester Market Shifts to 5¼ in. Drives," *Mini-Micro Systems*, February 1981, p. 85.
47. Simpson, "Product Profile: Half-Height 5¼-inch Disk Drives." Disctron, founded in 1980, achieved its higher density by employing a thin film medium together with a closed-loop servosystem, using a linear voice-coil actuator to allow more precise head positioning.
48. Thin film media employ a coating of metal film on the polished aluminum substrate in place of the conventional iron-oxide coating. The key difference between the two lies in the homegeneity of the metal film, which consists of a uniform magnetic layer in contrast to the iron oxide particles which are randomly suspended in an adhesive binder. The

homogeneity allows for up to 50 percent greater recording densities. Since the magnetic layer of metal film media is about one-tenth that of the oxide layer and also smoother, recording heads can fly closer to the disk surface. Thin film is also more durable. It is more expensive to manufacture per disk, but not per byte.

49. "Technology Exchange Seen Pushing Thin Film Heads," *Mini-Micro Systems*, January 1982, p. 18.
50. Andrew Roman, "Firing Up the Mini Winnie Market," *Mini-Micro Systems*, October 1983, p. 31.
51. James F. Moore, "Disk-Drive Distribution and Technology," *Mini-Micro Systems*, February 1982, p. 181.
52. IBM, "Historical Narrative Statement."
53. Brock, *The Computer Industry: A Study of Market Power.*
54. IBM, "Historical Narrative Statement."
55. Datapro Research Corporation, *Datapro 70*, March 1984.
56. For two products that IBM priced with small profit margins, the 2310 and 5440 cartridge drives, no plug-compatible competition emerged in the end-user market, although a large market for similar disks developed among OEMs supplying minicomputers (Moore, "Disk-Drive Distribution and Technology.").
57. *Datapro 70*, March 1984.
58. Brechtlein, "Comparing Disk Technologies."
59. Pettebone, "A Removable Lynx."
60. "The New Entrepreneurs," *Business Week*, April 18, 1983, p. 78.
61. In addition to the dichotomy between Winchester and floppy disks, there are 8-, 5¼-, and 3½-inch disks and below (as well as a few 9- and 10-inch Winchesters), half height and full height. Three main divisions of the 8-inch Winchester market alone had emerged by the 1980s. IBM and Fujitsu were the volume leaders in the over-40M bytes/inch range, which were supplied primarily by firms known for high-performance technology in the large Winchester sector. At the opposite end of the scale, Shugart led in the 5M to 20M bytes/inch range, followed by Memorex, while a mixture of firms, most of them well established, occupied the middle territory (International Data Corporation, "Winchester Backup Alternatives.")
62. There are, for example, a wide variety of different ways of achieving a given storage capacity. One may employ double- or single-density disks, double- or single-sided disks, one or more disks per spindle, one or more spindles per drive, and hard or soft sector formatting. The choices determine compactness, access speed, and cost. Small disk drives can serve a variety of different functions, including secondary storage, Winchester backup storage, or program loading, for systems ranging from small microcomputers to large minicomputers, supplied by a range of different vendors and operated in single-user or multiuser environments.

63. Carl Warren, "IBM Sets Storage Standard with 1.6M-Byte Flexible Drive," *Mini-Micro Systems*, November 19, 1984, p. 19.

64. Ibid.

65. Paul Freiberger and Michael Swaine, *Fire in the Valley* (Berkeley, Calif.: Osborne, McGraw-Hill, 1984).

66. Bowers, "Floppy Disk Drives and Systems."

67. Trifari, "Winchester Drives Focus of Attention."

68. Porter, "Rigid Disks;" George Stollman, "Selecting 8-in. Floppy Disk Drives," *Mini-Micro Systems*, November 1982, p. 315.

69. "8-inch Disks Come of Age."

70. Robert Schmidt, Nashua Corporation, telephone conversation, April 1984.

71. International Data Corporation, "Winchester Backup Alternatives."

72. A case in point was Dastek's agreement with Information Magnetics to permit the latter to offer a second source of its new thin film head. In return, IM provided Dastek with expertise on grinding and lapping of heads and systems assembly production (Roman, "Firing Up the Mini Winnie Market.").

73. Moody's *OTC Industrial Manual, 1980.*

74. "8-inch Disks Come of Age."

8 INTEGRATED CIRCUITS: HISTORY AND TECHNOLOGY

In this and the following chapter we examine the semiconductor industry, tracing its development and the pattern of innovative enterprises from the invention of the point-contact transistor at the Bell Laboratories of American Telephone and Telegraph (AT&T) in 1947 along the path that led to the digital integrated circuit and, by the early 1980s, to the 32-bit microprocessors and 256K random access memory (RAM) chips. Developments in linear circuits, power circuits, and other semiconductor devices that strayed from this path will be set aside. The present chapter examines, the history of the industry and the technology, and Chapter 9 analyzes the market.

The semiconductor industry is not, strictly speaking, part of the computer industry except insofar as the microprocessor is a computer's central processor on a chip. There are nevertheless two good reasons for including integrated circuits among the industry sectors to be analyzed. First, innovations in the industry have been the most important force behind the speed and direction of technological advances in the computer industry since the late fifties and, second, the patterns of development in the two industries display parallels and contrasts whose analysis sheds light on the conditions that influence the contribution of new enterprises to innovation.

THE SEMICONDUCTOR AND COMPUTER
INDUSTRIES COMPARED

The coincidence of events in the two industries began in September 1947 when the point-contact transistor was invented at AT&T's Bell Laboratories in Murray Hill, New Jersey, an accomplishment for which John Bardeen, Walter Brattain, and William Shockley were awarded the Nobel Prize in physics in 1956. The transistor uses semiconductor material to amplify or switch an electrical signal. (A semiconductor such as silicon or germanium, as the name implies, conducts electricity but not as well as conductors like metal.) Its main purpose was seen in 1947 simply as a replacement for the large, power-hungry vacuum tube. As it happened, the year before at the University of Pennsylvania, Eckert and Mauchly had put the finishing touches on ENIAC, the first fully electronic, programmable digital computer. The transistor turned out to be an ideal circuit element for digital systems, which require very large numbers of active circuits in contrast to analog systems.

Transistors were in commercial production at AT&T's manufacturing arm, Western Electric, in 1951,[1] the year that Remington Rand launched UNIVAC I, the world's first commercial stored-program computer. The transistor and the computer, coming onto the market as they did side by side, sparked a technological revolution. By the end of the fifties transistorized computers, the so-called second generation, were on the market, yet the two inventions occurred quite independently.

It is almost impossible to imagine where the computer would be today were it not for the transistor. The ENIAC used 18,000 vacuum tubes, occupied 3,000 cubic feet, weighed 30 tons, and required 140 kilowatts of power. Today's desktop computer, based on a microchip about a half centimeter wide, is "20 times faster, has a larger memory, is a thousand times more reliable, (and) consumes the power of a light bulb rather than a locomotive."[2] A single VLSI (very-large-scale integration) chip, which may contain anywhere from 100,000 to 500,000 transistors, can implement an entire system the size of a 1970 mainframe.

The transistor, like the computer, emerged after years of scientific research conducted in government, university, and industrial laboratories. Bell Laboratories, probably, the largest and most prestigious industrial research laboratory in the world, employed over 2,000 professionals in the late 1940s. The collaboration that achieved the breakthrough took place in its solid state physics laboratory, where 20 to 30 scientists were assigned to the project.[3] AT&T, in search of an electronic replacement for mechanical relays in its telephone switches, had conducted fundamental research on the properties of semiconductor materials since the 1930s, when several solid state physicists, including Shockley and Brattain, were brought to Bell Labs. Members of their matallurgy department also played an important part in producing pure crystals of semiconductor material.

Although the efforts were in no way linked together, both the transistor and the computer benefited from the results of research that the U.S. government had supported during and after World War II and from its role as a major customer thereafter. But the transistor at Bell Laboratories did not receive government assistance nor did the most profound advances in solid state technology that followed over the next three decades.

The U.S. military had funded research on semiconductor devices during World War II aimed at improving the reliability of radar detectors, none of it at AT&T. By that time it was recognized that what was needed was a better understanding of the materials used in order that impurities could be more effectively controlled and their quality improved, and the two semiconductor materials picked for analysis were silicon and germanium; the Radiation Laboratory at MIT was selected to organize the research, and 30 or 40 laboratories were assigned to the task. One of them, the physics department at Purdue, came close to inventing the transistor, but as soon as the war was over it abandoned its pursuit of the practical and returned to fundamental research.[4] It was at about that time that Bell Laboratories assembled a team of scientists to work on problems of solid state physics, drawing on the results of wartime research in the United States and Great Britain, with the primary aim of producing a solid state amplifier, or transistor, although improvements in rectifiers and other devices were also hoped for.[5]

When the transistor was invented, experts at Bell Labs did not foresee a great future for it beyond replacing the vacuum tube in its current operations. The response was similar to Thomas J. Watson's at the birth of the electronic computer. The idea that advances in semiconductor and computer technology would extend the market for computers into millions of factories, offices, and homes was understandably beyond the powers of contemporary imaginations. Like the computer, the transistor started a new industry. By 1980, semiconductor sales of U.S. companies alone amounted to $6 billion,[6] a figure that does not begin to account for the growth that the technology sparked in computers, telecommunications, digital timepieces, calculators, scientific instruments, industrial controls, and other industries.

The two industries, with their singularly synergistic relationship, paralleled each other in their very rapid rates of growth and seemingly limitless opportunities for innovation during the next three decades. There were important differences in market structure, however, which are described in Chapter 9. They account for the fact that, from the outset, new enterprises gained important shares of the semiconductor market and were responsible for critical innovations. By the 1980s, however, the structure of much of the semiconductor industry had come to resemble the mainframe industry in important dimensions that affect entry.

THE TECHNOLOGY

During the industry's first decade, effort was devoted primarily to finding a better way to make semiconductor devices rather than to designing better devices.[7] The basic problem of manufacturing was, and still is, twofold: first, to obtain semiconductor material of sufficient purity, and second, to control the introduction of new impurities. Contributions from materials science, physics chemistry, and electronics were called for. A number of companies contributed to the early advances in manufacturing techniques, among them AT&T, GE, RCA, and Philco. But the event that most firmly laid the foundation for future process development was the planar diffusion process introduced by Fairchild Semiconductor in 1959. The planar process made the integrated circuit, which was invented at about the same time, a commercially viable product. Although they may vary in detail, all current technologies for manufacturing ICs are direct descendents of the planar process. Because the complexity of the manufacturing process in this industry is an essential ingredient of market structure, a brief account of it appears in the appendix to this chapter.

There are currently two basic classes of integrated circuit devices: bipolar and metal oxide semiconductor (MOS). The bipolar transistor, which came first and is still in use, consists, in its simplest form, of three layers of monocrystalline semiconductor material.[8] The first such material to be used was germanium but by the mid-1960s silicon had taken over.[9] Through a process called "doping," a controlled number of atoms of another substance, such as phosphorus (to create an excess of electrons) or boron (to create a shortage), is introduced into each of the three semiconductor layers of a bipolar transistor in order to alter its electrical properties. The three layers in this way are made to be either p,n,p (positive, negative, positive) or n,p,n, with the properties of each layer chosen in such a way that an electrical current passing through the three layers can be strongly influenced by a much smaller current applied to the middle layer. Different types of transistors can be designed with special properties for specific applications. (Before the transistor, a vacuum tube performed the function of altering a current as it passed through an enclosed space that contained either a vacuum or an inert gas, in contrast to semiconductors, whose current alteration depends on the structure and conductivity of solid state materials.) In the planar transistor, invented at Fairchild in the mid-fifties the p,n,p regions were made on the surface of the silicon crystal rather than between layers of crystal.[10]

The original transistor was a discrete component that replaced only a single vacuum tube. It was expensive in relation to the tube, and could not operate at high temperatures or frequencies or with large currents. Its main advantage was its size (200 times smaller) and limited power consumption. In addition, it was more rugged. It is not surprising that hearing aids were for some time its most promising commercial application. Despite the fact that the transistor represented a monumental scientific breakthrough, it was a "manufacturer's nightmare."[11] The first transistors were neither reliable nor uniform, and their life expectancy was short.

Advances in process and design techniques led by the end of the fifties to the integrated circuit (IC), a single silicon chip containing a number of interconnected transistors or other elements such as diodes or passive components. Early ICs contained only a few transistors, but their functional density doubled every year for the next two decades, following what has come to be known as Moore's law (based on a prediction made by Gordon Moore of Fairchild in 1965). By 1980, VLSI chips contained more than 100,000 components on a single piece of silicon about a half centimeter wide.

It was not until 1970 that the MOS (metal oxide semiconductor) became a viable product. The MOS is based on the field effect technology (FET) rather than bipolar. In it, current flows between two regions of negative (or positive) material on the surface of the chip rather than through an n,p,n (or p,n,p) sequence of regions. An electrode, or gate, situated above the current path between the two negative or positive areas, determines whether or not current is allowed to pass, depending on whether the electrode emits a negative or positive voltage. The advantages of the MOS chip was that it could be made smaller and, at least in the beginning, cheaper and, although it is slower than bipolar chips, its power consumption is sufficiently low that many more circuits can be crammed onto a single chip. It is ideal for calculators and small terminals but, more importantly, it is the technology by which large-scale and later very-large-scale integration were effected, along with dramatic reductions in cost per function or per binary digit (bit) of storage. The cost per bit for the nMOS dynamic RAM, for example, fell from about 0.2 cents for the 1K to about 0.02 for the 64K within a few years.[12]

DEVELOPMENT OF THE SEMICONDUCTOR INDUSTRY

The Beginning

When the transistor was introduced, eight well-established manufacturers of vacuum tubes for the merchant (noncaptive) market stood in a position to capitalize on the innovation that was eventually to supplant their market. GE, RCA, and Sylvania claimed three-quarters of tube sales and the remainder went to Raytheon, Philco, CBS, Tung-Sol, and Westinghouse.[13] Their situation was in some ways analagous to that of IBM and other large office machine companies when the electronic computer arrived at about the same time, but, as it turned out, only one of them, RCA, was among the top 10 producers of integrated circuits by the 1970s, and it was number 9. (Sales do not necessarily include production for the "captive" market.) Table 8–1 shows the ranks of the leading U.S. merchant manufacturers for selected years from 1955 to 1979.

As early as 1953 the eight vacuum tube manufacturers, along with six newcomers to the field, had started to make transistors. Notable among the newcomers were Texas Instruments (TI), a geophysical services company since 1930 which transferred to this field, and Motorola, whose main product line had been mobile radios. In the late seventies they were respectively numbers 1 and 3 among U.S. makers of ICs (Table 8–1). TI held 20 percent of the merchant market as early as 1957, about the same share it held in 1980. Also among the participants was a new firm by the name of Transitron, founded in 1952 by a former physicist at Bell Laboratories and his brother. It became the second largest producer of semiconductors at one stage during the fifties by producing a gold bonded diode for the military. Bell Labs had developed the diode but Transitron overcame the tough production problems to increase yields sufficiently that their price was competitive with the point-contact diode then in use.[14] However, Transitron failed to survive into the era of ICs, possibly because of insufficient investment in R&D.

Raytheon became the most heavily involved of the vacuum tube companies in producing transistors in the fifties, almost all for the hearing aid market. Although it dominated this field, like Transitron it was never able to extend its dominance into ICs. The failure of the established vacuum tube companies to achieve sutained leadership in the new industry can be traced to the very early years of the semiconductor market. By 1957 companies that were new to the market ("new" meaning they had not produced vacuum tubes) claimed 64 percent.[15] Eleven of those percentage points were, however, claimed by Hughes, an established producer of diodes and rectifiers. But by 1963, when the industry was little more than 10 years old, Hughes was no longer a significant factor and the newcomers' share had risen to 68 percent. Of the remaining 32 percent, 7 percent was supplied by AT&T's manufacturing arm, Western Electric, leaving 25 percent to the tube companies. Western Electric sales, by a 1956 consent decree, were limited to its sister companies and to the government. If performance is measured in terms of value of sales or market share, the established vacuum tube companies as a group fell behind new entrants soon after the semiconductor industry was born; and the gap grew with time as the industry moved into the age of large-scale ICs.[16]

Classes of Semiconductor Companies

For this analysis it is useful to divide U.S. firms into five classes:

1.   AT&T in a class by itself,
2.   companies new to the electronics industry,
3.   established vacuum tube companies,
4.   established companies from other branches of electronics, and
5.   producers for their own captive markets.

AT&T was, of course, a captive manufacturer, but it stands as a class by itself in terms of the role that its research arm at Bell Laboratories and its equipment manufacturer, Western Electric, played in the

Table 8–1. Leading U.S. Merchant Manufacturers of Semiconductors Ranked by Share of World Market, 1955–79.

	Valves	Transistors (1955)	Semiconductors (1960)	Semiconductors (1965)	Integrated Circuits (1975)	Integrated Circuits (1979)
RCA	1	7	5	6	8	9
Sylvania	2	4	10			
General Electric	3	6	4	5		
Raytheon	4			10		
Westinghouse	5	8				
Amperex	6					
National Video	7					
Ranland	8					
Eimac	9					
Landsdale Tube	10					
Hughes		1	9	9		
Transitron		2	2	8		
Philco		3	3			
Texas Instruments		5	1	1	1	1
Motorola		9	6	2	5	3
Clevite		10	7			
Fairchild			8	3	2	5
General Instrument				4	7	10
Sprague				7		

	Valves	Transistors (1955)	Semiconductors (1960)	Semiconductors (1965)	Integrated Circuits (1975)	Integrated Circuits (1979)
National Semiconductor					3	2
Intel					4	4
Rockwell					6	
Signetics					9	6
American Microsystems					10	
Mostek						7
American Micro Devices						8

Source: Ernest Braun and Stuart MacDonald, *Revolution in Miniature* (Cambridge, England: Cambridge University Press, 1982), p. 123, based on I.M. Mackintosh, "Large-Scale Integration: Intercontinental Aspects, "*IEEE Spectrum* 15, no. 6 (June 1976):54, and *Dataquest*, February 20, 1980. Copyrighted © Cambridge University Press. Reprinted with permission.

industry's innovation. Moreover, the company pursued a liberal licensing policy from the beginning of the transistor era. An antitrust suit brought by the Justice Department which threatened to require divestiture of Western Electric was resolved in the 1956 consent decree and two of its restrictions had long-lasting and significant implications for the direction in which the semiconductor market was to develop. AT&T was required to license all of its existing patents pertaining to transistors free of charge and all of its future patents in the field at reasonable rates, which turned out to be between 2 and 5 percent of the sales value of the product. (At the time, the market for semiconductors was relatively insignificant and its future was not foreseen.) Coincidentally, this was the year in which a Justice Department suit against IBM was resolved in a consent decree with consequences that helped the computer industry develop without patent restrictions that posed serious barriers to entry. But there was a significant difference: whereas IBM was allowed to market its patented products with impunity, AT&T was restricted to supplying its captive market and the U.S. government, and it was constrained from entering the market for computers.

Had AT&T been allowed and chosen to compete, the semiconductor market might have shaped up quite differently, but AT&T had already waved license fees on the first commercial transistor as a memorial to Alexander Graham Bell and, after 1954, it did not assess royalties on transistors for hearing aides.[17] AT&T continued to be a major innovator in the following decades but, beyond that, it took steps, through a series of technical symposiums and publications in the fifties, to disseminate the new technology and to encourage its development. As a potential consumer of semiconductors, it stood to benefit from advances in the field, of course.

Companies New to Electronics.   The most important group of firms to the industry's growth and ultimately to the speed and direction of technological advance consisted of newcomers that had not participated in any branch of electronics before they entered the semiconductor market. With the exception of Texas Instruments (TI), all of the important members of this class got their start in semiconductors. For purposes of analysis TI is treated here as one of the new companies.

Before the end of the 1950s, two members of this group, TI and Fairchild Semiconductor, stood head and shoulders above the others as innovators. While TI went on to become the world's leading merchant producer of integrated circuits, Fairchild was to remain consistently among the top 10 throughout the sixties and seventies. In the very first decade both firms made fundamental innovations of profound importance to the future of the industry and they continued to contribute significantly to advances in technology in succeeding decades. Almost as important as Fairchild's innovations was its propagation of new companies. Most notable was Intel, but at least 80 other companies in Silicon Valley trace their lineage in one or more steps back to Fairchild.[18] On top of new spin-offs, teams of technical personnel who left Fairchild were responsible for the take off of National Semiconductor almost a decade after it was founded and for Motorola's successful entry into semiconductors.

Fairchild Semiconductor was founded in 1957 as an independent division of Fairchild Camera and Instrument by Robert Noyce, Gordon Moore, and six colleagues who left the semiconductor company that William Shockley had established in Palo Alto, California a few years earlier. Noyce had come to Shockley from Philco, where he helped to develop the surface barrier transistor.[19] Reportedly, the group of eight felt that work on new processes held more commercial promise than the new devices on which Shockley was concentrating, and they founded Fairchild with the aim of improving upon the oxide and diffusion process for manufacturing transistors that was then in use. By 1959 they had developed the planar diffusion process that laid the foundation for all subsequent developments in the manufacturing process of ICs.

TI is a firm that is difficult to classify. It is treated here as a new company. It had been in business under the name of Geophysical Services Inc. (GSI) since 1930, the year it commercialized an innovative seismographic instrument that the founder had invented, and had begun to provide geophysical exploration services as well.[20] When Western Electric offered to license the transistor to anyone for $25,000 in 1951, TI made its first plunge into electronic components, sending off a check followed the next spring by a contingent to Bell Laboratories' eight-day symposium on transistor technology. A small group was set up at TI to start building transistors and an organization.[21] Its first director of research was Gordon Teal, who had developed the process for growing single crystals of germanium at Bell and had grown high-purity single-silicon crystals. TI's first major innovation was the silicon transistor, in 1954, which was subsequently to replace the germanium device.[22]

Dozens of other companies have populated this class over the past three decades and there has been lots of turnover in the ranks. Transitron, once number 2, virtually vanished from the scene. But, along with TI and Fairchild, two other companies founded in the first decade of the commercial semiconductor industry rose to top rank. National Semiconductor, started in 1959, eventually climbed to second place in the industry, and Signetics, which spun off from Fairchild in 1961, rose to sixth place.

Between 1966 and 1972 there was a surge of new entrants, lured by prospects for development of the MOS chip, which led to the microprocessor and ultimately to very-large-scale integration (VLSI). More than 30 new merchant manufacturers entered the field, almost all settling in or near California's "Silicon Valley" and all but six of them spinoffs from other semiconductor manufacturers, as shown in Table 8–2. (Four others entered between 1974 and 1976.) The peak years of entry were 1968 and 1969, when three companies started up that were to join the four newcomers mentioned to account for over 60 percent of the value of production of U.S. merchant manufacturers by the late seventies.[23] They were Intel, formed by Noyce and a group from Fairchild in 1968, Mostek, a spin-off from TI in 1969, and Advanced Micro Devices (AMD), dating from 1969. Every one of these seven new companies is credited with at least one, and usually more than one, significant innovation. By the late seventies, their semiconductor sales ranged from well over $1 billion to $50 million for AMD. The only other contender for an important share of the market by then was to be Motorola, which entered from the electrical equipment industry. However, many small companies continued to populate the market.

The number of new entrants fell off sharply after the early seventies and in a wave of more than 15 acquisitions by large international equipment companies during the last half of the decade three of the eight most successful newcomers were bought out: Fairchild by Schlumberger of France, Mostek by United Technologies of the United States, and Signetics by Philips of Holland. Siemens of Germany purchased a 20 percent interest in AMD, and in the eighties, IBM acquired a 20 percent interest in Intel. The chief motivation behind these acquisitions lay in the increasing complexity of ICs, which put a premium on the capability of systems houses to design and manufacture their own devices. In addition, as the market for ICs boomed, equipment companies wanted to assure themselves of a supply of devices. IC houses such as TI and National Semiconductor integrated forward into calculators and computers for another reason as well, namely the search for higher profit margins in the less price competitive equipment markets. A resurgence of new entries began in the eighties, spurred by the demand for custom and semicustom chips, as the complexity of circuitry made standard designs less cost effective for some purposes.

Other U.S. Companies. The relatively small and steadily declining role of the vacuum tube companies is evident in Table 8–1. Only RCA ranked among the top 10 producers of semiconductors in the seventies and it was in ninth place by the end of that decade. But, along with RCA, GE and Philco had each been responsible earlier for important innovations.

Hughes was the most successful early member of the group that entered semiconductors from a branch of the electronics industry other than vacuum tubes and was briefly number 1 in the fifties. It was replaced as the sole distinguished member of this class by Motorola, which rose to second place a decade later and has remained close to the top ever since.

IBM is the leading captive producer of semiconductors aside from AT&T. As early as the late fifties, it manufactured some of the transistors for its mainframes and, beginning with the System 360 family of computers in the early sixties, it made "hybrid" integrated circuits, starting down the path that led it to become the largest manufacturer of ICs in the country, supplying a major portion of its own needs. Hybrid circuits were a compromise between monolithic ICs and discrete transistors, which IBM decided to install in its System 360 computers in order to avoid the risk of experimenting with a totally untested component in such an enormous undertaking. By the eighties, at least a half dozen other computer companies built some of their ICs but, except for DEC and Hewlett-Packard, none had developed a strong capability. Others in communications, automobiles, and instruments, most prominently General Motors' Delco Division, did the same.[24] GE withdrew from the captive market around 1970 but subsequently reentered.[25] As a general rule captive producers did not sell in the merchant market. Because of the proprietary nature, innovations of captive producers, other than Western Electric, are not easy to identify, but IBM is reported to have been first in the development of more than one generation of RAM chips and it invests heavily in basic research.

The importance of a large and diverse group of merchant suppliers of semiconductors (suppliers on the open market) as a precondition to entry of new firms into the computer industry cannot be overemphasized. Had the semiconductor market developed, instead, along the lines that it followed in Europe and Japan, dominated by large, integrated firms, a serious obstacle to entry of new firms into the computer industry

Table 8–2. U.S. Semiconductor Companies Founded between 1966 and 1976.

Company Name, Date Founded	City	Previous Employment of Founders, Number of Founders
American Microsystems (1966)	Cupertino	Philco-Ford (4)
Electronic Arrays (1967)	Mountain View	Philco-Ford (4), Bunker-Ramo (2)
Intersil (1968)	Sunnyvale	Union Carbide (3)
Avantek (1968)	Santa Clara	Applied Technology (4)
Integrated Systems Technology (1968)		Philco-Ford (3)
Nortec Electronics Corp. (1968)	Santa Clara	Philco-Ford (2)
Intel (1968)	"	Fairchild
Precision Monolithic (1969)	"	"
Computer Microtechnology (1968)	"	"
Qualidyne (1968)	Sunnyvale	Intersil (1), Fairchild (2), Leher (1)
Advanced Memory Systems (1968)	Sunnyvale	Fairchild (1), IBM (2), Motorola (1), Collins (1)
Communications Transistor Corp. (1969)	San Carlos	National Semiconductor (3)
Monolithic Memories (1969)	Santa Clara	IBM (1)
Advanced LSI Systems (1969)		Nortec (1)
Mostek (1969)	Carrollton, Texas	Texas Instruments
Signetics Memory Systems (1969)	Sunnyvale	Signetics (2), IBM (2), Hewlett-Packard (1)
Spectronics (1969)	Richardson, Texas	Texas Instruments
Advanced Micro Devices (1969)	"	Fairchild (8)
Four Phase (1969)	Cupertino	Fairchild (6), General Instruments (2), Mellonic (1), other (1)
Litronix (1970)	"	Monsanto (1)
Integrated Electronics (1970)	Mountain View	Fairchild (2)

Company Name, Date Founded	City	Previous Employment of Founders, Number of Founders
Varadyne (1970)		Texas Instruments (2), Nortec (4)
Caltex (1971)	Sunnyvale	Signetics (3)
Exar (1971)	Santa Clara	Intersil (2)
Micropower (1971)	Hauppauge, New York	Four Phase (1), Electro-Nuclear Labs (1), Nitron (1)
Standard Microsystems (1971)		
Antex (1971)	Cupertino	Caltex (1)
LSI Systems (1972)	Newport Beach	Signetics (1)
Nitron (1972)	Sunnyvale	CMI (3), AMI (4), Fairchild (1)
Frontier (1972)	Santa Clara	Intel (2)
Interdesign (1972)	Cupertino	National Semiconductor (2)
Synerteck (1974)	Sunnyvale	Fairchild (1)
Zilog (1974)	''	
Maruman (1975)		
Supertex (1976)		

Source: U.S. Senate, Committee on Commerce, Science, and Transportation, *Industrial Technology* (Washington, D.C.: Government Printing Office, 1978) p. 91, reproduced in Joint Economic Committee, U.S. Congress, 97th Congress, 2nd Session, *International Competition in Advanced Industrial Sectors: Trade and Development in the Semiconductor Industry*, February 18, 1982, pp. 30–31.

would have existed. On the other hand, the industry might have been better organized to contend with competition from the Japanese in the eighties.

Foreign Producers.   A number of large, integrated foreign companies entered the market in the late seventies. The main European contenders were former vacuum tube manufacturers whose production was geared mostly to consumer electronics and telecommunications rather than to data processing, which absorbs more than half of U.S. production. This focus is consistent with the relatively modest development of the computer industry in Europe. Between 1975 and 1980 European companies acquired several American semiconductor manufacturers.

Japanese companies, on the other hand, posed a serious competitive threat to U.S. manufacturers of RAM chips by the end of the seventies. By 1980 they had captured over 40 percent of the 16K RAM market and 70 percent of the 64K RAM market.[26] U.S. firms still claimed 60 percent of the worldwide merchant market for ICs, however, and a much larger share when captive production is included. Six large, vertically integrated firms that were well established in the electronics market prior to their entry into ICs, accounted for 80 percent of Japanese semiconductor sales.[27] By the mid-1980s they were to hold over 90 percent of the 256K RAM market, while American firms retained most of the merchant market for 32-bit microprocessors, logic, and specialty chips.

INNOVATIONS AND INNOVATORS

Table 8–3 presents a list of 41 innovations in the semiconductor industry, starting with the point contact transistor and ending with the 64K dynamic RAM chip in 1980.[28] Attribution of innovations is especially hazardous in this industry because of the exceptionally large gap between development of the concept for a new product and manufacture of the product with adequate yields to make it viable in the market. Some are clearly of more fundamental importance than others and probably some are left out that ought to be included. Nevertheless, I am confident that the list adequately reflects the relative contributions of different classes of firms.

The innovations are of two distinct sorts: improvements in the fabrication process and improvements in the structure or circuit design of the device. The letter "p" next to an innovation in Table 8–3 designates it as a process innovation.

The First Decade

The era of the semiconductor began in 1947 with the invention at Bell Laboratories of the point-contact transistor, which was in commercial production at Western Electric by 1951. The first decade was crowned with the display by TI's Jack Kilby of a crude and cumbersome integrated circuit at the Institute of Radio Engineers' show in early 1959. In 1961 it became a marketable product, thanks to the planar process, developed at Fairchild in 1959. During the 10 years between the transistor and the IC, the industry was preoccupied mainly with improving the process of manufacturing semiconductors, and that is where most of the innovations in that generation are to be found. Technological development concentrated primarily on increasing the product yield, either by reducing the density of defects or reducing the dimensions of the chip.[29]

By far the largest number of technological advances during this decade by any single firm or by any one of our five classes of U.S. firms, was contributed by Bell Laboratories and Western Electric, both of AT&T. Three vacuum tube companies, GE, RCA, and Philco, made one or more contributions, along with TI and Fairchild, which were responsible for major technological breakthroughs.

By 1951 William Shockley at Bell Laboratories had constructed the first grown-junction transistor out of germanium, a significant advance over the point-contact transistor. It was in production at Western Electric the next year. In it, action was achieved by sandwiching n-type semiconductors between p-type semiconductors, as described earlier. It replaced the point-contact transistor with one in which the action occurs in the body of the semiconductor and, in doing so, pointed the way to modern solid state electronics.[30] The junction transistor was the first to be used in hearing aids, where its low weight, small size, and low power consumption gave it a decided advantage over alternatives.

Controlling the level of impurities in the semiconductor was critical to the functioning of the grown-junction transistor. Work at Bell between 1951 and 1954 made possible the process of zone refining for removing impurities from germanium and soon thereafter brought the process within the capabilities of other semiconductor manufacturers. It was quickly adopted throughout the industry.

Pure silicon was much harder to obtain than pure germanium because of its higher melting point, but in 1954 Gordon Teal at TI announced

Table 8–3. Semiconductor Innovations Leading to Developments in Digital Integrated Circuits, 1947–80.

Date		Innovation	Company
1947		Point-contact germanium transistor	Bell Labs
1950	p	Zone refining	Western Electric, AT&T
1951		Grown-junction germanium transistor	Western Electric
1952	p	Alloy process	GE/RCA
1954	p	Jet etching technique	Philco
1954		Silicon transistor	Texas Instruments (TI)
1956	p	Oxide masking and diffusion	Bell, TI, GE
1958		Integrated circuit	TI
1959	p	Planar process	Fairchild
1960	p	Epitaxial process	Bell Labs
1961		RTL bipolar circuit	Fairchild
1962		DTL bipolar circuit	Signetics
1963		ECL bipolar circuit	Motorola
1964		TTL bipolar circuit	Pacific, Sylvania
1962		Metal oxide semiconductor (MOS)	various
1963	p	Silicon on sapphire	Autonetics, various
1967		64-bit ROM	Fairchild
1968		1K ROM	Philco-Ford
1968		CMOS	various
1968		MOS FET	Bell Labs, Phillips
1968	p	Nitride chemical vapor deposition	General Instr.
1969	p	Glass chemical vapor deposition	Bell Labs
1969	p	Collector diffusion isolation	Bell Labs

Date		Innovation	Company
1970		Shottky TTL	TI
1970		1103 1K MOS dynamic RAM	Intel
1971		Microprocessor	Intel
1971	p	Ion implantation	Bell Labs, Mostek
1971		EPROM	Intel
1972		Bipolar 1K RAM	Fairchild
1972		8-bit microprocessor	Intel
1972		Bipolar MOS combination	RCA
1973	p	Polysilicon deposition	Intel
1974		CMOS microprocessor	RCA
1974		Computer on a chip (TMS 1000)	TI
1974		16-bit microprocessor	National Semiconductor
1975		16K dynamic RAM	Intel, Mostek, TI
1975		Bipolar 4K RAM	Fairchild
1975		CMOS memory chip using silicon on sapphire	RCA
1975		Merged transistor integration injection logic	IBM, Phillips
1976		16-bit dynamic RAM	Intel, Mostek
1980		64K dynamic RAM chip	various Japanese

Sources: See text of Chapter 8.

p = process innovation.

that he had succeeded in making a silicon transistor using the grown-junction technique. It could operate at much higher temperatures than the germanium transistor because of its higher melting point, and was greatly in demand by the military, although it had been developed without government assistance.

GE's major contribution during this era, sometimes credited also to RCA, was the alloy-junction transistor in 1952. It yielded transistors with increased frequency and superior digital switching capabilities which encouraged the development of second generation computers. The process required very demanding manufacturing tolerances, however, and Philco met this demand in 1954 when its jet-etching technology produced the surface barrier transistor. It was faster and had a higher frequency response than earlier devices. But it was soon outmoded by the oxide masking and diffusion process of wafer fabrication, developed at Bell Labs and also GE in 1956, and shortly thereafter, by Fairchild's planar process. Philco developed the first automated production line in the industry to manufacture its surface barrier transistor and was able to slash prices, temporarily gaining a substantial share of the market.[31] But rapid obsolescence of its production facilities drove it out of the semiconductor market.

Both Bell and GE contributed to development of the oxide masking and diffusion process in 1956, which converted fabrication partially to a batch process and paved the way for the planar process. The impurity to be introduced into the semiconductor was diffused from its vapor, and by carefully regulating time and temperature its penetration could be accurately controlled, while photomasking determined where diffusion occurred.

Kilby's integrated circuit, in 1959, consisted of two circuits on one piece of germanium, each performing the function of several discrete components. Components had to be connected by hand. Kilby had joined TI in the same year from a company called Centralab, where he had been working along similar lines.[32] The idea that a complete circuit of amplifiers, resistors, and capacitors could be realized within the body of a single piece of semiconductor material had been foreseen soon after the invention of the transistor by W.G.D. Drummer in England, and the concept had been further developed by several investigators.[33] But Kilby was the first to overcome the engineering problems involved in fashioning a transistor, resistor, capacitor, and diode out of the same piece of silicon. TI received what Kilby described as critical support in further developing the concept and the manufacturing technique from the U.S. Air Force.[34]

Robert Noyce had been thinking along similar lines at Fairchild and it was his planar process that made the IC commercially practical by making it possible to connect the components of circuits using the batch process of oxide diffusion, (described in the chapter appendix) rather than by hand. The flatness of the planar transistor meant that all connections could be made on its surface. TI and Fairchild disputed patent rights to the IC all the way to the U.S. Supreme Court. Kilby's IC was first but Noyce's was in many ways better. In the end both were granted patents which they cross licensed and in 1959 both began to manufacture ICs, using the planar process, which were available in production quantities two years later. 1962 marked the beginning of mass IC production, at first almost entirely for military and space programs. ICs were expensive, costing between $50 and $100 each, compared with about a dollar a piece a decade later.

The epitaxial process developed at Western Electric in 1960 further reduced production costs and improved the frequency range of ICs. It permitted silicon vapor to be deposited on a single crystal silicon substrate, which made it possible for components to be formed in the deposited silicon without interfering with the substrate. This eliminated the undesirable electrical characteristics of a thick base region. It overcame a fundamental weakness of the planar process—its inability to produce high-frequency, high-power transistors because of the high resistance of the collector material.

The Second Decade

When the sixties decade opened, efforts were underway to develop and produce the metal oxide semiconductor (MOS), which was to pave the way for the microprocessor and for the 1K RAM chip at the beginning of the next decade, and for the successively more powerful memory and logic chips that followed. The MOS chip, which controlled the flow of current by use of a metal gate that was typically insulated from the silicon by a layer of silicon dioxide, lent itself especially well to IC fabrication and made it ultimately possible to pack many thousands of components onto one chip.

MOS technology was first developed at RCA, where work that began on it in 1959 culminated in 1962. In addition to consuming much less power so that a far greater level of integration was possible than on bipolar devices, the MOS required only about half as many processing steps. But production was plagued with oxide defects and other problems that manufacturers' experience with bipolar devices had not schooled them to deal with, and RCA eventually shifted back to bipolar. Fairchild, which had also started to work on the MOS chip, abandoned it after process difficulties. Two new firms, General Microelectronics, which spun off from Fairchild in 1963, and General Instrument, were the only companies making MOS chips in 1965. They, too, faced serious production problems while many large companies took a wait-and-see attitude.[35] Then, in 1969, MOS production took off and by 1970 sales exceeded $100 million. It is impossible to attribute the innovation to any particular firm or group of firms. There were many contributors building on each others' failures as well as their successes. The idea was first conceived by Shockley at Bell,[36] but it was not feasible to construct it out of germanium, the semiconductor medium that was current at that time. A number of different MOS technologies can be distinguished, including nMOS and pMOS. In 1968 several of the former vacuum tube companies came out with the complementary MOS (CMOS) chip, which gained importance because the low steady-state dissipation of the circuit makes it ideal for applications such as battery-powered equipment.[37] By 1984 CMOS appeared to be the wave of the future for VLSI chips because of its low power consumption.[38]

From the beginning of the sixties, advances were also made in the design of bipolar (as distinct from MOS) logic circuits. These circuits are usually classified into families based on common design features. The first bipolar ICs were Fairchild's resistor-capacitor-transistor logic (RCTL) and TI's direct-coupled transistor logic (DCTL), but both had weaknesses and were soon supplanted by RTL, pioneered by Fairchild. This, in turn, was quickly replaced by diode-transistor logic (DTL), introduced by Fairchild and Signetics and perhaps other companies. Fairchild's 930 DTL emerged as the industry leader in the mid-1960s as a result of very aggressive pricing. But just when the DTL was at its peak, Sylvania came out with its Sylvania Universal High-Level Logic (SUHL), the first of the transistor-transistor logic (TTL) family.[39] One source attributes this design to a small company named Pacific Semiconductors,[40] and another reports that Fairchild invented TTL in 1964 but did not market it for three years.[41] Its advantage was fast switching speed, and demand grew very rapidly. TI came out with a proprietary TTL chip and others quickly second-sourced the two companies. Newer circuit designs were introduced, based on the TI design, that could cram increasing numbers of functions onto a chip, and soon what is now known as medium-scale Integration (MSI), which integrated hundreds components on one chip, was born. Sylvania suffered from low yields and TI took over as leader of bipolar logic while Sylvania withdrew from the market in 1970. In that same year, TI introduced the Shottky TTL, which greatly increased the speed and improved the performance of bipolar logic.

In the late sixties, custom large-scale integration (LSI), using MOS technology and containing a thousand or more elements on a chip, came to be regarded as the wave of the future and competition developed to devise the least costly design. Although much effort and ingenuity went into the race, in the end the arrival of the microprocessor in 1971 made the concept obsolete for the time being.[42] A decade later it was revived when computer-aided design helped to bring semicustom-tailored circuits into the marketplace for equipment manufacturers willing to pay the price.

Various organizations are credited with the first silicon-on-sapphire chip (SOS), which had lower power requirements and higher density possibilities. In the hunt for an insulator substrate to replace silicon, attention focused on sapphire because its crystalline structure was known to be similar to that of silicon, an advantage when it came to using it for a base on which to grow silicon crystals.

The first read-only semiconductor memory (ROM) was marketed in 1967 by Fairchild, containing 64 bits of storage. A year later, Philco-Ford upped the capacity to 1,000 bits (or 1K).

The incredibly rapid fall in the price of ICs from $50.00 when they first appeared to about $1.00 a decade later testifies to the very substantial advances in the production process that were taking place during the decade. The fall in price was accompanied by a growth in sales of discrete equivalents of ICs from 100 million in 1963 to 8.6 billion in 1967 and to 40.6 billion in 1971. The cost reduction of about 28 percent for every doubling of output was the product of steady improvements in production processes leading to higher and higher yields. Among them were new methods of chemical vapor deposition, introduced by General Instrument (founded in 1967 as a wholly owned subsidiary of an older company by the same name) and Bell Laboratories. Clean-room technology began to be installed in the early sixties, the forerunner of the superclean rooms that would be needed for LSI production in the next decade. New lithographic techniques for mask making, were introduced, often pioneered by instruments manufacturers, and computer-aided design was commonplace by the end of the decade, both essential to LSI technology in the future.

Less fundamental were advances in packaging of ICs. TI's "flat pack," a package with ribbonlike leads coming out of two sides, was introduced in 1962 and became the industry standard. Fairchild's dual-in-line package (DIP), with two rows of pins on opposite sides, was an ingenious variation that was widely accepted. The next year Fairchild or GE (depending on the source) introduced plastic encapsulation as an alternative to ceramic or metal. Western Electric's beam lead technique, using gold metalization to connect gates of the chip and also to provide beamlike leads to the external circuitry, was another packaging advance.[43]

The Memory Race of the 1970s

The developments of the 1960s were capped in 1970 by the production at Intel of the 1K dynamic RAM chip, based on MOS technology and named the 1103. It was the device that led to the replacement of the computer's magnetic core memory by the semiconductor memory. A RAM, or random access memory (RAM), chip contains memory cells that can be reached independently, rather than by following a sequence.[44] The technology that underlies its production has become a driving force in the industry. A static RAM is faster than the dynamic RAM but requires six transistors per cell rather than one; thus, it is more expensive and its density has increased less rapidly.

Semiconductor memories had been produced earlier, but around 1968 a surge of new companies went into business with the aim of producing a low-cost, high-performance semiconductor memory that could replace the computer's core memory.[45] Among them were Intel, Mostek, and Advanced Memory Systems. Core memory was satisfactory for mainframe computers, but as minicomputers (and later microcomputers) came along it did not meet their need for smaller, more compact, and less expensive internal storage capacity.[46] The RAM chip helped to pave the way for small computers.

Better established semiconductor houses, like TI, Fairchild, and Motorola, evidently decided to hold back at this stage from an all out commitment to the new technology. Intel's success in developing polysilicon MOS technology (in which a polysilicon electrode "gate" replaced the aluminum electrode that had afforded only very low yields) broke the technological barrier and led to volume production of the 1K

RAM.[47] Advanced Memory Systems actually beat Intel to the market by three months, however, with a 1K RAM that was faster but not as easy to use.[48] The 1103 became established as the market prototype and other companies followed with similar products.[49] Two years later Intel introduced the very important erasable, programmable read-only memory chip (EPROM).

Three years after the 1K RAM, Intel, Mostek, a recent spin-off from TI, and TI each brought out 4K RAMs, TI having sat out the 1K round. Mostek had a unique 16-pin design to replace the traditional 22 pins, which allowed greater packaging density with a simpler layout. Although it was not a major innovation, it was regarded as a bold stroke for a new firm and became the industry standard. By 1976, Intel, Mostek, and TI had a combined share of more than 80 percent of the dynamic RAM market, but many other companies joined them with proprietary designs or by second sourcing. Fairchild introduced a 4K nMOS chip in 1975 that was reputed to be twice as fast as the others, based on a special application of the planar process. In 1972 Fairchild announced the first bipolar 1K RAM, more expensive but much faster than the MOS-based memories, and three years later followed with the 4K bipolar RAM.

In 1975, Mostek, Intel, and TI once again led the pack in quadrupling memory cells with the 16K RAM (one source says that Intel was first), but all three failed to expand fast enough, due either to production or cash flow problems, leaving the door open for the Japanese to seize over 40 percent of the market by 1979. A more significant intrusion of Japanese competition began, however, with the 64K RAM. Historically, Japanese firms had proved to be capable followers. They had not led American firms in product development but this time they beat them to the market. They were able to cut the price of 64K RAMs sold in the United States from $28.00 at the beginning of 1981 to $8.00 a few months later.[50] One cannot be certain, however, that the price cut was entirely a reflection of cost reductions.[51] With the arrival of the 256K RAM a few years later, Japanese vendors were to take over the lion's share of the memory chip market. Memory chips are commodity devices where quality control and cost control are of the essence. American firms continued until the mid-1980s to dominate logic and specialty chips where design is the critical factor. By 1980 the state of the art in memory chips included, in addition to the 64K dynamic RAM, a variety of ROMs, the PROM (programmable read-only memory), introduced by Intel, and 16K static RAMs.

The Microprocessor

The other technological triumph that changed the course of the semiconductor (and the computer) industry in the 1970s was the microprocessor, invented in 1971, once again at Intel, in the same year that it came out with the PROM and a year after its 1103 RAM. A microprocessor is a computer's central processor on a single chip. When it is combined with memory and input and output circuits it is a complete computer. It created a virtual revolution in microelectronics applications.

The precursor of the microprocessor was the calculator on a chip, which includes four functions: add, subtract, multiply, and divide. According to one source,[52] it was first produced by Mostek shortly after its founding in 1969, but another source credits TI, National Semiconductor, and others with near simultaneous production of the single-chip calculator.[53]

The invention of the microprocessor at Intel was the serendipitous outcome of a request from a Japanese calculator company, Busicom, for a range of calculator chips of different designs. At that time, 1969, Intel was a brand new company developing memory chips. The job was assigned to Ted Hoff who, in an environment free of preconceived notions or manufacturing constraints to limit his imagination, conceived the design of a programmable chip to meet Busicom's needs. (A microprocessor differs from a dedicated calculator chip in that it can be programmed with software.) Neither Intel nor Busicom at first perceived the full import of the idea.[54] It was simply a better way to meet Busicom's needs. Intel subsequently renegotiated its contract in order to retain marketing rights and at the end of 1971 the first microprocessor, the 4004, was born. It had a 4-bit word length, and when combined with other chips containing a memory, additional registers, and an input/output device, it would become a microcomputer opening up vast new markets.

Intel brought out the 8-bit 8008 in 1972 and later the 8080, which became the industry standard. Other companies followed with variations or improvements, including Motorola's very popular 6800. By the late seventies virtually all major U.S. semiconductor manufacturers were making microprocessors and most of the industry had shifted emphasis away from dedicated logic circuits.

The 8-bit microprocessor was followed by National Semiconductor's 16-bit device in 1974 and in 1981 Intel introduced a 32-bit microprocessor that integrated 200,000 transistors and was built on three chips.[55] Throughout the 1970s, competition and learning curve economies drove the price of microprocessors steadily downward.

TI was the first to make an entire computer on a chip.[56] Working on simplification of the connections between different parts of the microcomputer, it invented a "bus" to serve as a trunk line for carrying signals between the different units of the computer (processor, memory, I/O) and to avoid impossibly complex networks of interconnections. In 1971 the feasibility of the single-chip computer was demonstrated by TI and a patent was eventually granted. The device reached the market the next year and in 1979 over a million of these chips were sold for use in calculators, toys, computer games, and simple control systems.

By the end of the 1970s, custom design of LSI chips, which had been more or less abandoned earlier as too costly, resurfaced in the form of semicustom tailored chips. For some purposes they are superior to LSI microprocessors whose programming costs can be prohibitive.[57]

Summing Up

The conclusion appears to be justified that the most innovative company during the early history of the industry was AT&T, the parent of Bell Laboratories and Western Electric, a firm that was unique in its commitment to research in general and its special involvement with the semiconductor industry. The technological leadership of companies that entered the electronics industry after the invention of the transistor—what we call new companies—all of them with the exception of TI starting up on their entry into the industry, was critical at each stage in the evolution of the industry. Several of them, individually, were responsible for more than one innovation of profound importance and collectively they can probably be said to have outperformed AT&T after the first major advances in the technology. Certainly, they were far more innovative as a group than the other vacuum tube companies. Some of the latter were important innovators in the first few years of the industry but thereafter, aside from RCA, their contributions waned. Established firms from other branches of electronics are, with the exception of Motorola, scarcely noted in the annals of semiconductor innovation.

The innovative newcomers of the 1950s, particularly TI and Fairchild, remained at the forefront of new technologies as they grew and matured into the seventies, but their most dramatic advances in technology were typically made when they were relatively new. Intel, like Fairchild, was only two or three years old when it made a succession of stunning contributions. It is of more than passing interest that Robert Noyce was a founder of both of these companies.

APPENDIX: THE MANUFACTURING PROCESS FOR INTEGRATED CIRCUITS

The manufacture of integrated circuits (ICs) involves three distinct stages: first, circuit design and mask making, second, fabrication of the circuit on a silicon chip and last, packaging and testing of the circuit.

Circuit Design and Mask Making

The process of making an IC begins with designing the circuit to meet given specifications, usually aided today by computer tools in such tasks as modeling circuits, checking logic, and simulation. As ICs came to contain many thousands of components, the design of logic chips became exceedingly complex. The next step is to generate the circuit patterns that will be transferred to a set of glass plates that form the "masks" to be used in the fabrication process. Hundreds of identical circuit patterns are etched onto the glass mask, a process that requires several complicated steps and specialized optical and lithographic machines.

Fabrication

Fabrication of integrated circuits involves a number of complicated and delicate stages. It begins with the production of very pure crystalline silicon in the form of a rod, currently 3 to 5 inches in diameter, compared with 1 inch when the technology was first developed. During the process, "dopants" are introduced into the silicon melt to give the desired n- or p-type semiconductivity. The process up to this point is generally performed by independent chemical companies. The rods are then sawed with diamond-edged cutters into thin, round wafers, which are in turn polished and cleaned. Each wafer will accommodate several hundred identical ICs. The fabrication process begins when the IC manufacturer next oxidizes the wafer at temperatures as high as 10,000 to 12,000 degrees Centigrade to create a layer of silicon dioxide on the surface. Silicon dioxide is a perfect insulator. It is in turn covered with a layer of photosensitive material, called resist. The next step is to transfer the pattern of hundreds of identical IC designs from the glass mask to the silicon wafer.

The mask, which is opaque in the regions that are not to be doped, is placed on top of the silicon wafer and subjected to ultraviolet radiation. The photosensitive resist that has been exposed is then developed and removed and the oxide layer beneath it is etched away to expose the silicon layer below. At this point the resist layer is removed from the remaining surface of the wafer, leaving an oxide layer covering all of the area that was shielded by the opacity of the mask and leaving "holes" in the areas that were not. In this way a wafer is obtained that is covered with an oxide layer except for several openings in each IC that give access to the silicon.

A batch of such wafers is placed in a high-temperature furnace in a controlled atmosphere containing the desired impurities, or dopant. Temperatures, the concentration of impurities, and the duration of exposure must be very carefully controlled at this stage. A diffused layer of the dopant deposits itself in the holes that have been etched out of the oxide layer, making contact with the silicon. Now, the remainder of the oxide layer is removed and usually a new layer applied and the entire process repeated one or more times using different dopants until the desired arrangement of n and p regions has been created.

In the final stage of fabrication, a thick layer of oxide is spread over the surface and, using the same etching process as before, this time a layer of metal is evaporated on the surface to make contacts with the silicon. The desired pattern of conductors is made by etching away the undesired metal.

The fabrication process, which is presented here in a rather simplified sketch, will vary depending on the particular type of IC, but the fundamental characteristics of the process will be similar. The process is generally carried out by manual operators under highly controlled conditions in the plant of the IC house. Much of the technological knowhow of the company resides in these plants along with most of its physical capital, invested in equipment and ultraclean rooms.

Testing and Assembly

The fabrication process results in a number of 3- to 5-inch in diameter wafers, each containing many copies of the same IC. The wafers are tested with complex and specialized equipment and then cut up into "chips," each containing a single IC. Next the chip is glued to a frame containing the pins and the IC is connected with the pins using gold wires. The package is then housed in a plastic or ceramic container and usually retested. It is now ready to be shipped. This stage of the process typically makes use of large amounts of relatively unskilled manual labor and for this reason most U.S. companies perform it overseas where labor is less expensive than in the United States. IBM and Japanese companies, however, have chosen instead to automate this phase.

NOTES

1. Ernest Braun and Stuart MacDonald, *Revolution in Miniature* (Cambridge, England: Cambridge University Press, 1982).
2. Ibid.
3. G.W.A. Dummer, *Electronic Inventions and Discoveries*, 2d ed. (New York: Pergamon, 1978).
4. Braun and MacDonald, *Revolution in Miniature*.
5. Dummer, *Electronic Inventions and Discoveries*.
6. The Editors of Electronics, *An Age of Innovation: The World of Electronics, 1930–2000* (New York: McGraw-Hill, 1981).
7. Braun and MacDonald, *Revolution in Miniature*.
8. As its name implies, semiconductor material has electrical properties intermediate between those of an insulator and a conductor. Free charge carriers are not usually present, but they can be generated with the application of a small amount of energy. The term *semiconductor* has come to apply to the entire range of passive and active electronic components made out of semiconductor material.
9. Nico Hazewindus and John Tooker, *The U.S. Microelectronics Industry: Technical Change, Industrial Growth, and Social Impact* (New York: Pergamon, 1982).
10. Ibid.
11. Braun and MacDonald, *Revolution in Miniature*.
12. Robert N. Noyce, "Microelectronics," *Scientific American*, September 1977, p. 63. See figure on p. 69.
13. Braun and MacDonald, *Revolution in Miniature*.
14. John E. Tilton, *International Diffusion of Technology: The Case of Semiconductors* (Washington, D.C.: The Brookings Institution, 1971), p. 67.
15. Tilton, *International Diffusion of Technology*, p. 66.
16. Reports by Tilton (*International Diffusion of Technology*, Table 4–5) do not always agree with the numbers in Table 8–1 concerning the

market shares of GE, RCA, and Sylvania among the top three of the vacuum tube companies, but they do agree on the fact that the shares of TI and at least one other newcomer were always greater.

17. Braun and MacDonald, *Revolution in Miniature.*

18. "Silicon Valley Genealogy," chart (Mountain View, Calif.: Semiconductor Equipment and Materials Institute, n.d.).

19. Robert W. Wilson, Peter K. Ashton, and Thomas P. Egan, *Innovation, Competition, and Government Policy in the Semiconductor Industry* (Lexington, Mass.: Lexington Books, 1980).

20. Subsequently it went into exploration on its own and acquired substantial oil assets before the geophysical services branch was bought out by four employees in the early forties. The name GSI was later changed to Texas Instruments. During World War II it sold instruments to the military that were akin to its seismographic equipment, and by 1950 its total annual sales from manufacturing had risen from about $1 million in 1947 to over $7 million.

21. John MacDonald, "The Man Who Made T.I.," *Fortune*, November 1961.

22. Braun and MacDonald, *Revolution in Miniature.* The company soon managed to produce large quantities of silicon by chemical methods. The replacement of germanium with silicon increased the temperature and frequencies that the transistor could withstand and opened up a large military market to TI.

23. Hazewindus and Tooker, *U.S. Microelectronics Industry.*

24. Ibid.

25. Douglas W. Webbink, "The Semiconductor Industry: A Survey of Structure, Conduct and Performance," Staff Report to the U.S. Federal Trade Commission, Bureau of Economics (Washington, D.C.: U.S. Government Printing Office, 1977).

26. Hazewindus and Tooker, *U.S. Microelectronics Industry.*

27. Joint Economic Committee, U.S. Congress, 97th Congress, 2d Session, "International Competition in Advanced Industrial Sectors: Trade and Development in the Semiconductor Industry," February 18, 1982.

28. The list has been drawn from a variety of sources. Unlike the sectors of the computer industry studies, where it was necessary to ferret out individual innovations from a large body of literature, innovations in the semiconductor industry have been surveyed by a number of independent sources, covering different periods in history. I have drawn freely on these lists as well as from conversations with Professor Richard B. Adler, associate head of the Department of Electrical Engineering and Computer Science at MIT. Occasional disagreements among sources concerning the date or originator of an innovation are noted in Table 8–3 and also in the text.

29. Noyce, "Microelectronics."
30. Braun and MacDonald, *Revolution in Miniature*.
31. Richard C. Levin, "Innovation in the Semiconductor Industry," in *Government and Technological Change: A Cross-Industry Analysis*, ed. Richard A. Nelson (New York: Pergaman Press, 1982).
32. Braun and MacDonald, *Revolution in Miniature*; The Editors of Electronics, *An Age of Innovation*.
33. Noyce, "Microelectronics."
34. Levin, "Innovation in the Semiconductor Industry."
35. The Editors of Electronics, *An Age of Innovation*.
36. Conversations with Professor Richard B. Adler, associate head, Department of Electrical Engineering and Computer Science, Massachusetts Institute of Technology, Spring 1984.
37. Hazewindus and Tooker, *U.S. Microelectronics Industry*.
38. Arthur L. Robinson, "CMOS Future for Microelectronic Circuits," *Science*, May 15, 1984, p. 705.
39. Wilson, Ashton, and Egan, *Innovation, Competition, and Government Policy in the Semiconductor Industry*.
40. The Editors of Electronics, *An Age of Innovation*.
41. Wilson, Ashton, and Egan, *Innovation, Competition, and Government Policy in the Semiconductor Industry*.
42. Ibid.
43. The Editors of Electronics, *An Age of Innovation*.
44. Each of the thousand cells on a 1K chip contains storage capacity for one bit of information and a transistor to let the information in or out. "Dynamic" means that the chip must receive continuous electric pulses or lose its memory. Unneeded data can be instantly erased and replaced with new information on the dynamic RAM, and it can be mass produced more cheaply than static RAMs and ROMs (read-only memories).
45. Wilson, Ashton, and Egan, *Innovation, Competition, and Government Policy in the Semiconductor Industry*.
46. Braun and MacDonald, *Revolution in Miniature*.
47. Gene Bylinsky, "How Intel Won Its Bet on Memory Chips," *Fortune*, November 1973, p. 142.
48. Wilson, Ashton, and Egan, *Innovation, Competition, and Government Policy in the Semiconductor Industry*.
49. AMS spokesmen have blamed their loss to Intel on Intel's very effective marketing. Bylinsky reported in *Fortune* ("How Intel Won Its Bet on Memory Chips"), however, that the key was Intel's ability to live up to performance objectives with one of the toughest monitoring and quality control systems in the industry.
50. Gene Bylinsky, "Japan's Ominous Chip Victory," *Fortune*, December 14, 1981, p. 52.

51. IBM had been using the 64K chip two or three years before it was on the market in the United States, according to Richard B. Adler (conversation, 1984). But evidently it was not a success.

52. Joint Economic Committee, "International Competition in Advanced Industrial Sectors."

53. Braun and MacDonald, *Revolution in Miniature*. The calculator contains most of the features of a computer for performing arithmetic operations, but in it all possible operations are permanently wired with route selection dependent on key depression. In the computer and the microprocessor, by contrast, routes and sequences of routes can be programmed. Instead of a limited number of fixed-wire routes, it has a large number for the programmer to select from.

54. Ibid.

55. Ibid.

56. The Editors of Electronics, *An Age of Innovation*.

57. "The Boom in Tailor Made Chips," *Fortune*, March, 1981.

9 INTEGRATED CIRCUITS: MARKET ANALYSIS

It is evident from the previous chapter that the doors of entry into the semiconductor market were wide open to small, new companies until after the middle of the 1970s, and they exploited the opportunities for growth and innovation to the exclusion of all but a handful of companies that antedated the solid state revolution. The most notably exceptions, AT&T and later IBM, produced for their captive markets. In the late seventies, capital requirements escalated until it became virtually impossible for new firms to enter the major sectors of the market. Between 1976 and 1981 at least 15 acquisitions gobbled up many of the industry's outstanding young firms, as equipment manufacturers sought their own captive sources of ICs and smaller semiconductor houses were beset with problems in financing growth. But we observed that by 1980 some fresh opportunities for new companies had emerged in the custom and semicustom circuit markets.

The ability of new enterprises to enter and innovate during the first two decades of this industry, in contrast to the computer industry, which got its start in the same year, was a result of relatively low initial capital requirements and more limited product differentiation barriers.

ABSOLUTE COST BARRIERS

As in the other industries in this series of studies, the two potentially significant absolute cost barriers to entry of innovative new firms were restricted access to the requisite technology and to capital.

Access to Technology

Because process technology was as critical as product design, limited access to patents or unpatented information, if they related to semiconductor production, could deter entry.

Patents.   The discussion of patents here pertains to their coverage of both process and product design. Their role was not much different from their role in the computer industry: they provided at best modest barriers to imitation. In the early fifties, the patents that mattered were owned by AT&T and that company followed a liberal licensing policy from the beginning. In 1953 its maximum rate of royalties was lowered from 5 to 2 percent, possibly under the influence of an antitrust suit that had been instituted against it in 1949, and the 1956 consent decree that followed required the company to continue the liberal policy. AT&T patented everything that was patentable in order to prevent other companies from obtaining the patent and to serve as a bargaining chip in cross-licensing agreements, but its liberal licensing policy set the tone that the industry was to follow. With the arrival of the integrated circuit (IC), patent rights were disputed and the legal settlement in 1966 awarded both TI and Fairchild rights to license the patent for the next 10 years, thereby assuring competition.[1]

The number of patented technologies that are essential to production of an IC has virtually guaranteed widespread cross licensing, and, beyond that, infringements were widely ignored in the industry. According to Tilton, a firm with few or no patents to exchange was charged royalties of anywhere from 1 to 6 percent of sales, but "In fact, most new companies can infringe patents with impunity until they become important enough to make a suit worthwhile. Even then, the normal outcome is an out-of-court settlement whereby the infringing firm agrees to accept a license."[2] Levin pointed to the anomaly that large-scale ICs could not be patented because there is no way to specify the precise layout of the circuit other than by a diagram, and diagrams were not acceptable for patent purposes. Production processes that depend on subtle manipulation of conditions during the fabricating process, which are absolutely critical to success in the industry, are not really susceptible to patenting, nor would a firm risk the loss of secrecy entailed in patenting them.

Technical Know-How.   The lack of potency of patent control in the industry was balanced by the importance of access to unpatented technical knowledge and know-how. When the transistor came into the world, most of what was known about the physics and chemistry of solid state electronics resided in the minds of a few individuals, most of them at AT&T's Bell Laboratories. But, to make matters worse, the key to a company's success in delivering reliable devices at competitive prices was knowing how to increase yields by improving the production process, and it is generally agreed that the main source of this knowledge comes from experience in production.

Almost from the beginning, the secret of bringing down the cost of semiconductors was to increase the yield from a given batch of wafers. In 1975, the "cumulative" yield for a mature circuit such as the 11-year-old TTL was as low as 20 percent while the yield on Intel's 5-year-old 1103 was under 9 percent.[3] Fabrication is a batch process with virtually all costs fixed per batch. Thus, if yields can be increased from 10 percent to 20 percent, the fabrication cost of a circuit can be almost cut in half. The problem of yield is the main obstacle to increasing the functional density of circuits at ever decreasing costs per function. Yields can be increased either by reducing the density of defects on the silicon wafer or by increasing the density of the circuitry. The first requires meticulous attention to process control and cleanliness. The second is accomplished by crowding more and more circuit elements into a given space through improvements in the resolution of the photoengraving process. Reducing the size of the circuit elements not only reduces cost but improves the basic performance in terms of speed and power consumption.[4] Because of the importance of managing and improving upon the very complex and delicate production process, experience with production is key to a firm's success in the industry, and the 25 to 30 percent decline in cost of an IC with each doubling of the industry's output has generally been interpreted to imply that the learning curve is very steep.[5] A very steep learning curve, under ordinary circumstances, would erect an absolute cost barrier that could result in a natural monopoly. There are several reasons why this did not happen in semiconductors, which, indeed turned out to be highly competitive.

First, all of the 25 percent cost reduction is not necessarily due to experience. Part accrues with the passage of time from new processes and equipment that are developed outside of the firm and made available to all comers. Second, some of the reduction in cost that is due to learning within the firm is not appropriable by the firm. The focus of efforts to increase yields is mainly on the fabrication process where skilled engineers and circuit designers work together to modify products, to experiment with exposure times and temperatures used in the preparation of crystals, and to control crystal contamination. The learning that takes place within the firm is not an automatic by-product of production but is produced by deliberate efforts of the firm and often a large amount of R&D.[6] Some of this learning becomes a public good available to other firms, but often only with technical assistance from someone who has the experience. This helps to explain the high rate of job transfer among engineers within the industry and also the proliferation of spin-offs. Most new semiconductor companies are founded by defectors from other semiconductor firms, presumably bringing with them critical know-how.

But the most important reason, it seems to be agreed, that a steep learning curve did not provide a strong advantage to older companies was the rapid change in technology, which meant that a new learning process had to be undertaken every couple of years if a firm was to remain competitive. Each new product provides an opportunity for some firm to get a head start in raising yields. Each new IC precipitates a race to see who will get ahead. "Any time there is a generation jump, there is a new ball game," says Noyce. "The score you racked up before doesn't count for much." Although, he adds, "The experience your players got in the earlier game is still valuable in the new one."[7]

A head start that puts it further along the learning curve than competitors offers an advantage to the innovator that patent rights do not generally afford in this industry. But the rapid obsolescence of process technology for many years prevented older companies from outperforming new competitors merely on the basis of experience, and established companies often ran into trouble trying to produce new products. At the same time the critical value of state-of-the-art knowledge that resides in the minds of experienced individuals has been an impetus to their founding of new companies. Companies, new or old, who could attract individuals with talent and know-how had a competitive advantage;

relatively new or small companies showed themselves in this industry to be better able than large, established firms to attract and utilize such individuals, and the consequence was the most rapid rate of spin-offs and job swapping of any industry on record.

A new wrinkle in the learning-curve effect emerged with the arrival of VLSI chips, however. The slope of the curve is much steeper in the mass production of standardized memory chips than in microprocessors and logic chips, and the learning is transferable from one to the other. Large-scale manufacture of commodity RAM chips therefore became the preferred route of entry into other major sectors of the market, creating a strong push toward diversification from memory into the other chips. With their capture of the 64K and higher RAM markets the Japanese threatened to dominate other markets as well.

Capital Requirements

The capital market was unusually hospitable to new semiconductor firms over much of the industry's lifetime, but the total amount of capital that a new company could hope to secure was, as always, limited. It was significant, therefore, that the minimum efficient investment for a firm in the industry's formative years was quite low. But by end of the 1970s it had risen to a virtually prohibitive level for small new firms in the major sectors of the market. The predictable decline in their rate of entry was further encouraged by a sagging venture capital market and a nationwide recession.

In the early 1950s, General Transistor, could start up with only $250,000, while Transitron, for a time number 2 in the industry, required only $1 million. Fairchild invested no more than $350,000 per year during its first two years and TI sank just $4 million into semiconductors before production became profitable.[8] Many large vacuum tube companies invested substantially more with only modest results. As late as 1968, Intel's start-up required first-stage support from a venture capital company of only $2.5 million together with $250,000 of the founders' capital, which was followed by another $10 million. Levin estimates that by the early 1970s state-of-the-art technology cost $10 million,[9] but that was before competition had come to be based on very efficient mass production of LSI or VLSI memory and micro processor chips of extremely high quality. By the late 1970s, $50 million was required for entry into commodity chips and by 1985 the figure had more than doubled for the 256K RAM. Small firms can have trouble also finding the capital to keep up with expansion in the market and changes in technology, a factor that contributed to the wave of mergers in the late seventies.

Optimum scale was attained at a fairly low level of production in the forties and fifties, before it reportedly doubled from 10,000 three-inch wafers per month in 1970 to 20,000 four-inch wafers a decade later.[10] As the industry matured in the late seventies, dramatically escalating fixed costs of manufacturing, R&D, and circuit design increased minimum optimal scale of production at the same time that the amount of capital required for any given level of production mounted steeply. Combined with increasing advantages of vertical integration and of diversification (because of the transferability of learning from RAM production), the result was to raise the capital costs of entry in most sectors of the industry beyond the level that a new firm could manage.

Fixed Plant and Equipment.   Manufacturing was relatively labor intensive in the formative years of the industry. Automation was slow to take hold because of the very rapid rate of obsolescence, evidenced by the 25 percent or more decline in the price of ICs every year. Over half of the transistor types marketed in 1966–68 were less than two years old.[11] Philco was badly burned in the 1950s when it automated a plant for the production of its surface barrier transistor, a device that was quickly overtaken by the integrated circuit. Most U.S. firms performed assembly and testing overseas where cheap labor was available rather than automating these operations at home.

The emergence, in the seventies, of MOS technology, and the extraordinarily fine lithography needed to make high-density chips, increased the need for cleanliness in the environment and for high-precision optical equipment. Temperature control became more critical; additional steps were involved in the fabricating process, and costly special procedures, such as ion implantation, were employed. By the end of the seventies, fabrication had become an integrated, computer-controlled process and photomasking equipment, electron-beam writers, and clean-room environment for the production of LSI chips had increased capital costs of plant and equipment many times over. By then, some large American companies were also finding it economical to follow the Japanese in automating the assembly stage rather than performing it overseas. Expensive retooling was necessary with each new generation of chips, and companies that did not keep up with the evolving technology could not achieve the 15 to 20 percent per year reduction in price of ICs.

Research and Development and Circuit Design.   R&D is required in this industry not only to innovate but just to stay abreast of advancing technology (many firms invest more than 10 percent of revenues in R&D). Although as late as 1969–70 it cost Intel only $1 million for each of two years to develop its 1103 RAM chip, during the four years 1972–76, R&D expenditures by the top nine semiconductor companies ranged from $6 million for AMD to $193 million for Fairchild. Motorola and TI spent still more, but they produce equipment as well as semiconductors. Innovative firms have not always had to start out by innovating, however. R&D can be postponed. Second-sourcing afforded new entrants opportunities in the sixties to start out conservatively until their fortunes permitted them to plow back resources into new product or process development. National Semiconductor and AMD both followed this strategy successfully.[12]

Knowledge from R&D in this industry, just as in computers, has historically been transferred from competitors by defecting employees who are hired by or start new firms and by reverse engineering. Most new companies since the late fifties have spun off from potential competitors. The semiconductor industry has been characterized from its inception by an extraordinary degree of individualism, aggressiveness, and competition, together with an ethic that condones pirating personnel and supports a large number of "head-hunting" organization who facilitate and promote job swapping. Technology transfer runs a risk of challenge in the courts, however, and it became less manageable as circuit design became more integrally involved with the production process. As Richard Levin wrote in 1982, "It has become increasingly difficult for a small number of employees to carry away sufficient knowhow to easily establish a viable and highly competitive advanced production capability."[13]

The manhour cost of circuit design increased five fold in the seventies with the coming of LSI, and by 1985 designing a VLSI circuit could take more than a year. But there emerged an expanding niche in the market for a second tier of specialized semiconductor houses that design fairly small batches of custom or semicustom chips, and a number of new companies entered this market after the late seventies to serve the special needs of users who were willing and could afford to pay the higher prices.[14] By 1981 they made up somewhat less than 10 percent of the IC marketplace. The impetus behind the demand for their services was the increasingly high density and complexity of chips that carry thousands of "gates," or logical elements, in place of hundreds several years ago, with the cost per gate running much less than on the lower density chips. The result has been a demand by equipment manufacturers for greater specialization. A fully customized chip can cost up to $500,000 to design. Because the microprocessor, which is an alternative, can be wasteful of space and of computing power, for many customers semicustom circuits have come to the rescue, with the help of computer-aided design.[15]

Vertical Integration.   Important benefits from investment in vertical integration did not appear until well into the seventies. Indeed, until then the industry was fragmented in the extreme, served by an infrastructure of subcontractors and producers of equipment, materials, and services, similar to the minicomputer industry described in Chapter 5. Some IC houses did integrate upstream into silicon wafer production, but those who chose not to obtained supplies at competitive prices from merchant producers, typically chemical companies. IBM integrated upstream from computers to semiconductors in the fifties, but semiconductor companies did not begin to integrate forward until considerably later.

Forward integration became compelling in the late seventies for two reasons. As margins on high-volume chips fell under aggressive pricing pressures, integrating forward seemed to promise IC houses the higher rewards of systems manufacturing, a promise that was not always fulfilled. But, more important, LSI and VLSI greatly enhance the value of marrying systems design and the design of certain critical custom chips. The leading IC houses, including TI, Fairchild, Intel, National Semiconductor, and Motorola, became diversified electronics systems manufactuers, producing calculators, microcomputers and other final products at the same time that some large systems houses integrated upstream into semiconductors to become captive producers of custom components.[16] By the mid-1980s some analysts were arguing that the highly diversified and integrated structure of the Japanese industry for commodity chips gave it a competitive advantage that the historically fragmented merchant manufacturers of the United States would not be able to contend with.

Lag in Revenue Collection.   Semiconductor houses do not require capital to support leasing policies common to the mainframe industry, but there is a counterpart in what is known as forward pricing. The predictably rapid fall in the cost of a new device means that unit cost at the outset greatly exceeds what it will be once experience has been acquired. The optimum pricing strategy is, therefore, in theory, to charge below average cost in the beginning and make up the loss by charging more than average cost as it falls. The loss at the outset can be viewed, alternatively, as an investment in the learning process which is recovered on sales of chips at a later stage. Forward pricing, to the extent that it is followed, raises capital requirements for entry.

Measures of Capital Intensity

The ratio of value-added to payrolls in the semiconductor industry, a rough indicator of the capital intensity of production, was 40 percent lower than in manufacturing as a whole from 1963 to 1976.[17] In both semiconductors and all manufacturing the ratio rose about 40 percent during that period. Between 1970 and 1976 the ratio of value of gross fixed assets to payrolls escalated 50 percent, after remaining stable beween 1963 and 1967 but it remained below the average for all manufacturing. (This was before the more spectacular increase in semiconductor capital costs later in the decade.) The amount of capital required to produce a dollar's worth of ICs, according to another source, rose from 40 cents in the first half of the 1970s to 55 cents in the latter half, and to 70 cents by the early 1980s.[18]

PRODUCT DIFFERENTIATION

Product differentiation barriers to entry were not significant until the arrival of LSI and VLSI. Price competition has always been strong and the fact that every producer must guarantee a second source, which is often supplied by several manufacturers, is testimony to the substitutability of the devices of different suppliers. Some firms invest heavily in "reverse engineering" of new circuits, and many unauthorized imitations find acceptance in the marketplace. In fact, there are companies that specialize in this service and a "second source" is frequently an unauthorized copy.[19]

Customers do not rely on suppliers for the servicing and technical support that provide opportunities for product differentiation in some computer sectors, nor is advertising a factor in the market where customers are, generally speaking, technically sophisticated and few in number. Nevertheless, because confidence in a vendor's ability to produce devices that will perform according to specifications and to deliver on schedule is critical, an established semiconductor house with a record of performance has a competitive advantage, all else being equal. But, historically, the lack of a track record did not stand in the way of new entrants with products that offered price and performance advantages over their predecessors or who could deliver when others failed. Their ability to compete with established companies was enhanced by the fact that the latter had their share of production problems. The availability of one or more alternative sources of a device helped to alleviate customers' anxiety in dealing with a new firm at the same time that second sourcing served as a route of entry that permitted new firms to build track records and sometimes to assemble the capital to develop new products.

Customer confidence in the vendor became increasingly critical, however, as the growing complexity of circuits made them as difficult to test and debug as a mainframe computer. In another respect, as well, the structure of the industry in the late 1970s took on aspects of the mainframe industry: the compatibility of chips, both microprocessor and logic, that performed different functions in a computer system became a necessity (a PC market emerged analogous to what we witnessed in computers), systems builders became critically dependent on the continued ability of the vendor to supply their families of microprocessor and logic chips and on to assure a potential for upward migration. Considerations such as these fortified the competitive positions of firms with established records of performance.

THE ROLE OF GOVERNMENT

Procurement and R&D Support

Because of its significant and early support for R&D and production of transistors and later ICs, the manner in which the U.S. government disbursed its funds necessarily influenced opportunities for new companies to gain a foothold in the industry. Although the government did not contribute to its development at AT&T, the military was the first customer for the transistor. According to Braun and MacDonald, "Of the 90,000 transistors produced in 1952, mostly point-contact devices from Western Electric, the Military bought nearly all."[20] Although hearing aids quickly became a major source of demand, between 1955 and 1962, the share of U.S. semiconductor production claimed by the military ranged between 38 and 48 percent,[21] and it continued to claim an important share of the market until well into the seventies.

The government supported the semiconductor industry in three different ways during the 1950s. First, it provided production refinement programs through the Signal Corps and, second, direct R&D funds. The former were designed to increase production capacity for transistors and other semiconductor devices and improve their performance and reliability. The earliest firms to benefit were Western Electric and the established vacuum tube companies.[22] Although newcomers like TI and Transitron gradually gained support, their share of the total was not proportional to their sales. As for R&D support, by the end of the decade new firms had captured 63 percent of the transistor market but only 22 percent of government R&D funds.[23]

But what made the difference for the newcomers was the third source of government support: the market that it created for transistors. By 1959 when demand from the Defense Department accounted for 45 percent of the market, 69 percent of their contracts went to new firms.[24] Military purchases of semiconductors amounted to $180 million in 1959, compared with R&D and production refinement support of $7.3 million.[25] The value of the government market was not only in its size. It lay in the military's insistence on the highest quality components, its lack of concern for cost, and the fact that it was the main customer for embryonic devices. It effectively financed the vendor's investment in gaining the experience that was critical to success in this industry.

Military and space contracts provided the sole sources of demand for the first ICs. Both programs offered opportunities for companies to gain valuable experience in production until the price fell sufficiently to open up the commercial market, and new enterprises were particularly well positioned to benefit. As Utterback and Murray argue, though the volume of direct sales to the government was only a fraction of total miltiary sales, the volume of sales far understates its influence.[26] Defense demand in the early stages of a component's life cycle provides an essential first market and often the only demand. Golding reports that in the early sixties, quite apart from cost considerations, equipment designers hesitated to make use of unproven ICs and two decisions were responsible for the breakthrough that led to their acceptance.[27]

One was NASA's announced intention to use ICs for its prototype Apollo spacecraft guidance computer and the other was the U.S. Air Force's intention to make maximum practical use of ICs in the guidance mechanism of an improved version of the Minuteman I intercontinental ballistic missile. TI was awarded the original Minuteman II development and preproduction contract at the end of 1962 and later similar contracts were awarded to Westinghouse and RCA. In 1963, the Apollo contract for ICs, which went to Fairchild, exceeded Minuteman demand in volume, but not in value. The success of these two programs encouraged weapons systems contractors to incorporate ICs into additional projects and the surge in demand supported the original suppliers and made room for new contenders such as Motorola and Signetics.

In contrast to its role in procurement, the government had no direct role in supporting reearch that led to the major technological breakthroughs of those years, most importantly, the transistor at Bell Laboratories, the silicon chip at TI, the planar process at Fairchild, and the integrated circuit at either of the latter two companies. (Soon after Kilby, working at TI, had demonstrated his "solid circuit" in 1959, however, he received a series of air force contracts which were important in sustaining development through the critical years.[28] Nor was the government to have a role in the important memory and microprocessor advances of the 1970s. Throughout the history of the industry, the companies themselves continued to supply most of the R&D funds. During 1970–76, direct government funding of R&D amounted to only $17 million out of a total of $1,351 million for the industry.[29]

On balance, we are led to conclude that the U.S. government was close to neutral in influencing opportunities for new enterprises relative to established companies, in the sense that it did not discriminate on the basis of noneconomic considerations. In the important area of procurement, it awarded major contracts to firms, like TI and Fairchild, that had demonstrated superior technological capability to perform the job. Though it was less evenhanded in allocating research funds, those funds were insignificant in both size and impact compared with procurement contracts.

Had private equipment suppliers, rather that the U.S. government, been the main customers for early ICs, the speed and development of the industry might have been quite different. Certainly the rate of acceptance of new technology would have been slower and the slide down the learning curve less precipitous. But there is no compelling reason to believe that new enterprises would have been either more or less favored. Nevertheless, small, new enterprises stand more in need of the generous cash disbursements that flowed from government sources than do better established companies and such generosity would not have been forthcoming from civilian customers. To this extent, the government market made it possible for some new firms to exploit a talent for innovation that might otherwise have languished for lack of funding.

Regulation

A second important instrument by which the federal government influenced opportunities for new enterprises was antitrust action. By barring from participation in the merchant market the company with the most substantial financial and technical commitment to the industry, it made way for new entrants that might otherwise have been crowded out. By obliging AT&T to make its patents available on easy terms to all applicants, it helped to remove a potential barrier to entry, although some say the company would, in any event, have followed a liberal licensing policy.

WHERE WERE THE VACUUM TUBE COMPANIES?

Why did established electronics companies that antedated the new technology fail, on the whole, to make a significant contribution to growth or innovation in the industry? With the exception of AT&T, most dropped out of semiconductors during the fifties and sixties, although all had at least a brief fling at them. Three possible explanations deserve consideration.

First, the former vacuum tube companies (AT&T excluded) miscalculated the potential of the industry in the beginning and, before they recovered, new entrants had gained a strong foothold in the market. The transistor was regarded as, at best, a substitute for the vacuum tube in the beginning, with the chief advantage of smaller size, but not as a device that would open vast new fields of applications. It was expensive and unreliable, and meanwhile the vacuum tube business continued to thrive. It was 1959 before the value of sales of semiconductors exceeded that of receiving tubes and it was the following year before they exceeded those of receiving and power tubes combined. Even then, receiving tubes alone remained more than a $300 million a year business. Thanks to a robust replacement market, sales did not fall off seriously until the 1970s.[30] While companies like TI were aggressively pushing their way into the transistor market, some tube manufacturers were busily advancing the traditional technology. Moreover, solid state technology opened up new markets that had not been served by the vacuum tube manufacturing.

Second, the solid state physics of the transistor was a new technology, completely novel to most tube manufactuers. Because semiconductor research was, at the outset, science based and process oriented, it did not mix comfortably with the established engineering research departments of older electronic firms.

> The transistor was so radically different from the valve (vacuum tube) in the way it worked, in the way it could be manufactured and sold, and in its apparent potential, that it could not be comfortably accommodated within the existing electronics industry without changes that the industry was then unwilling or unable to make. In its typical subjugation of semiconductor development, manufacture and marketing within valve departments, the established electronics industry demonstrated that it was largely unaware of the impact the innovation could have.[31]

Finally, the necessary scientific and technical expertise was in short supply and older companies were not always in the best position to attract it. Their vacuum tube departments were evidently less than eager to employ young blood that threatened established positions. In sum, the established vacuum tube companies had no strong competitive advantage in the development, production, or marketing of semiconductors over potential newcomers. On the contrary, new companies may have had greater motivation and better adapted organizational structures for pursuing new innovative technologies.[32] The established vacuum tube companies did not fail for lack of financial effort. They invested substantial sums in R&D in the 1950s and, we saw, were responsible for some significant innovations. Braun and MacDonald believe they failed to realize that success lay in the ability to attract and make use of the right individuals.[33]

The absence of one established electronics company from the merchant market needs no explanation. Had AT&T's Western Electric been free from the outset to sell transistors in the open market, there is no certainty that new enterprises such as TI and Fairchild would have been able to gain a significant share of it. On the other hand, such companies often beat AT&T to the market with innovations in spite of its tremendous investment in research. IBM avoided the merchant market by choice. Had either company competed in the merchant market, it might have shaped up rather differently for new enterprises.

NOTES

1. Richard C. Levin, "Innovation in the Semiconductor Industry," in *Government and Technological Change: A Cross-Industry Analysis,* ed. Richard R. Nelson (New York: Pergamon, 1982).
2. John E. Tilton, *International Diffusion of Technology: The Case of Semiconductors* (Washington, D.C.: The Brookings Institution, 1971), p. 77.
3. Douglas W. Webbink, "The Semiconductor Industry: A Survey of Structure, Conduct, and Performance," Staff Report to the Federal Trade Commission, Bureau of Economics (Washington, D.C.: U.S. Government Printing Office, 1977), Table 111-1, p. 440.

   "Cumulative" yield refers to the percentage of potential output of devices that pass the test of usability after all stages of production have been completed. The stage where the yield is lowest is wafer fabrication. In the cases of the two ICs referred to above, the yield of the fabrication process was 40 percent for the older and only 20 percent for the newer one. Yields can be as low as 1 percent for early batches. They tend to be higher in the volume production of RAM chips [Robert W. Wilson, Peter K. Ashton, and Thomas P. Egan, *Innovation, Competition, and Government Policy in the Semiconductor Industry* (Lexington, Mass.: Lexington Books, 1980).].
4. Robert N. Noyce, "Microelectronics," *Scientific American,* September 1977, p. 63.
5. Noyce, "Microelectronics"; Tilton, *International Diffusion of Technology.*
6. Tilton, *International Diffusion of Technology.*
7. Noyce, "Microelectronics."
8. Tilton, *International Diffusion of Technology.*
9. Levin, "Innovation in the Semiconductor Industry."
10. Nico Hazewindus and John Tooker, *The U.S. Microelectronics Industry: Technical Change, Industrial Growth, and Social Impact* (New York: Pergamon, 1982).
11. Noyce, "Microelectronics."
12. Wilson, Ashton, and Egan, *Innovation, Competition, and Government Policy in the Semiconductor Industry.*

13. Levin, "Innovation in the Semiconductor Industry."

14. "The Boom in Tailor Made Chips," *Fortune,* March 1981.

15. In CAD the computer stores many elements of a circuit in its memory, permitting engineers to assemble the circuit on a screen linked to the computer. While the process is not sophisticated enough to turn out fully customized circuits, it can shorten the time and reduce the cost of responding to demands for semicustomized chips which contain standard arrays of gates that can be linked together in the final stages of manufacturing to fit the customer's need.

16. Joint Economic Committee, U.S. Congress, 97th Congress, 2nd Session, "International Competition in Advanced Industrial Sectors: Trade and Development in the Semiconductor Industry," February 18, 1982.

17. U.S. Bureau of the Census, *Census of Manufacturers,* Table a.1., various years.

18. Hazewindus and Tooker, *U.S. Microelectronics Industry.*

19. Webbink, *The Semiconductor Industry.*

20. Ernest Braun and Stuart MacDonald, *Revolution in Miniature* (Cambridge, England: Cambridge University, 1982).

21. Tilton, *International Diffusion of Technology,* p. 90.

22. Braun and MacDonald, *Revolution in Miniature,* p. 70.

23. Tilton, *International Diffusion of Technology,* Table 4.10, p. 94.

24. Ibid., pp. 90, 91.

25. Ibid., Table 4.9, p. 93, and Table 4.7, p. 90.

26. James M. Utterback and Albert E. Murray, "The Influence of Defense Procurement and Sponsorship of Research and Development on the Development of the Civilian Electronics Industry," Center for Policy Alternatives, Massachusetts Institute of Technology, June 30, 1973, CPA 77–5.

27. A.M. Golding, "The Semiconductor Industry in Britain and in the U.S.: A Case Study in Innovation, Growth and the Diffusion of Technology," Unpublished Ph.D. thesis, University of Sussex, England, 1971, as cited in Utterback and Murray, "The Influence of Defense Procurement."

28. Richard R. Nelson, "The Link between Science and Invention: The Case of the Transistor," in National Bureau of Economic Research, *The Rate and Direction of Inventive Activity: Economic and Social Factors* (Princeton, N.J.: Princeton University Press, 1982), pp. 549–83.

29. Ibid.

30. Electronic Industries Association, *Electronic Market Data Book,* 1962, reference 18, Table 35, p. 44.

31. Braun and MacDonald, *Revolution in Miniature,* p. 63.

32. Wilson, Ashton, and Egan, (*Innovation, Competition, and Government Policy*) examined the internal organizations of a number of semiconductor companies and found in larger firms with nonautonomous semiconductor divisions a lack of the flexibility that facilitates rapid response to technological change as well as weak communication and interaction between R&D, production, and marketing functions.
33. Braun and MacDonald, *Revolution in Miniature.*

10 MARKET CONDITIONS FOR INNOVATION BY SMALL, NEW FIRMS: CONCLUSIONS

We have seen that innovation can occur under a variety of different market structures and that the structure of a market can play an important role in determining the kind of firm—whether large or small, new or old—that innovates. In some markets large, established firms were the engines of technological progress and in others new enterprises spearheaded innovation. Only in semiconductors was there much evidence of the two competing side by side. In computers, small, young firms were conspicuously innovative in new markets that established firms left unattended.

It is evident, empirically, that at any given time there may be significant opportunities for innovation of the sort that small, new firms can exploit in markets that they can enter with the expectation of earning a satisfactory return on investment. At the same time there will remain opportunities for innovation that can only be exploited by large firms in protected markets. Some opportunities for innovation that would yield a net benefit to society will remain unexploited by any type of firm whatsoever because their markets do not offer sufficient protection from competition to justify the investment required for their development. As significant as any finding of this study is the fact that many economically viable and socially desirable innovations would not have been undertaken at all, or without considerable delay, *but* for the entrepreneurship of small, new business.

223

The industry studies in the preceding seven chapters were intended as a step toward answering the question, what are the specific market conditions that determine whether small new enterprises have the ability and the incentive to innovate? Chapter 2 laid out an analytic framework to serve as a guide to understanding the contrasting performance of such firms as innovators in some industries as compared with others. It was argued that, in order to innovate, a firm must be in a position to develop, produce, and market a new product without serious cost disadvantages relative to potential competitors, whether they are in the same or other industries, and must have an incentive to invest in research and development, in addition to production, of the innovation and to assume the more than ordinary risks. This final chapter summarizes the findings of the industry studies and weighs their implications for the theory of innovation and market structure. It begins with a review of the pertinent characteristics of markets that permitted small, new firms to avoid or overcome market barriers, followed by an assessment of the sources of their incentives to innovate in such markets.

AVOIDING AND OVERCOMING BARRIERS TO INNOVATION

Chapter 2 described the barriers to entry that can confer significant competitive advantages on incumbents over potential entrants, large or small, new or old: economies of scale, absolute cost advantages, and advantages in differentiating products. It was argued that small, new firms may be deterred from entering a market to innovate, however, not only by their handicaps relative to incumbents but also relative to established firms in other markets who are potential entrants, and concluded that in order to innovate, a small, new firm must follow one or more of four strategies: 1) choose a market whose inherent characteristics offer at most limited cost advantages to established firms, incumbent or otherwise, over small, new firms; 2) develop a sufficiently superior new product to overcome any cost disadvantage; 3) enter a market in which incumbents maintain the price sufficiently above minimum average cost to permit a small, new firm to compete; or 4) enter a market in which large, established firms fail to compete.

The first of these was found to apply in all of the markets where small, new firms were successful innovators, whereas the other three operated from time to time and to varying degrees. The one market that conferred significant advantages on established firms from neighboring industries and on incumbents once they were established—mainframe computers— was never successfully penetrated by a small new company, not even one with the innovative talent, the experience, and the head start of an Eckert–Mauchly or an ERA.

There was no shortage of new firms that produced products sufficiently superior to those of established firms to surmount more modest barriers. Diablo's electronically controlled daisywheel printer and Mohawk's Keyed Data Recorder succeeded in competition with large, established computer firms, but examples were most notable in semiconductors, where new firms overcame the potential advantages of the established vacuum tube manufacturers by outperforming them as innovators and eventually dominated the market. The vacuum tube, for which semiconductor devices were a substitute, was produced in a concentrated market of large, established firms, but the revolution in production technology made the fixed capital and technical expertise of the old line producers obsolete; indeed, their commitment to a past technology probably slowed their response to the new one.

Small, new firms were able to enter some markets and survive, at least temporarily, because incumbents' prices were maintained sufficiently above minimum average cost. In the case of the plug-compatibles, IBM's "price umbrella" was the consequence of a deliberate strategy, which it abandoned when its market share shrank uncomfortably. An incumbent can sometimes maximize profits by charging a price that is high enough to encourage entry so long as it is confident that it can eliminate competition when it becomes too threatening, and for IBM that turned out to be the case. But antitrust pressures were also behind its restraint in discouraging entry. The inability of incumbents to meet all of the rapidly growing (40 to 50 percent a year) demand in minicomputers and small disk drives helped to make room for newer firms in those industries, and the technological gap associated with a rapidly changing technology often permitted firms to compete with market leaders by fielding more up-to-date products.

Finally, new computer firms were most successful in markets that they created by innovating, and in those sectors established firms rarely chose to compete. The innovators were generally followed only by other new firms, at least in the short run. Possible reasons for the absence of older firms are examined later. We review, now, the strategies that new firms followed to avoid markets that presented significant barriers or, alternatively, to overcome barriers.

Absolute Cost Barriers

Capital Cost Barriers.   Because of its limited availability, new firms were absolutely restricted to innovations that could be developed, produced, and brought to market with a relatively small amount of capital in a short period of time. When Gene Amdahl, with a sterling reputation and a product design well underway, managed to assemble close to $50 million in the seventies, most of it involving a joint venture with Fujitsu, he set a record for new firms in the industry. By that time $15 million counted as an unusually large sum for a start-up, and in earlier decades new innovative firms were typically established with amounts closer to DEC's $70,000 and less than $1 million for Fairchild Semiconductor. By contrast, hundreds of millions were sunk into general purpose mainframe systems by IBM and each of its handful of large-scale competitors in the fifties, and it took a decade or more for all but IBM to get out of the red. By the seventies, entry into that industry cost anywhere from $200 million to $1 billion.

Although government procurement contracts and an expanding venture capital market eased access to capital for many new firms, the amounts available were limited. New innovators were thus confined to markets where the overall advantages of large scale and of horizontal and vertical integration were slight enough that the total value added required to be competitive was relatively small at the same time that capital requirements per dollar of value added were low. Most (but not all) new computer firms reduced total value added also by concentrating on products at the low end of the price spectrum and marketing them without frills, beginning with minicomputers and followed by peripherals designed for mini- and later microcomputers. The three successful new computer companies described in Chapter 3 set the pattern, starting out with low-cost equipment that was marketed to "smart" customers without peripheral equipment, software, or service contracts, and distributed through third-party OEMs or to the U.S. government.

A firm that is among the first to enter a market need not at the outset achieve optimal scale, scope, or capital intensity but, in due course, it must acquire sufficient capital to optimize if it is to survive and grow as an independent firm. The alternative is acquisition by a firm that has the capital to finance expansion. New firms sometimes seek out small, specialized market niches that do not offer scope for exploiting economies of scale. The markets for minicomputers, small disk drives, and early integrated circuits offered superb opportunities for targeting small, specialized groups of customers because of the diverse needs of customers and the numerous tradeoffs to be considered. In larger markets, the speed with which investment in fixed capital dedicated to large-scale production becomes a prerequisite to success depends on the rate at which the product cycle unfolds to allow standardization of products and stabilization of production processes. (It also depends on the degree of competition from firms with better access to capital.) For some low-capacity disk drives, standardization of the product and production techniques occurred almost overnight, while in semiconductors, where production technology was a major source of technological advance, it took more than two decades.

It was a fortuitous circumstance for small, new innovators that the computer and semiconductor industries, during most of their history, were extremely fragmented in the sense that a very high degree of vertical disintegration of the production process was possible without significantly increasing unit costs. This allowed them to curtail the total size of their operations in terms of value added, but it had another salutary ramification for computer firms: production processes that were capital intensive in the use of plant and equipment could be spun off. The manufacture of computers and most peripherals could be conducted essentially by putting together components and subassemblies in labor intensive shops. By the mid-1960s, when new computer firms began to enter the market in force, semiconductor chips on the market contained much of the circuitry that was required, and microcoding and other trends toward modular construction soon made it possible for minicomputer firms like Prime Computer and Tandem to purchase almost all of their inputs from independent vendors.

The typical small new computer firm started out in a low-cost facility (sometimes the owner's garage) where circuit boards and other components were assembled by hand, and the manufacture of many small new disk drives and printers, too, was conducted economically by assembling off-the-shelf parts. The environs of Boston and "Silicon Valley," where the majority of new firms got their start, teem with job shops, circuit board manufacturers, and suppliers of components, subassemblies, services, and materials. Even newcomers who designed low-cost peripheral equipment for mass production (Seagate, Shugart, Sanders Technology, Diablo) used off-the-shelf components.

Semiconductor firms, too, were in a position to practice a high degree of vertical disintegration, purchasing silicon ingots, specialized equipment, services, and chemicals from independent vendors. But the batch production process almost from the beginning meant some scale economies were available. The absence of pressure to exploit them with capital intensive production techniques reflected the extremely rapid advances in process technology that militated against any firm's investing heavily in automated facilities and the lack of a market for mass produced standardized chips. But the arrival of large-scale integration and of the microprocessor in the seventies changed matters. With them, the market for customized chips was drastically curtailed in favor of commodity chips, at the same time that very costly production equipment—clean-room environments, high-precision lithography, and so on—became imperative. Together with the greatly increased fixed cost of designing LSI and later VLSI chips, these developments dictated both large-scale and capital intensive production in major sectors of the semiconductor industry.

Until the mid-1970s, the advantages of integrating computer production with component production lay chiefly in secrecy, quality control, and a guaranteed supply of components rather than in technical efficiency. This changed when the emergence of very-large-scale integration created complex interrelationships between the design of computers and of custom integrated circuits that made a marriage of the two functions attractive, if not imperative, in the large systems industry. Nevertheless, Amdahl and Cray did not find it necessary to invest in the production of most components for their supercomputers. Forward integration on the part of semiconductor manufacturers like Texas Instruments in the seventies was motivated more by the higher profits that they anticipated in the product market than by technical considerations, expectations which were not always confirmed. By the eighties, however, it was beginning to appear that the Japanese manufacturers' integration of semiconductor and computer operations had perhaps given them an advantage with which the fragmented American industries could not effectively compete.

The fixed cost of R&D and of circuit design in semiconductors and software design in computers is a potential source of economies of scale and scope and of insurmountable threshold capital costs to innovators. New computer firms focused on innovations that required a relatively small R&D effort, and not infrequently its cost was little more than the deferred wages of a few engineers. The transfer of technology (by DEC, Amdahl, Transitron, Shugart, and many others) that had been developed at academic, industrial, or government laboratories, usually by transferring personnel, helped to minimize R&D costs in both industries.

With notable exceptions like the supercomputers of Cray, CDC, and Amdahl, small new innovators in computers and peripherals focused on scaling down and simplifying more complex and proven technologies to meet user demand for economy, and on adapting technologies to meet specialized needs. Such firms generally led the way in substituting electronic for mechanical functions and also in adopting new generations of semiconductors.[1] The extraordinary advances in IC technology in the sixties and seventies, not least of all the microprocessor, provided ready-made opportunities for them to innovate. By supplying a single product rather than a complex integrated system or family of systems, and purchasing components off-site, R&D could be narrowly focused. Amdahl testified that by purchasing most components he vastly reduced R&D costs compared with IBM's costs for similar projects, and we saw that the relative simplicity of their products made it possible for SDS and Data General to beat mainframe vendors to the market with new generations of computers. IBM, on the other hand, judged it advisable to defer the use of integrated circuits when it developed its very large and complex System 360 family of computers even though other computer manufacturers were already exploiting the new technology.

In both semiconductors and computers the R&D of new firms was weighted on the side of development, leaving research aimed at a fundamental understanding of new principles to academic or large industrial laboratories. But semiconductors contrasted with computers in that small new firms did introduce fundamentally new products and processes such as the silicon chip, the planar process, the integrated circuit, the 1K RAM chip, and the microprocessor. None, however, required an investment in R&D that was beyond the limited means of young companies, a few million dollars or less. Their success in attracting highly qualified and experienced personnel may help to explain their superior performance as innovators compared with better established firms in that field who invested far more heavily in R&D.

Other Absolute Cost Barriers.   Restricted access to either critical production techniques or resources was rarely a deterrent to entry of large or small firms with the important exception that production experience offered an advantage in semiconductors, where the delicate and complex fabrication process was critical in lowering costs and increasing circuit density of chips. The advantage of experience acquired by an innovating firm in that industry was generally short-lived until the 1970s, however, because of the rapid obsolescence of technology as well as the frantic transfer of personnel among companies. It did not, therefore, offer incumbents long-term protection from competition by newer firms. Indeed, the pace of technological change, combined with the first mover's experience helped newcomers to compete with established companies from the neighboring vacuum tube industry by rendering old technologies obsolete. By the late 1970s, circumstances had changed radically: the steepness of the learning curve in the mass production of commodity RAM chips made experience with that process almost a prerequisite to low-cost production of logic or microprocessor chips, and firms without the capital to support large-scale, capital intensive RAM production and the ability to compete in that very price and quality-sensitive market were in danger of being frozen out of the commodity market altogether. Moreover, the affinity between production of RAM chips and other types vastly increased economies of scope.

The production of some disk drives also required sophistication and experience, as a result of which new firms were very often founded or staffed by defectors from IBM's disk drive division. On the other side of this coin was the acquisition by established equipment companies of innovative new enterprises as a substitute for experience, the route followed by all of IBM's major competitors when they entered the computer market and by large equipment manufacturers who acquired semiconductor firms in the late 1970s.

Patents rarely restricted the use of production technology. In the computer industry, process technology was not where the action was. In semiconductors, the rapid rate of obsolescence of process technology, and producers' desire for secrecy militated against the effectiveness of patents for this purpose, and, at the same time, advances in technology that emerged from experience in the production process were not generally susceptible to patenting. In both computers and semiconductors the imperatives of cross-licensing and action, or the threat of action, by the Antitrust Division of the Justice Department caused the leading vendors to follow liberal licensing policies.

Professional personnel with specialized talent or knowledge were, in all of these industries, a critical factor of production whose scarcity value conferred advantages on companies that could attract it without paying the scarcity rent. But the ability of firms to attract it was, perhaps, less a matter of scale, maturity, or incumbency than of idiosyncracies of individual firms. If anything, newly founded companies were better able to lure talent by virtue of the advantages of ownership and profit sharing that they could offer. In the most striking instances, unusual talent resided in the founders of firms (Eckert, Mauchly, Norris, Noyce, Olsen, Cray, Amdahl, et al.). There is also a strong suggestion that when a dramatic change in production processes occurs, as in the shift from vacuum tubes to transistors, new firms are more willing to employ individuals schooled in the new technology. It was TI that hired Gordon Teal, who had developed the process for growing single crystals of germanium at AT&T, and William Shockley who employed Robert Noyce (although Noyce soon left to found his own firm). The mindset of established producers can be an obstacle in adapting to a revolution in technology.

Contributing to the ability of new firms to hire specialized technicians and to the transfer of technology that they often brought with them was what surely must be a uniquely individualistic, aggressive, and competitive climate in the two communities that have supported most of the growth of new electronics enterprises—Boston's Route 128 and California's Silicon Valley—together with an ethic that made job swapping a way of life. It is unlikely that ever before has the rate of turnover among engineering and managerial personnel in a region or an industry approached the scale that those areas experienced.

Product Differentiation Barriers

Patents were no more effective in deterring imitation of products than of production processes, and for most of the same reasons. On the other hand, proprietary knowledge of the circuitry and operating system of a computer that a competitor would need to design compatible equipment was a significant barrier in the mainframe sector where a large share of the market was locked into IBM early in the game by the formidable costs of software conversion.

At least as important as the physical product differentiation in the mainframe industry was the subjective product differentiation associated with the brand image of a long-established producer. IBM's worldwide reputation and dedicated customers in the office equipment market at the inception of the computer industry combined with a number of characteristics of the product to mount an almost inpenetrable barrier to new firms. In the face of the mainframe's high cost, complexity, and novelty, and the customer's demand for long-term servicing and future enhancements, purchasing agents in the information processing industries turned readily to the familiar brand names of well-established vendors to validate their decisions. But credit must go also to IBM for the skill and vigor with which it exploited its reputation from the time that it entered the mainframe industry. Few other firms would have succeeded in transforming an image from one industry into such a formidable barrier to entry in another.

Small, new innovators in the computer industry avoided the formidable product differentiation barriers by targeting customers who were not served by the large, established vendors and who, at the same time, had less cause to depend on the vendor's reputation. On rare occasions a new company succeeded in direct competition with IBM by introducing superior peripheral equipment, but the vast majority of new innovators created new markets, followed other new firms into them, or carved out specialized niches. Minicomputers and their peripherals were not replacements for products that had formerly been marketed by large equipment companies. They also cost less and could be more easily evaluated by potential customers than mainframes, being less complicated and less novel when they arrived on the scene, and more specialized. At the same time customers were generally more technically sophisticated and did not depend to the same degree on the vendor for software, maintenance, and other support services. Nor were products typically marketed through personal sales representatives.

Product differentiation barriers were more modest during the first two decades or more in the semiconductor industry than in mainframes, and small newcomers did, indeed, compete directly with established vacuum tube manufacturers. The potential customers for the early devices had not always been previously served by the vacuum tube vendors, and the problem of compatibility between different vendors' devices did not arise until after the arrival of the LSI logic and microprocessor chips in the seventies. Earlier, devices could be more easily tested and evaluated by customers and future supplies of compatible devices were not a significant issue.

Significant opportunities for differentiating semiconductor devices lay, however, from the outset, in establishing a reputation for prompt delivery and reliability. The willingness of the U.S. government, the major customer for the first integrated circuits and for many embryonic devices until the seventies, to bet on small companies like TI and Fairchild gave them a chance to earn a track record. Customers' demand for a second source of every device created opportunities for other new entrants, many of whom developed track records by producing authorized or unauthorized copies of other vendors' devices. But, while product differentiation barriers were at first relatively low in semiconductors they were not absent. New companies were conspicuously successful in hurdling them by producing new products that were demonstrably superior to those of established firms, a feat that they accomplished with relatively little capital and a great deal of ingenuity. Getting a new device to the market first was often the key to successful entry.

The Effects of Industry Maturation

As new industries matured and young firms grew and became established, barriers emerged to create difficulties for later generations of firms to enter those markets, although many continued to carve out specialized niches for themselves. Some innovators were pressed to merge with large, better established companies to obtain broader financial or product bases. Merger did not prevent successful innovators, like Shugart (in disk drives) and Mostek (in semiconductors), from serious market losses and even bankruptcy in the eighties, however. Mergers and acquisitions also provided established companies with the technological bases with which to enter a market. This was conspicuously the case in mainframes where all of IBM's competitors from the office machine industry got their start in the fifties by acquiring small, new computer firms. It was not uncommon later in minicomputers and disk drives.

Although maturation was slow to arrive in semiconductors, toward the end of the 1970s, barriers to entry began to resemble those in the mainframe industry at its beginning. The extraordinarily high fixed costs of LSI and VLSI circuit design, like R&D in mainframes, presented formidable capital cost barriers to new firms, and, in addition, semiconductor fabrication demanded extremely high plant and equipment outlays. At the same time, customers now sought compatibility among their standardized logic or their microprocessor chips, locking themselves into the supply of a single vendor or one of its second sources, analogous to the compatibility requirements in the mainframe industry that had generated a plug-compatible industry. Also as in mainframes, customers now required greater assurance that a vendor would be able to supply devices and product enhancements in the future.

THE INCENTIVE TO INNOVATE

According to the analysis in Chapter 2, in order to have an incentive to invest resources in R&D and assume the more than ordinary risk of innovation, a firm must expect to appropriate enough of the consumer and producer surplus generated by the innovation to earn a return on the investment as good as could be expected if the resources were invested elsewhere at similar risk. The larger the potential surplus, the smaller the proportion that needs to be appropriated, and the size of the potential surplus, it was argued, depends on opportunities for innovation that are exogenous to the firm. The proportion of the surplus the innovator can appropriate is a function of his unit cost of production relative to the unit cost to other firms of developing and producing a close substitute that consumers regard as equally desirable once the innovation is on the market. Only to the extent that the latter costs exceed the former will the innovator receive any compensation for its investment in R&D. The question, then, is, How, in the relatively competitive markets to which small, new firms have access, can an innovator that lacks the advantages of size and maturity hope to prevent other firms from reproducing an innovation and marketing it at a price that will preclude its earning and adequate return? The barriers that deter new firms from innovating in some markets are, after all, the main sources of the monopoly power that Schumpeter saw as essential to provide the necessary return on investment in innovation.

It was concluded in Chapter 2 that the primary source of the cost advantage that the small, new innovator must count on is the leverage gained by being first. The first mover may benefit from a temporary monopoly of the innovation and from the opportunity to gain a greater long-run market share than any competitor. In either case, its R&D investment (and other fixed costs) will be spread over a greater cumulative output to achieve lower unit costs than its competitors'. The innovator's unit cost of R&D will also be lower than theirs in the unlikely event that imitators must spend more to replicate the innovation than it cost the innovator to originate it. In either case, assuming potential imitators' costs of production are at least as high as the innovator's, the market price will not fall below the level that allows the innovator a rate of return as great as competitors would demand on their investment, although, to be sure, followers will often incur less risk. What can be said about the extent to which these factors in practice operated to allow small, new innovators to appropriate sufficient surplus to justify their investment, as they patently did in a large number of cases? We consider next the effects of the seven potential first mover advantages that were outlined in Chapter 2.

First Mover Advantages

1. It takes time for competitors to develop an imitation of an innovation and, except in the case of simultaneous invention, the arrival of competition is therefore delayed, allowing the innovator a short-term monopoly. The time lag depends on the complexity of the invention, the ease with which it can be reproduced, and on how far competitors have gone toward developing similar products of their own when the innovation is first marketed. Not many examples were found in this study of innovations by small, new firms that took the originator more than a year, or at the outside two, to develop, and presumably an imitator would require less time. Often, of course, the innovator gained a jump on competitors by virtue of research results brought from a previous place of employment. But competitors had an advantage in the functioning model that was available to be emulated, sometimes by reverse engineering. Moreover, they were often already well along in developing a similar product. In semiconductors, where the average product life is only about two years, a monopoly of a year was not trivial. On the other hand, before LSI, new semiconductor devices could be reverse engineered rather quickly, and the fact that several firms were likely to be working simultaneously to develop a new generation device (for example, the MOS chip, and new generations of RAMs chips) could virtually eliminate the innovators "honeymoon."

2. Time is required also for competitors to mobilize resources and arrange for production and marketing of an imitation once they have developed the prototypes. In order to exploit the delay in arrival of competition, the innovator must mobilize the resources and organize production to meet demand. Thus, the speed with which the first mover can increase production relative to the speed with which all potential competitors combined can do so is critical. An incumbent with a large market share to begin with can sometimes exploit an innovation, whether its own or someone else's, more expeditiously than a new firm by virtue of having production and marketing facilities in place, a customer base, and access to capital, but success is not guaranteed, as we witnessed when solid state technology replaced the product of the large vacuum tube companies. Nevertheless new innovators commonly had to struggle to assemble the capital for growth, usually failing to meet all of the demand that they had generated, often by a wide margin. In semiconductors, minicomputers, and small disk drives, dozens of firms typically

moved in quickly to capture a part of the surplus for themselves. Innovators without the financial staying power to capture a significant share of the market often realized significant returns by selling out to larger firms once the innovation's potential had been demonstrated.

3. If an innovation requires a specialized resource that is very limited in supply, the first mover may have a chance to monopolize the supply or secure it at a lower price than can followers. No specialized resources were critical in the industries examined with the exception of talented individuals, who turned out to be highly mobile. But uniquely talented individuals were more often than not among the founders of innovating firms and at least for some time unavailable to competitors. While innovators in electronics industries are fortunate in not requiring other specialized resources that are either closely held or widely disbursed, it is worth digressing here to point out that in an industry like much of American agriculture, by contrast, where farmland is distributed among hundreds or thousands of individual holders (the classical atomistic industry), the incentive for a producer to innovate is severely, perhaps fatally, limited by the inability to assemble the resources that would be required to appropriate more than a miniscule share of the surplus.

4. A first mover may protect an innovation through patents or trade secrets. In general, patents proved not very effective in deterring entry, but they should not be ruled out altogether as a means of capturing surplus. Developers of new printers, disk drives, and integrated circuits profited from licensing of patents, and a patent could be used to improve the terms of cross-licensing agreements. Costly legal battles were waged over patent rights from time to time, for example, TI versus Fairchild over the integrated circuit and RCA versus MIT over the core memory.

First movers in the computer industry employed trade secrets especially effectively to achieve a product differentiation advantage based on complementarities between their hardware and their customers' software. This was most conspicuously a barrier in the large mainframe industry. In the 1970s, Intel and Motorola gained a similar advantage in marketing, respectively, their 8800 and 6800 microprocessor chips to computer manufacturers who became committed to employing devices of a given family throughout their systems. An analogous advantage accrued to the first mover in the personal computer industry (not examined in this study) from the marketing by commercial software houses of thousands of software packages that could be run only on Apple computers, whose interfaces were proprietary. It took a firm with IBM's clout to break that barrier.

5. When the production process is characterized by a steep learning curve, the first mover may for a time enjoy lower unit costs than followers. In the semiconductor industry, where the delicate and complex production process was critically important and constantly advancing, production experience gave the first mover a decided advantage. Before the arrival of LSI, the advantage was unusually short-lived, however, in part because some of the learning could be transferred to competitors who hired the innovator's personnel but, more important, because technology typically became obsolete within about two years. But, by the same token most of the surplus from a short-lived innovation had to be captured within a couple of years. When the market shifted to mass-produced commodity chips in the late seventies, experience gained in the production of RAM chips became critical to mass production of logic and microprocessor chips, and the market leaders in the very capital intensive RAM sector were poised to achieve a potentially decisive advantage in the industry as a whole.

6. When the market for a new product is so limited that one small firm of optimal scale can serve all of the market (a natural monopoly), the so-called percentage economy of scale barrier may protect the first firm in the market from competition. Both minicomputers and disk drives offer extraordinary opportunities for tailoring products to meet specialized needs of diverse groups of customers, and these small market niches were a frequent path of entry for new firms. When larger, better established firms can exploit economies of scope in diversifying into such markets, the first mover's protection is limited, however. DEC often followed innovators into new sectors of the minicomputer market after they had demonstrated their promise. On the other hand, when diseconomies of scale or of scope (economies of specialization) are significant, they may prevent any innovator's capturing a sufficient share of the market to justify investment in innovation. Such factors could account for the low rate of technological progress in some industries, for example construction.

7. The subjective product differentiation advantage of the first mover has been specifically considered by economists in the context of marketing "experience" goods, goods whose characteristics are best appreciated through purchase and use.[2] While not ruling out competition for new customers, a head start in the market for such a product can translate into a permanently larger market share than that of any follower, along with a greater opportunity to exploit scale economies. The greater the risk involved in experimenting with a product relative

to its cost, the more effective the barrier to firms that would follow. Customers rely on experience to evaluate the quality of a product when other means of gathering the information are more costly or less reliable. One alternative is to rely on the experience of other customers, but this, too, gives an advantage to a first mover that attracts many satisfied customers to begin with. Another approach is to rely on the reputation of the producer, rather than that of the specific product. It is, in practice, not always possible to separate the first mover's advantage in building the reputation, or image, of the firm from its advantage in building customer experience with a product. When products obsolesce quickly, the former is bound to be more effective than the latter, but in either case the first mover may gain an advantage.

The more technically complex the product, the less technically sophisticated the buyer, the harder it is for the customer to experiment with competing brands, and the less frequently the customer purchases the product, the greater is likely to be the tendency to choose a product initially on the basis of the image of the product or the firm and to stick with the initial choice, even at some sacrifice in price, so long as the product is satisfactory. General purpose mainframe computers are a superb example of experience goods, and IBM benefited mightily from this fact in exploiting its world wide and long-standing image. IBM was not, of course, the first mover but it captured a major share of the market early on. Later, the computers and peripherals offered by most small, new innovators, beginning with minicomputers, were more easily evaluated by customers in advance of purchase, the products being simpler and more specialized and the customers generally more sophisticated. Nevertheless, assessing quality was far from costless, and the first mover had a chance to tie customers to its product before competing products were on the market. As the market would grow, competitors could hope to attract customers new to the market, but the innovating firm's head start was often instrumental in its gaining a larger long-term market share than any of its followers.

Early semiconductor devices were more easily evaluated by customers than either computers or the large-scale integrated circuits that came later, which could be as complex as a mainframe to test and debug. But from the beginning a first mover that demonstrated a capacity to deliver reliable devices on schedule gained an advantage in claiming market share over rank newcomers.

A first mover's subjective product differentiation advantage cannot necessarily withstand competition from firms that have established reputations in other markets, as evidenced by the transfer of IBM's image from office machines to mainframes and later from mainframes to personal computers. But more often than not, in these studies, the first mover ended up with a greater market share than any of those that followed on its heels and maintained it, if not permanently, for a considerable period of time. It is probably the case that the innovator's head start in winning the loyalty of customers and gaining market share was, in general, more critical to earning an adequate return on investment in R&D than were other potential first mover advantages, most of which were pretty slim or short-lived most of the time.

Other Contributing Factors

While it is tempting to point to the success of DEC, CDC, Cray, Fairchild, TI, and Intel as evidence of first mover advantages in gaining market share, it is possible that each of these firms would have earned its status even had it been a follower. None sustained its position by resting on its laurels. Success depended on the ability to continually stay on top of rapidly evolving technologies. (Some first movers, like Transitron, who stood second in the semiconductor market early on, could not sustain their leadership.) Many first movers may simply be firms that are more capable than others of continuing innovation, whose initial success gives them access to the capital to exploit their rare capabilities. To some degree, they have a monopoly on talent. The founders of DEC, CDC, and Cray remained in charge throughout most of their firms' histories (Norris gave up his directorship of CDC in 1986, and Noyce remained with Fairchild until he went on to found Intel).

Although the first mover's opportunity to gain the largest share of the market for an innovation and a head start in exploiting it permits R&D to be spread over a greater cumulative volume of output, an imitator whose total R&D cost is substantially less than the innovator's may still be able to undersell him. It is easier to reproduce some innovations than others. Data General's effort to build a 32-bit minicomputer to compete with DEC's VAX 11/780, chronicled by Tracy Kidder in *The Soul of a New Machine*,[3] is a reminder that following an innovator can involve a substantial investment of resources. On the other hand, many new products have been reverse engineered at relatively little cost, as indicated by the small industry that developed to produce unauthorized "second sources" of integrated circuits in the seventies.

In searching for the basis of the incentive to innovate in these extremely competitive markets, it is difficult to avoid the conclusion that the explosion of very highly valued exogenous opportunities for innovation that could be developed with only modest amounts of capital permitted innovators to appropriate sufficient surplus to justify their investment in spite of only limited protection from competition. The innovator's share of surplus did not have to be very large to make the investment worthwhile. In many other industries or at different times, greater market power would no doubt be necessary.

THE LIMITED COMPETITION FROM ESTABLISHED FIRMS

In assessing the conditions that permitted small new enterprises to innovate successfully, attention must be paid to the noticeable absence in their markets of competition from large, established firms. One cannot help but be impressed by the consistency with which firms already established in neighboring industries failed to compete in the industries that new firms created, either before or after their profitability had been demonstrated. When established computer firms did enter markets like minicomputers, it was often to field a product that would support their own systems. (This does not apply to "new" companies like DEC who diversified into niches in their own markets that had been created by later arrivals.) Evidently their potential advantages were not as great as one might have expected or they chose not to exploit their potential. In either case, new questions are raised regarding the market conditions under which one or the other class of firm can be counted on to innovate.

A possible reason for an established firm not to compete in a market that attracts new firms is that its opportunity costs are higher than those of new firms. Markets in which large, established companies operate typically afford them some protection from competition, whereas the markets that new firms can enter are often intrinsically competitive. At the same time, the industries in which the most likely candidates for entry into the new markets were already established themselves experienced rapid growth and offered unusually attractive opportunities for investment.

Investment in a potentially profitable new product may be rejected by a going concern, moreover, because it does not fit into its current product line or marketing strategy. (The high-powered mainframe that Amdahl worked on at IBM is an example.) Established management may be more risk averse than founders of new enterprises, or inclined to sit back and wait for a new product to emerge on the theory that it has little to lose by making a late entry (as we saw in the memory chip race). Established firms refrain from innovating for fear of depreciating their investment in production equipment and inventories as well as their customers' installed equipment, especially when the firm has leased it to them (the introduction of new fault-tolerant mainframes, for example, would have forced customers into costly software conversion).

But while one can think of numerous reasons that established corporations with potential cost advantages might choose not to enter or innovate in a market where they would have a competitive advantage, it is also possible that their competitive advantages are not as great as they at first appear. Small firms may be better organized and staffed to perceive and act on opportunities for innovation. There is conclusive evidence that established computer firms simply failed to appreciate the possibilities for the minicomputer and later the personal computer. New firms are often more facile in exploiting opportunities for innovation because of the personnel they can attract. The large companies that made vacuum tubes did not fall behind in the semiconductor race for lack of financing or effort, and the same can be said for IBM's attempt to produce a supercomputer to compete with CDC's 6600 in the 1960s. On the other hand, numerous entrepreneurs got their start by exploiting concepts for products that had been rejected by their previous employers.

THE SCHUMPETERIAN HYPOTHESIS AND BEYOND

In this study few simple rules have been found to separate the kinds of industries in which small, new firms have both the ability and the incentive to innovate from those in which they do not. The characteristics that distinguish industries in this respect are both complex and subtle. The one firmly grounded generalization that can safely be made is that small, new enterprises cannot innovate where the threshold cost of capital exceeds the limited amount that is available to any such firm, whether capital is needed for R&D, production, or marketing. (The same would apply to an industry in which critical productive resources were controlled by one or more established firms.) For some innovations, either R&D or production cannot be accomplished at all without a major investment of resources and they must be left to firms that can assemble the capital. But it is not always possible in advance to identify the industries in which innovation will require such an investment, in part because small, new enterprises have shown themselves to be ingenious in economizing on R&D, not infrequently by borrowing it. Beyond the absolute capital cost barrier, generalization becomes more treacherous. Not only may the ingenuity or luck of an innovator in perceiving a market or developing a new product overcome its cost disadvantage but firms with potential advantages may fail to compete. Indeed, virtually all of the barriers to innovation by small, new enterprises, other than threshold resource requirements, must be viewed as conditional.

In spite of the hazards of prediction, the structural characteristics of an industry remain a fairly reliable guide and a useful tool in understanding, after the fact, why small, new firms either were or were not among the innovators. It is tougher to use market structure as a basis for predicting their innovative performance. That is because the nature of most innovative opportunities is hard to foresee and because innovations can create totally new markets or transform the structure of old ones.

This book began by referring to the opinions of two economists on the eve of the solid state and computer revolutions to the effect that the small entrepreneur operating in a competitive environment could not be counted on to help drive the wheels of technological progress. For Galbraith, research and development had become so costly and sophisticated that it could be carried on only by a firm that had the resources associated with considerable size,[4] whereas Schumpeter perceived that only a firm with considerable market power would be willing to risk the investment.[5]

Galbraith's assertion is the easier to respond to. It is simply a fact that was unforeseeable at that time that opportunities for innovation that could be developed with very small amounts of capital, probably unprecedented in number and value, were just over the horizon. Whether or when such a wealth of opportunities might occur again is largely a matter for speculation. It was a happy circumstance for small, new innovators that many of those opportunities fell in markets that did not require large-scale, capital intensive production and marketing facilities nor technology and resources that were monopolized.

But still, as Schumpeter recognized, small competitive firms are at a disadvantage in protecting their innovations from competition sufficiently to induce them to risk the necessary investment. The high value of exogenous opportunities for innovation, as measured by the surplus they were capable of generating relative to the investment in R&D, was no doubt instrumental in providing the necessary incentive. A short-term monopoly was often sufficient to allow a new firm to appropriate the surplus needed to provide a satisfactory return on investment. But, while this situation may have been peculiar to a particular stage in industrial history, it was aided and abetted by another phenomenon that was not unique. Schumpeter drew attention to the crucial role of innovation in creating new industries. Indeed, this was the most desirable consequence of what he called the "perennial gale of creative destruction." A frequent side effect of the creation of new industries that Schumpeter did not specifically mention is a more hospital environment for new firms.

All of the industries examined here were newly created by innovations that took place during the period that was studied; they either employed categorically new technologies or adapted technology to fill the needs of customers that were not being served by established firms, or both. In mainframes and semiconductors there was an overlap between customers of the new product and one or more earlier products, but the technology was completely new. In minicomputers, supercomputers and small peripherals, the technology was often derivative but the potential customers were not yet served by established companies. The result was in each case the growth of an industry that was not coterminous in its structure or its membership with any previously existing industry.

Schumpeter recognized that:

> the impact of the creation of new things—new technologies for instance—on the existing structure of an industry considerably reduces the long-term scope and importance of practices that aim, through restricting output, at conserving established positions.[6]

But in a newly founded industry there are as yet no established positions and, when new kinds of knowledge and experience, new production facilities, new customers, or all three are called for, established firms are likely to find their ability to extend market power more limited still. The ground on which new firms stand relative to established firms is, therefore, higher in new markets, to some extent protecting them from the most threatening sources of potential competition. Beyond that, innovators, regardless of size or age, typically find first mover advantages stronger the greater the gap between the new product and competing ones. Also, in an industry with no incumbents, a new firm need not at once achieve optimal scale or optimal capital intensity of production to be competitive while, at the same time, the optimal degree of capital intensity is generally lower in the early stage of the product cycle than later on. Finally, even when established firms stand on higher ground, they can, as we saw, be slow to enter industries that are not closely allied to their old ones.

Much remains to be learned about the characteristics of industries that encourage innovation by small, new enterprises and the specific roles that such firms play in the innovation process. More studies, covering additional industries are needed for this purpose. But also needed is an effort to understand the kinds of innovations that are not likely to be undertaken at all, or without considerable delay, *except* for such firms. The evidence suggests that a large number of innovations that leap the boundaries of existing industries to appeal to new groups of customers or to employ broadly new technologies are candidates for this classification. Established firms were observed to concentrate on innovations that served or enhanced their traditional customer bases and were slow to pioneer with technologies that required the abandonment of traditional production techniques.

There are, thus, complementary roles for large established firms and small, new enterprises in advancing technology, a complementarity that is augmented by a mutual dependence in gaining technical knowledge and know-how. This was manifest by a tendency for established firms to obtain expertise by acquiring newer firms at the same time that other new firms transferred technology and know-how from the research laboratories and production facilities of established firms. These observations lead us back to the conclusions of Jewkes and his collaborators that were cited in the very first chapter of this book: "It may well be that there is no optimum size of firm but merely an optimum pattern for an industry, such a distribution of firms by size, character and outlook as to guarantee the most effective gathering together and commercially perfecting of the flow of new ideas."[7] To determine that blend and how it can best be achieved remains a challenge to economic research.

NOTES

1. R&D in computers contrasts with industries like pharmaceuticals and biotechnology in terms of the time it takes to bring a new product to the

market and the certainty of success. A research chemist may have little more than a working hypothesis regarding the effects of a new entity until it is synthesized, and numerous unanticipated factors can halt its advance toward the market, not least the regulatory factor. [David Schwartzman, *Innovation in the Pharmaceutical Industry* (Baltimore: Johns Hopkins University Press, 1976).] The originator of a computer, on the other hand, usually has a fairly good idea how it will work before the prototype is constructed, and the transition from prototype to quantity production follows a relatively short route (in contrast, think of penicillin, polymers, and Watt's steam engine)..

2. R. Schmalensee, "Product Differentiation Advantages of Pioneering Brands," *American Economic Review* (June 1982):349–65.
3. Tracy Kidder, *The Soul of a New Machine* (Boston: Little Brown, 1981).
4. J.K. Galbraith, *American Capitalism* (Boston: Houghton Mifflin, 1956).
5. Joseph A. Schumpeter, *Capitalism, Socialism, and Democracy,* 3d ed. (New York: Harper & Row, 1950).
6. Ibid., p. 87.
7. John Jewkes, David Sawers, and Richard Stillerman, *The Sources of Invention,* 2d ed. (New York: Macmillan, 1969), p. 168.

INDEX

A.B. Dick, 132
Absolute cost barriers, 19, 26–30, 226–231; and cost of capital, 27–30; defined, 26; and factor supplies and prices, 26–27, and access to technology, 27, and mainframes, 66–70; and magnetic disk storage, 162–174; and minicomputers, 115–118; and printers, 137–183; and scale economies, 20–21, 38; and semiconductors, 206–214; see also Capital requirements, Experience curve, Patents, Personnel, professional
Acquisitions, 52–53, 56, 182, 205, 226, 230, 233, 244
Addressing systems, 75, 97, 112
Adler, Richard B., 201 n. 28, 203 n. 51
Advanced Memory Systems, 98, 194, 195, 202 n. 49
Advanced Micro Devices (AMD), 182, 211
Advanced Scientific Computer (Texas Instruments), 97
Advertising, 68, 214; scale economies, 24, 40–41 n. 30

Age of firm: and cost of capital,24, 28; and product differentiation, 31; and size of firm, 10–11; see also Size of firm, New firms
Aiken, Howard, 44
Alloy-junction transistor, 190
AM International, 132
Amdahl, Gene M., 92–93, 94, 96, 99, 226, 228, 229, 231, 241
Amdahl Corporation, 92, 157
American Capitalism (Galbraith), 3
American National Standards Institute, 78
American Research and Development, 48, 115
American Standard Code for Information Interchange (ASCII), 78
American Totalisator, 48
Amlyn, 153, 160, 161, 164, 167 n. 35
Analex, 125
Anderson, Harlan, 60, 103
Antitrust regulation, 5, 59, 71, 78–79, 230; and AT&T, 5, 79, 180, 206, 217; and IBM, 5, 59, 71, 78–79, 94, 96, 180, 225
Apollo Corporation, 116

ABOUT THE AUTHOR

Nancy S. Dorfman received her doctorate in economics from the University of California at Berkeley in 1967 after serving as an economist with the Federal Reserve Board of Governors and other governmental agencies. Subsequently she has been an economist with consulting firms in Cambridge, Massachusetts, and Washington, D.C., and with the Massachusetts Institute of Technology, where she began work on this study as a Research Associate with a grant from the National Science Foundation. She has served as a member of governmental panels on health policy and nuclear waste disposal. Her professional publications cover environmental, energy, and transportation economics and the evolution of Boston's Route 128 high-technology economy. She is presently affiliated with the Center for Policy, Technology and Industrial Development at the Massachusetts Institute of Technology and practices as an economic consultant in Belmont, Massachusetts.